Effective
Handgun Defense

FRANK W. JAMES

©2004 Frank W. James

Published by

Gun Digest®Books
An imprint of F+W Publications
700 East State Street • Iola, WI 54990-0001
715-445-2214 • 888-457-2873
www.gundigestbooks.com

Our toll-free number to place an order or obtain
a free catalog is (800) 258-0929.

Library of Congress Control Number: 2004113663

ISBN-13: 978-0-87349-899-9
ISBN-10: 0-87349-899-2

Designed by Paul Birling
Edited by Kevin Michalowski

Printed in United States of America

To: Cathy,
for your encouragement

TABLE OF CONTENTS

ACKNOWLEDGMENTS

The author and publisher would like to thank the following individuals and organizations for their help and assistance in the preparation of this book: Accurate Arms Company, Rob Adam, Paul Adamowski, The Advanced Tactical Group, Black Hills Ammunition, Beretta U.S.A. Corporation, Browning, Joe Bunczk, Dick Burg, Mike Bussard, CCI-Speer, Jonathon Arthur Ciener, Jim Cirillo, Colt's Manufacturing Company, Eagle Grips, Chris Edwards, Federal Cartridge Company, the late Tom Ferguson, Steve Galloway, Glock, Inc., Frank Harris, Harris Publications, Heckler & Koch Inc., The International Training Division of HK Inc., Richard Heinie, Kurt J. Hindle, Jeff Hoffman, Hogue Grips, Hornady Manufacturing Company, Kevin Howard, George Huening, Bob Hunnicutt, the International Practical Shooting Confederation, J. Allan Jones, J. D. Jones, Mike Jordan, Ken Jorgensen, Kahr Arms, Harry Kane, Jerry Lee, Marty Liggins, Gene Lumsden, Tom Marx, Josh Markowitz Photography, John Meyer Jr., Ichiro Nagata, the National Rifle Association, The 1911 Society, Wayne Novak, Chris Pollack, Publisher's Development Corporation, Lane Raab, Remington Arms Company, Dennis Reese, the late George von Rosen, The United States Secret Service, Shotgun News, Sig Arms Inc., the Sig Arms Academy, Raj Singh, Carolyn Sizer, Clint Smith, Heidi Smith, Smith & Wesson, Steve Snyder, Dean Speir, Craig Spegal Custom Grips, Springfield Armory USA, Sturm Ruger & Company, Steve Sweat, John Taffin, Taurus International, the Texas Ranger Museum, Paul Thompson, the Thunder Ranch Training Facility, Jack Weigand, Syl Wiley, Winchester-Olin Ammunition.

Ichiro Nagata's photographs are used with the kind permission of Publisher's Development Corporation, the Firearms Marketing Group and their late founding publisher George E. von Rosen. Their cooperation is greatly appreciated.

I want to thank my close friend, R. Walter Rauch, for his help and advice during the research and writing of this work. I also want to thank my editor, Kevin Michalowski, for his patience and kindness throughout the preparation of this book.

I want to thank my wife, Cathy, for her help in editing and correcting my printed 'thoughts', but mostly I want to thank her for the support a writer needs when preparing a book, especially one that was written during trying times.

FOREWORD

Even after being Frank James' good friend for many years, I still need to "read" his work to truly appreciate the depth of research and effort he puts forth when he addresses a topic.

When Frank and I travel together the talk, of course, does turn to firearms and tactics, but more often than not this modest Indiana farmer is content to discuss those things that he holds most dear to himself: his family and farm.

Frank can hold his own among the best of the firearms experts, of course, but he never seeks out the spotlight on center stage. However, if the group discussion should falter on a technical question, Frank is often the one who supplies the correct answer.

Effective Handgun Defense aptly demonstrates once again Frank's deep commitment to his writing craft in the firearms field. He provides the reader with an informative blend of history, practicality and technical data; a book that will certainly quickly become a much-used reference work in the dedicated shooting enthusiast's library.

Walt Rauch

INTRODUCTION

Most people when they read the title of this work, Effective Handgun Defense, will think immediately of a relatively small, easy-to-conceal handgun of some description. While there is no argument such a handgun would fit the popular definition of a concealed carry self-defense handgun, it is not the standard or definition I used when I began this project. For more years than I care to remember I have been carrying handguns of various descriptions and calibers either as an essential piece of equipment for the job or simply as a part of my ordinary daily wardrobe. The vast majority of the time all of the handguns I've carried were relatively large and powerful revolvers or pistols, and the reason was simple – it often takes a large powerful handgun to neutralize a living, breathing target. There are exceptions, of course, as there are for most every hypothesis, but the failures I've experienced in terms of stopping what I was shooting were most often associated with poor marksmanship, or small caliber and medium-bore handguns. The poor marksmanship was my problem, but the experiences gained with so many handguns gave rise to my opinions and ultimately this book.

No, I have never had to engage another human being with gunfire and for that I am eternally grateful. I have taken my share of wild, feral and domestic creatures, large and small, with handguns and this experience, gained over many decades, has left me with a number of beliefs and, perhaps to a few, some pointedly narrow-minded ideas

I will state unequivocally here and now I believe in big-bore handgun calibers. I also believe that handguns firing cartridges with a muzzle velocity greater than 1,000 fps work better than those of a like caliber and kind that don't.

Yet, I am not an advocate of the Super Heavy handgun calibers like the .500 Magnum or its lesser-powered equivalents. When I say that I'm not trying to create controversy or animosity, it's just that my experience has not yet indicated I have a physical need for such powerful calibers in a handgun.

Because of these noted preferences I tend to be something of a revolver aficionado, but that doesn't mean I don't appreciate a good auto pistol. I even appreciate many of the smaller small-caliber auto pistols that have been made in the last 100 years. This book is not intended to be the last word on self-defense handguns or even concealed carry pistols. My arrogance is not that great. My intention is at best to create an overview and for some a reflection or reminder about some of the handguns many of us have used over the years for both serious social purposes and for the far more enjoyable recreational shooting.

The 'Concealed Carry' movement is a recent phenomenon in our country and it is to my mind one of the greatest indicators of our individual freedom. The number of states in our nation that grant the individual citizen the right to carry a concealed self-defense handgun stands at 31. The right to carry a tool capable of lethal force for self-defense

is an immense responsibility, but it is also a measure of the trust each state government places in the individual who exercises these rights. I am grateful to have been born and raised in a nation and particularly a state where these rights have been exercised for many years.

This book is meant for the person who has received a concealed carry permit or is thinking about the subject. The truth is the concealed carry self-defense handgun will always be something of a contradiction. Of all the weapon systems available, the handgun is probably the least efficient in terms of its potential for successful deployment against armed aggressors. Yet, it is also the tool that can prove most convenient in terms of being available in our daily lives. The handgun, because of its size, weight and overall ergonomics, is the tool that will probably be the only firearm available if the unthinkable happens.

In a perfect world, there would be no need for lethal force instruments to defend ourselves, because in a perfect world there would be no criminals and no criminal assaults. In a perfect world, there would be no rapes, no armed robberies, no carjackings and no kidnappings and no murders, but as we all know the world in which we live is not perfect.

This book is intended for those who have chosen to research the lethal force instruments of yesterday and today in order to help them understand the nature of these instruments and tools.

This book is also intended for those of us who have developed a love for these instruments, not necessarily for what they can do or can't do, but because many of them represent some of the finest engineering available in small portable consumer goods. Yes, firearms and handguns are inanimate objects completely incapable of returning affection or adoration, but for many readers the handguns shown in the following pages will remind them of another time and place when the reader may have been younger, stronger and in some cases placed in great physical jeopardy because of events beyond their control.

It is my firm belief that for many the presence of a concealed carry firearm made the difference between going home or not going home at all.

Frank W. James
May 1, 2004

CHAPTER ONE

The History Of The Fightin' Handgun

The rebuke would not go unanswered. Two armed men faced each other with determination and resolve. Onlookers retired to the safety of the surrounding storefronts as the drama unfolded in the dusty street. The gunfight that followed was brief, decisive, swift and real.

The participants, described by many citizens as "desperadoes", had been acquaintances for years. Their disagreement after a 'friendly' game of cards was apparently over the exact amount of the debt owed by one to the other. The true cause of the conflict was never clear. Regardless of its origin, the disagreement rose to the point where honor demanded satisfaction and satisfaction was found in deadly violence.

The time was July 21, 1865, and the location was Springfield, Missouri. The participants in this gunfight were Davis K. Tutt, a man the world would little note, and James Butler Hickok. A man the world would recognize for all eternity as "Wild Bill".

Hickok was already known at this stage in his life for being "a man of action". He would later die violently in a town named Deadwood at a poker table holding what was immortalized as the Deadman's Hand. (The cards were the two black aces and two black eights. Legend has left the fifth card obscure, but many historians believe it was either the jack of diamonds or the queen of diamonds.)

You know who won this gunfight in Missouri, but the details are fascinating to those who study such things for a number of reasons.

The first important fact about this event is it was one of the very few documented instances of a walk-and-draw gunfight in the Old West.

Secondly, the distance at which the two gunfighters drew and fired at each was extremely unusual, both then and now. One eyewitness placed the distance between the two men at a startling 100 paces.

And lastly, only two shots were fired. Again, eyewitnesses recorded that although each man wore two pistols they drew only one pistol each. The shots were simultaneous. One witness said he thought that only one man had fired until he saw smoke coming from the pistols of both participants.

Hickok's aim and speed won the day. Dr. Edwin Ebert stated subsequently in sworn testimony before the coroner that a bullet had entered Tutt's body between the fifth and seventh rib on his right side and exited between the fifth and seventh rib on his left side. The examination was only superficial being without autopsy, leaving the doctor to conclude the specific cause of Tutt's death was blood loss.

Hickok was immediately arrested and charged with murder, but later the charge was reduced to manslaughter. The trial lasted two days, ending with Hickok's acquittal. The jury ruled he acted in self-defense because Tutt was the aggressor. Tutt had worn Hickok's watch, which he had kept as security for Hickok's gambling debt, in public. Hickok had specifically warned Tutt against doing so until Hickok settled the debt.

In a legal sense, this only gives evidence, if not emphasis, to the critical difference between murder and self-defense in any gunfight. The time differential between the two legal judgments can be measured in micro-seconds, or by a far wider, but infinitely more elusive measurement of public perception as to who actually was the aggressor.

Hollywood Western films have often depicted some variation of this type of gunfight with actors like Gary Cooper, John Wayne, and countless others. The main point, however, is seldom do gunfights happen in public with plenty of impartial witnesses. Even the

During the summer of 1844, fifteen Texas Rangers under Captain Jack Hays used Colt Paterson firearms to good advantage against eighty Comanche Indians. The Colt Paterson revolvers and carbines gave the Texas Rangers a decided technological edge which they exploited to the fullest. The engagement between the Rangers and the Indians became known in history as "Hays Big Fight" and left a lasting impression on the Indians. It left an even bigger one on the Texans.

Gunfight at the OK Corral almost two decades after the Tutt/Hickok gunfight was never cut and dried as to who was actually at fault or guilty of a crime.

Yet here, two men with a disagreement, decided to settle it with a duel in the late afternoon sun and they did it using the most modern technology available at the time – six-shot revolvers.

Prior to the introduction of the revolver, about the closest thing to a fighting handgun was the dueling pistol, but dueling was fought according to a code, the Code Duello, and was a formal, almost institutionalized affair created to settle injustices, both real and imaginary.

Dueling pistols were specifically made for fighting according to the code, but today they would be classified as "target-grade" firearms and not rough-duty, everyday service pistols. The service pistols from that period were more often than not extremely inaccurate and often made heavy enough to be used as clubs once their single round had been expended.

This fact alone gives some explanation as to why the Bowie Knife proved so popular during the same period on the American frontier.

Prior to the six-shot revolver, pistols were too unreliable in accuracy or function to depend upon for self-defense. Formal dueling with pistols was characterized by the fact it occurred primarily between men of social stature; i.e. "gentlemen."

The rough frontiersman of the expanding American West had little use for social titles, or the orderly rules of fighting a duel. Although fighting a duel according to a code of honor was a common practice in the South prior to the Civil War, inhabitants of the developing West changed the practice of armed fighting to what was available in terms of equipment and what suited their individual temperaments.

In many parts of the world today, this questionable attribute of human nature

Designed by Joe Wesson, son of D.B. Wesson -- founder of Smith & Wesson, the Safety Hammerless Double Action was an early attempt to provide a self-defense pistol that would not snag or 'hang-up' during the draw stroke from inside a coat pocket. Available in .32 and .38 calibers these revolvers proved popular with both citizens and law enforcement officers concerned about self-defense prior to 1900.

continues, and explains the real-world need for a continued interest in fighting handguns, but they should be concealed fighting handguns regardless of size for reasons of civil social interaction, as well as legally mandated requirements. This need is not a modern one. In different parts of the American Frontier, as well as east of the Mississippi River, many did not approve of the open carrying of sidearms following the American Civil War. It is well to remember the initial source, if not the root cause, of the Gunfight at the OK Corral was the misdemeanor violation of the Tombstone ordinance prohibiting the open display of firearms by the Clanton cowboys.

By the late 1850s, technology had perfected the first true fighting handgun. Some commentators may question this conclusion, but prior to the introduction of the percussion cap revolver, handguns were always carried in combination with a suitable fighting knife and the reason was simple. The pistol lacked the firepower necessary to stop a fight reliably unless the fight was conducted according to an agreed code. Otherwise, the knife was essential for victory, meaning survival, when there were no rules other than the bounds of one conscience.

Actually, little has changed in the world during since those pre-Civil War days.

WHAT IS A FIGHTING HANDGUN?

The fighting handgun by definition is a reliable and trustworthy weapon. It can be large, which may make it difficult to conceal and carry daily, or it can be small, which in contrast usually means it is limited in its terminal effectiveness. But its main attribute is its reliability. It must always work and that means more than mere reliable functioning. This firearm must deliver sufficient force to end the conflict in a manner or means favorable to its owner.

In plain language, it must be decisive and it must be decisive in a way that is independent of the aggressiveness of the antagonist. For instance, a few individuals when faced with the certainty of deadly force from the pointed muzzle of a gun will comply with most any demand. However, this is not a trait one can expect from most criminals, especially those with a history of criminal violence.

The 1851 Colt Navy revolver proved highly popular with military officers, frontiersmen and scouts and was used by both sides in the American Civil War, but James Butler Hickok, also known as 'Wild Bill' Hickok proved the value of these fightin' handguns when he used an 1851 Colt revolver to kill Davis Tutt at a distance of 100 paces in the first 'walk and draw' gunfight in Springfield, Missouri on July 21, 1865.

The Walker Colt revolver was a six shot .44 caliber monster that weighed four pounds, nine ounces and it proved itself immediately in terms of reliability and power. An army officer, Colonel R.B. Marcey, upon witnessing an encounter between his troops, most of who were armed with .36 caliber Navy pistols and two of whom were armed with Walker .44s, and a grizzly bear noted upon skinning the dead animal it was the projectiles from the Walker Colt revolvers that killed it and not the Navy revolvers. He resolved "...thenceforth to carry the larger size."

The decisiveness of any defensive weapon depends upon a combination of four factors inherent with its design and operation. They are power, accuracy, speed of deployment, and mechanical reliability. The first three factors are secondary in importance to the last. Mechanical perfection, which seldom exists in anything made by man, will not however win the fight by itself.

Hickok was known to carry two Model 1851 Navy Colt revolvers. These cap-and-ball handguns fired a .36 caliber ball of soft lead. Hickok considered reliability so important that he reportedly fired, cleaned and reloaded each gun every morning upon rising to guarantee they would work as designed – if needed that day.

It was Sam Colt who really created the class of firearm that proved the concept and the advantages of the fighting handgun, even the concealed carry fighting handgun. The Colt revolver offered a sixfold increase in ammunition capacity while at the same time improving the reliability and accuracy of the fighting handgun.

During the summer of 1844, 15 Texas Rangers under Captain Jack Hays used Colt Paterson firearms to good advantage against 80 Comanche Indians. Normally, the Indians held the advantage due to their horsemanship and the ability to rapidly fire arrows. The introduction of Colt Paterson revolvers and carbines gave the Texas Rangers a decided technological edge which they exploited to the fullest.

Previously, horsemen had to dismount to shoot and reload their muzzleloaders during battle. Thus, they were little more than mounted infantry, but these Texas Rangers were able to fight from horseback, which at the time was new for white men. This engagement became known as "Hays' Big Fight" and left a lasting impression on the Indians. It made an even bigger one on the Texans.

The success of Hays proved welcome news to Colt because even though his design was good, problems had hindered government sales and his first commercial arms endeavor, Patent Arms Mfg. Co., failed. After failure of his arms company, Sam Colt worked on waterproof ammunition and underwater harbor mines. Colt returned to arms manufacturing when Captain Samuel H. Walker of the Texas Rangers wrote to Colt requesting "...the most perfect weapon in the World..." for use by "people throughout Texas".

The product of this request was the Walker Colt revolver. It was a six-shot .44 caliber monster that weighed 4 pounds, 9 ounces and it immediately proved reliable and powerful.

An Army officer, Colonel R. B. Marcey, wrote about the greater penetration and power of the .44 Colt over the smaller bore revolvers. He related how a full-grown grizzly bear was killed by his troops during the spring of 1858. Many of his men were armed with .36 caliber Navy revolvers and they scored several hits upon the bruin, but it was the two balls from the .44 caliber Dragoons, or Walker Colt revolvers, that killed the beast. Upon skinning the animal, the soldiers found projectiles from the smaller caliber Colt revolver had only penetrated an inch or so past the thick hide of the bear. Colonel Marcey ended his description of events by stating "...and I resolved thenceforth to carry the larger size."

The Colt revolver was a key tool of the American Civil War and used by both sides, especially mounted troops. The revolver changed warfare by giving men unprecedented firepower when compared to the standard infantry rifle which fired one round that had to be loaded through the muzzle, a time-consuming and involved process. The mounted warrior of the Civil War was mobile and heavily armed often carrying carry five or six revolvers that were not reloaded until after the skirmish was won, or the raider escaped.

The classic example for the most efficient use of the revolver was demonstrated by the Confederate raider John Singleton Moseby. Moseby would write "I think I was the first cavalry commander who discarded the saber as useless..." The saber was really nothing more than a large knife. Moseby was one of the first military commanders to recognize the reliability of the Colt revolver and the advantage it offered over traditional cavalry weapons.

Moseby's men armed themselves with Colt revolvers – four to six per man. And the guns were used effectively. At the battle of Miskel's Barn in April of 1863, Moseby and seventy of his men engaged 150 Union troopers under the command of Captain Flint. The Union forces emptied their pistols prematurely and then charged the rebels with sabers. Moseby's men, literally, put the reins between their teeth and charged into the Union forces with Colt revolvers in each hand. The result was a rout. Flint was killed and nearly 100 of his men were killed or wounded as a result of the accurate short-range revolver fire from the rebels.

The American Civil War was fought mainly with percussion cap-and-ball weapons, but Rollin White, a former Colt employee, patented the bored-through chamber concept in 1855. The firm of Horace Smith and D.B. Wesson purchased the rights to this patent and in the process developed what would eventually become known as the .22 rimfire cartridge. Smith & Wesson gained recognition immediately for the quality of their arms as well as the innovation of the bored-through chamber.

The bored-through chamber gave birth to the metallic cartridge and firearms became even more reliable. The cartridge was self-contained and sealed. The cap-and-ball revolver was subject to malfunctions brought on by moisture and cap failure. The result was a leap forward for firearms technology, but the tactics and skills learned by the combatants during the Civil War carried over to the American West and gave precedence to the importance of a reliable fighting handgun.

The firm of Horace Smith and D.B. Wesson purchased the rights to the Rollin White patent which pioneered the bored-through chamber concept and in the process developed what would eventually become known as the .22 rimfire cartridge. The Smith & Wesson Model 1 was a popular choice among Union Army officers as a self-defense weapon even though it was in actuality the *first* .22 rimfire handgun.

Remington Arms produced this five-shot percussion revolver for concealed carry, self-defense purposes during the American Civil War. The Remington New Model Pocket revolver was a .31 caliber handgun.

The Reconstruction of the South characterized American history following the Civil War, as did the expansion westward into territories dominated by Native Americans and the continued violence in border states like Missouri. Guerilla fighters like Frank and Jesse James (no relation to the author) were never pardoned after the war, although Jesse James did swear an oath of allegiance to the Union on May 21, 1865 at Lexington, Missouri. Jesse was on his sickbed as a result of a severe gunshot wound. Many contemporaries of the former Confederate guerillas felt they were forced to continue their lawless actions after hostilities ceased because of the hangman's noose that awaited them. This was the result of the political ramifications of the Drake Constitution adopted by Missouri following the Civil War and the continuing animosities between the Radicals and the Conservatives of post-war Missouri politics.

Whatever their motivation, Frank and Jesse James learned the lessons of fighting quite well and utilized multiple handguns and thoroughbred horses in robbing corporate-owned trains, express companies and banks for more than 16 years following the Civil War.

By the time the war ended Jesse James had already learned some hard lessons; after being shot twice through the chest. The last incident was the result of a mounted encounter with a patrol of cavalrymen of the Third Wisconsin on Salt Pond road near Lexington, Missouri on May 15, 1865. Both the bushwhackers of which James was a member and the cavalrymen opened fire immediately upon seeing each other. Jesse was struck with a .36 caliber ball through his right side. It was fired from a Colt Navy revolver. The bullet missed the ribs, but cut through his lung and remained in his body the remainder of his life. There is even some dispute as to how long it took Jesse James to recover from this wound, even if many agree it almost proved fatal. Jesse used the incident as an alibi for many years when witnesses under a promise of anonymity would later say otherwise.

It is relevant to note that although Jesse James was a well-known racist and cold-blooded killer, he was never apprehended. He lived constantly as a fugitive from the moment the war ended until his death on April 3, 1882. Both friends and strangers protected him due either to sympathetic feelings or outright, unbridled fear of the James brothers and fellow Confederate veterans.

Frank James surrendered approximately six months after his brother's death. He was acquitted twice when he stood trial for murder and robbery and became an exception to the unwritten rule for most gunfighters and outlaws when he died a natural death on February 18th, 1915 at the age of 82. Frank James revealed the importance he placed on his gunbelt, holster and revolver when he surrendered and handed them to Governor

Introduced in the early 1880s, Smith & Wesson introduced their .44 caliber double-action revolver. It was developed at the request of the Russian government and built on a modified Number 3 frame. Chambered for the .44 Russian cartridge, a few were used as fightin' handguns on the American frontier.

Introduced in 1873 by Colt after the Rollin White Patent on the bored-through cylinder expired, the Colt Single Action Army revolver became the sidearm of the U.S. Cavalry as well as the revolver of choice for thousands of people exploring and settling in the American West.

Crittenden, saying, "No living man except myself has been permitted to touch (these) since 1861." The date was October 15, 1882. (It should be noted the revolver he surrendered was an 1875 Model Remington, so we must assume Alexander Franklin James was speaking metaphorically when he said this.)

The James Boys were not the only group of Civil War veterans that took to liberating banks, express companies and railroad trains. Their firepower was often multiple handguns and a large supply of ammunition. They thoroughly understood the principles of fighting. Both brothers were quick to embrace the new metallic cartridge technology when it was introduced and popularized with the 1873 Colt Single Action Army revolver. Although Jesse is often associated with Smith & Wesson revolvers of that time period, he was also known to carry Colt Single Action revolvers. Both men used Henry and later Winchester repeating rifles.

In fact, it is documented that members of the James-Younger gang tried to purchase repeating rifles in Northfield, Minnesota prior to their famed failed bank robbery on September 7, 1876. Fortunately for the citizens of Northfield, the hardware store of Anselm Manning had only shotguns for sale and the gang declined them. Most of the gang carried Smith & Wesson revolvers, in pairs, together with cartridge belts and abundant ammunition for this raid, but because the citizens of Minnesota seldom carried arms, the gang members made a concerted effort to conceal these somewhat large handguns under long linen dusters.

The Northfield Robbery brings out one other important element and that is the role of the engaged armed citizen. One authority on Jesse James, T.J. Stiles, feels the bank at Northfield, Minnesota was chosen because Adelbert Ames owned it. Ames, a graduate of West Point, had served the Union forces throughout the Civil War rising in rank to General. Following the war he was made military governor of Mississippi and worked faithfully to guarantee and protect the rights of African-Americans, but those forces opposed to freedom and basic rights for African-Americans proved greater, eventually forcing his resignation after he had been freely elected governor of the state. He moved to Minnesota to go into partnership with his father and his brother. Jesse James targeted the bank, it is believed, because of its owner's past history.

The James-Younger gang scouted Northfield over a period of several weeks prior to the robbery identifying themselves as cattle buyers, but even so, merchant J.S. Allen became suspicious of the strangers on September 7th, 1876 when they entered the bank. Allen approached to investigate. When one of the armed gang tried to grab him and take him hostage, Allen broke loose and ran for help, whereupon the robbers opened fire. The usual method employed by the gang was for two or more members to ride up and down the streets of the town discharging their pistols in an attempt to terrorize the citizenry and keep them out of their way.

Unfortunately for the James-Younger gang, Henry Wheeler, a young medical student working in his father's drug store grabbed a breech-loading carbine and ran to a second story window of the Dampier Hotel overlooking the street outside the bank and opened fire with the only two cartridges he was able to secure in his rush. On the same side of the street George Bates grabbed a shotgun and opened fire, but it was another shotgun-wielding Northfield citizen, Elias Stacey, who shot Clell Miller lethally in the face with small birdshot. This was followed by Wheeler's second shot, which dropped Cole Younger's horse and brought him to ground, face first. Younger then ran to Miller and upon finding him badly shot received a serious bullet wound to his left hip. Quick-thinking Younger pulled Miller from his horse while at the same time unbuckling Miller's gunbelt to get his ammunition and pistols.

Over 200,000 Colt Model 1860 Army revolvers were manufactured before production ceased. A large percentage of these revolvers were purchased by the Union Army during the Civil War and used by many in the years following the Civil War during the expansion and settlement of the American West. The Colt Model 1860 Army revolver was a six shot, percussion revolver in .44 caliber.

Another Northfield resident, J.B. Hyde, blasted away at the robbers with a double-barreled shotgun. The unarmed town marshal Elias Hobbs threw rocks at the mounted gunmen. Hobbs was not the only brave individual in Northfield that day. Bates discovered his shotgun would not open to reload. He grabbed a pistol, which proved to be empty, and he continued to aim it at the outlaws in an effort to draw their fire away from his fellow citizens. As for cowardice, Cole Younger at some point during the ensuing melee rode up to a drunk just leaving a basement saloon and shot and killed him on the spot. The man, Nicolaus Gustavson, was unarmed.

Hardware store owner Manning, hearing the gunfire, secured his Remington rifle. Using a corner of a building a short distance away from the bank as cover Manning was soon joined by an unarmed Adelbert Ames. Ames noticing that Manning's hands were shaking badly began coaching the store owner in a confident, calm tone of voice just as he had his troops during the war. Manning then shot and killed mounted gang member Bill Chadwell with one shot.

The Younger brothers began to focus their attention by this time on Manning and Ames. Just in the nick of time medical student Wheeler replenished his supply of rifle ammo and re-engaged the Youngers. His next shot shattered Bob Younger's right elbow. Bob switched his revolver to his left hand, but his brother Cole soon realized they were beaten. He yelled inside the bank. The robbers, Charlie Pitts and Frank and Jesse James, were forced to acknowledge defeat. Not before the leader of the gang, in all probability Jesse James, murdered the bank bookkeeper, J.L. Heywood, in cold blood by a shot to the head at point blank range.

As the gang organized to leave the town one other Younger brother was hit in the shoulder leaving all of the Younger brothers wounded by the efforts of a concerned citizenry of Northfield, Minnesota. In the two weeks following the attempted bank robbery, the Younger brothers would be captured. Charlie Pitts would be shot to death and the James brothers would establish an endurance record for physical torment and stamina under the worst of all physical conditions as fugitives escaping a multi-state manhunt.

Published reports concerning Jesse James in the years following the Northfield raid have said he often carried two fully loaded revolvers of significant caliber, while wearing three completely filled cartridge belts with still more spare cartridges in his pockets. In addition, he stuffed a Model 1873 Winchester lever-action rifle inside a large folded umbrella which he carried with him whenever he traveled. He also carried a valise full of spare ammunition to fit both the rifle and the handguns. (A rifle similar in description to this one was on display at the Clay County Museum near the original James homestead in Kearney, Missouri when the author visited the James farm several years ago.)

Some question if this amount of ammo could be true simply because of the sheer weight of all this ammunition. Even if only partially accurate it still conveys the importance Jesse James placed on multiple fighting handguns, as well as the additional carbine (which was concealed in the umbrella), and the ammunition necessary to keep these firearms functioning during a lengthy exchange.

In 1873, Colt Firearms introduced the Colt Single Action that would become known around the world as the Peacemaker. Smith & Wesson submitted the Schofield revolver for the government trials to select a new Army revolver. Colt eventually won the contract.

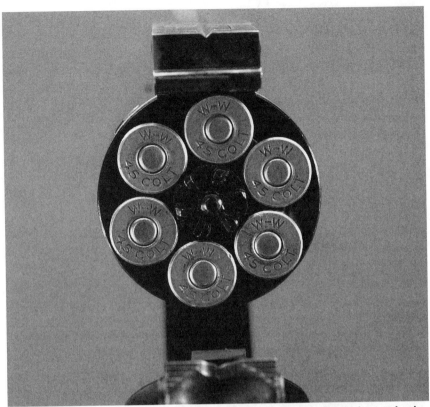

The advantage of the Smith & Wesson Schofield over the Colt Single Action was it was a break-open design that ejected all six spent cartridges at once. This made the Schofield faster to reload, unfortunately the Colt Single Action Army still proved more popular. The model shown here is a replica able to chamber the .45 Colt round.

On October 15, 1882 the outlaw Frank James surrendered to Missouri Governor Crittenden and handed him his gun, belt and holster saying, "No living man except myself has been permitted to touch (these) since 1861." The revolver he surrendered was an 1875 Model Remington (similar to the model seen here), so we must assume Alexander Franklin James was speaking metaphorically when he said this.

The popularity of the Colt Single Action Army has never died out. Bill Ruger capitalized on it by designing the Ruger Blackhawk revolver, a modern design that used music wire springs and a number of new manufacturing techniques to create a revolver that reminded many of the older Colt.

The Schofield was developed from a previous revolver Smith & Wesson introduced for commercial sale in 1870. The previous model was known as the Model 3. The Smith & Wesson Schofield and the previous Model 3 were tip-up designs that ejected all six empty cases simultaneously.

The Remington Company submitted a revolver to the same trial. The Remington revolver resembled in size and profile the Colt 1873 Single Action Army and it was in the opinion of many experts the better revolver. The biggest advantage of the Remington "Army" of 1875 was that the grip was integral with the frame which was forged. This design was protected by W.S. Smoot's patent. The Colt SAA employed screws to secure the grip portion of the revolver to the frame and over time or heavy use these screws often loosened or backed out.

All of these guns would see extensive use as fighting handguns on the American frontier, but it was the Colt revolver that would go on to garner the most praise. The Colt SAA revolver remains today the most recognized and the single best example of a fighting handgun for the time period between its introduction in 1873 and the introduction of smokeless powder before the turn of the century.

The Colt Single Action Army figured prominently in the history of the American West as well as the history of American law enforcement. Texas Ranger George Herold used

▶ **To many nothing is as beautiful as an engraved Colt Single Action, especially one which has been fitted with ivory grips. The beauty of this gun to the users of over 100 years ago was found in its dependability and reliable operation.**

Merwin and Hulbert revolvers were sound fightin' handguns seen during the latter part of the 19th Century. Merwin and Hulbert were not manufacturers as these revolvers were actually made by Hopkins and Allen of Norwich, Connecticut. Merwin and Hulbert revolvers came in both single action and double action mechanism designs due to their evolution over a period of years. The model seen here is one of the later models featuring a top strap over the cylinder and a double action trigger mechanism. The Merwin and Hulbert design was significant because after firing all six chambers, the barrel was rotated ninety degrees and the barrel and cylinder were then pulled *forward* to remove the fired cases from the cylinder.

The introduction of the Ruger Vaquero was a response by many participants in the fast-growing activity known as "cowboy shooting". Placing a heavy reliance on the correct period clothing this 'sport' allows the contestant to compete with replica firearms that are virtually identical to the ones used in cowtown gunfights all across the developing western United States prior to 1900.

one to kill the infamous bandit Sam Bass while attempting to apprehend the outlaw at Round Rock, Texas. Bass, wounded, lived to escape the gunfight that occurred in front of the bank Bass and his gang intended to rob. He was found a day later mortally wounded under a tree on the prairie a short distance from the scene.

Bat Masterson and Wyatt Earp were both known users of the Colt Single Action. It was a Colt Single Action Army that was used to kill Wild Bill Hickok in Deadwood, South Dakota. Jack McCall shot Hickok from behind. McCall obviously knew of Hickok's expertise and feared his prowess with defensive sidearms. McCall was charged with murder and brought to trial for this cowardly act, but amazingly he was found "not guilty" by the local jury. It turned out later this jury had no legal authority.

During a second trial in Yankton, South Dakota, McCall claimed he had been paid to kill Hickok. The man who allegedly paid him to murder Wild Bill was never found. McCall was found guilty of murder after this second trial and was hanged on March 1, 1877.

Like Hickok, Jesse James was shot and killed from behind, but in this instance it was by a member of his own gang. These two examples plus others like the deaths of Pat Garrett, the man who shot Billy the Kid, and John Wesley Hardin are more indicative of the manner and courage of most participants in Old West gunfights. This reality stands in stark contrast to the previously mentioned Tutt/Hickok walk-and-draw street fight. Few men or boys were foolhardy enough to challenge men who were renown for their skills with fighting pistols, concealed or otherwise, and their instinctive, immediate willingness to use them with deadly accuracy.

Although Hickok was alleged to have killed scores of men, the best estimate is he probably killed six men in both physical altercations and gunfights. Frank and Jesse James certainly murdered far more men, but just how many is unknown. Obviously, they used firearms to deadly effect during the war. The description and circumstances of their behavior after the war can only be characterized as murder.

Of course, this judgment runs counter to the acquittal of Frank James after his surrender, but many factors were important then that wouldn't be even considered currently. Who knows what influences the decision of a jury?

Today, the concealed carry fighting handgun is still a legitimate tool for defensive protection, but only when used in the narrow parameters set forth in the law.

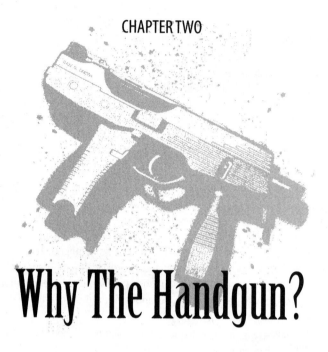

CHAPTER TWO

Why The Handgun?

O ne hundred years ago, the fighting handgun was not exactly a new device, but all the history surrounding its use in a fight was fairly recent. Many assumed the mere possession of a handgun regardless of caliber or condition provided the essential protection one seeks in a concealed weapon. To illustrate this thinking in terms of history one has only to examine the gun that really established the firm of Smith & Wesson.

The gun was the Smith & Wesson Model 1 (Second issue), the latter designation having been added by modern collectors to distinguish it from the First issue Model 1. The Model 1 was a seven-shot .22 caliber rimfire revolver of a tip-up design. Prior to the American Civil War Smith & Wesson had sold approximately 11,000 Model 1 revolvers during its three and a half years of production. (Smith & Wesson was also an ammunition manufacturer at the time and they pioneered the round that would become known as the .22 rimfire cartridge.) In early 1860, a redesigned Model 1 (the Second issue) began production and more than 115,000 were produced before it was dropped from production in 1868. Obviously, the Civil War spurred the sales of the Model 1, but think about it, the Model 1 was a seven-shot rimfire .22 caliber revolver and for all practical matters was little different in terms of power and effectiveness than many .22 rimfires on the market currently. While the .22 rimfire cartridge and corresponding firearms have much to recommend them, their lack of power is a serious concern for any self-defense consumer, both then and now.

However, one should never focus solely on the equipment if you are truly concerned about your personal safety or that of the family. Attention must be paid to the mindset essential for successful self-defense, regardless of the chosen weapon. And weapons often involve far more than mere firearms whether they are handguns or otherwise.

A HANDGUN WOULD APPEAR TO BE A POOR CHOICE...

Handguns on superficial inspection are probably the worst firearms one could ever use in defense of themselves and their loved ones. Handguns are far less powerful than rifles, and when compared to a shotgun, far-more difficult to master in terms of hitting the target. (Although the ease of hitting the target with a shotgun is often over-stated and misunderstood. Additionally, shotguns when used in a self-defense role are all too often loaded with the wrong ammunition for the situation presented. Self-defense shotguns probably require almost as much training to be used properly as the handgun, a point many commentators often overlook.)

However, the handgun is a great tool and it could be the almost ideal tool for self-defense because it can be readily available when worn daily and if one is prepared for violent trouble.

Notice I didn't say *anticipating* violent trouble. That's because authorities and the courts have historically taken a dim view of paranoia, no matter how much it is justified or deserved. Preparation, however, is another thing altogether and almost always involves extensive training.

Louis Awerbuck of the Yavapai Firearms Academy is seen here at the Boone County, Indiana Sheriff's Firing Range instructing a group on the proper use of the combat shotgun. The author feels Awerbuck is among the better firearms instructors in the United States.

If you are having concerns about being labeled a paranoid for investigating concealed carry handguns, ask yourself if the same people would tag you as frightened of fire because you purchased a fire extinguisher, or felt you were scared of driving because you purchased a car that received a good rating for crash-test durability? Preparation for personal safety comes in many forms and this book is addressing only one of them.

Luck has been defined as preparation meeting opportunity. Preparation requires training – frequent and thorough training. Many people, both police and civilians, who have survived violent encounters through their skillful use of a defensive, fighting handgun have been described afterwards as being 'lucky'. Good intensive training is a means of insuring luck. Obviously, many in history were lucky. Frank James was lucky. Bat Masterson and Wyatt Earp were equally lucky.

THERE ARE RULES TO HAVING A FIGHTING HANDGUN???...

Yes, there are rules to possessing a self-defense, fighting handgun. Everyone interested in these devices will soon become acquainted with the federal and state laws and ordinances concerning their possession in their respective areas. There are also rules reflecting the mindset of one who chooses to pursue and investigate this subject. Some of them are rather straightforward and sometimes they may even seem funny, but that doesn't mask the intent to create a mindset that makes one aware of their surroundings, their environment and, most importantly, their responsibilities.

The 20 rules that follow were collected and compiled originally by a close personal friend, Dean Speir, and they are available in their origin form on his website, www. TheGunZone.com. He credits a number of authorities as his sources and I would be remiss not to include them as well. They are the following: Mark Moritz, Clint Smith, John Farnum, Andy Stanford, Evan Marshall, Pat Rogers, Shalom Pam, James DeMarco, David Hackworth and Tim Burke. In a few instances, I have deleted or added and put my own interpretation in place on these rules, so if you find them irksome or troubling I accept full responsibility and you should hold the previously mentioned personalities blameless.

RULES OF GUNFIGHTING...

1. HAVE A GUN. This is the absolute First Rule of Gunfighting and can be properly attributed to Mark Moritz, an attorney living in Arizona.

a. If at all possible, have at least two guns and even better, make sure one of them is a long gun, preferably a rifle with a high-capacity magazine.

b. Bring all of your friends who have guns. (The United States Marine Corp performs this theory quite well and remains among its better practitioners.)

2. Anything worth shooting is worth shooting twice. Ammo is cheap. Life is valuable. When the prosecutor asks, "Why did you shoot the deceased twice?" the answer is "...because I was trained to do so!"

3. Only hits count. A miss with the most powerful gun you own is still a miss. Shoot and carry what you can hit with. (That is incorrect grammar, but it is perfect logic.)

The 20th Anniversary of the founding of the International Practical Shooting Confederation (IPSC) was celebrated by Colt Firearms with a series of commemorative pistols. The pistols, like this ornate 1911 .45 Automatic, featured many of the enhancements developed during the first 20 years of IPSC competition. The "DVC" seen engraved in gold lettering at the back of the slide stands for the Latin words; Diligentia, Vis, Celeritas. Translated they mean Accuracy, Power, Speed. This was the motto adopted by IPSC and first used by the South West Combat Pistol League.

4. Proximity negates skill. Distance is your friend. You can't go to the store and buy time, but you can create distance between you and your adversary through lateral or diagonal movement and achieve the same result as buying time. If you can create a distance greater than 21 feet between you and your adversary, the mathematical odds for increased survival weigh heavily in your favor.

5. Accuracy is relative. RELIABILITY IS NOT. You must use a gun that works All The Time – EVERY TIME. If it doesn't work, get a different gun or better ammo or both. No Excuses.

6. If your shooting stance is good, you're probably not moving fast enough or using cover properly.

7. Always cheat. Always win. The only unfair fight is the one you lose.

8. If you are not shooting, you should be communicating, reloading your weapon and moving.

9. Someday someone may kill you with your own gun, but they should have to beat you to death with it because it is empty.

10. Always Have A Plan.

a. Always Have A Back-Up Plan, because in all probability the first plan won't work.

This 'Thunder Ranch Special' 1911 Government Model from Wilson's Gun Shop, Inc. is a special tribute to both Thunder Ranch and effective handgun defense. It offers the user everything that's needed in a fighting pistol.

11. Use cover or concealment as much as possible.

12. Flank your adversary whenever possible, but protect your own flanks.

13. Decide to be aggressive enough, quickly enough.

14. Watch Their Hands. Hands Kill. However, once the weapon appears, this issue has been decided. Now move to the next issue and watch their eyes because their eyes may telegraph their future movement.

15. The faster you finish the fight, the less chance you will have of getting shot.

16. Always perform a tactical reload whenever possible and scan for threats; left, right and to the rear.

17. Carry the same gun in the same place All The Time.

18. Your number one option for personal security is a lifelong commitment to Avoidance, Deterrence, and De-Escalation.

19. Be Polite. Be Professional. Be Courteous to Everyone. TRUST NO ONE.

20. In 10 years nobody will remember the details of caliber, stance or tactics. They will only remember who lived.

TRAIN HARD TO FIGHT EASY...

Luck has little to do with successful survival when the survivor employed a handgun they practiced with often. The handgun becomes even more effective when used during intensive training from acknowledged experts, used continuously in stress-induced situations like competitions and then carried on a daily basis. Many police academies teach their respective instructors that students can learn in one or more of three learning modes. In the first, some people can learn a technique involving hand and eye coordination simply by reading about it from a book. Another method of learning is by watching others perform the drill or maneuver. Lastly, some people can only learn a hand/eye skill by practicing it themselves under careful tutelage. Because of this human learning behavior any worthwhile training should involve elements of all three techniques to insure everyone in the class is able to fully absorb the lessons being taught.

The Latin motto, "Diligentia, Vis, Celeritas" was used to indicate the importance in a self-defense pistol of accuracy, power and speed. Accuracy was necessary to hit the target. Power was necessary to neutralize the target, and speed was necessary to survive the alleged threat. The 1911 Government Model was often used because it offered the best combination of features to accomplish this multifaceted task.

Preparation involves training and training can be found in many different forms. People train with fighting handguns not out of a paranoid conviction of impending doom, but because they have assumed responsibility for their own welfare and are unwilling to leave their personal safety and that of their families and loved ones to others. Some even train, and train hard, because they enjoy the sheer act of training as a pastime and value its physical activity. The harder they train, the more demanding their physical exertion.

Training under properly supervised conditions should always involve some degree of fatigue. Why? Because things always work well when you are well rested and alert. Experience has shown however that few things in life go wrong when you are fresh, or if they do, the solution is often found quickly or thought to be easy. Life is never easy. If it is, you aren't old enough to be reading this book!

Among the things in life that can go wrong is a violent armed criminal assault and it will probably occur when you are just flat dog tired, if not ill from an occasional flu bug or cold. Like the skilled athlete in many sports, if you have to consciously think about what your reactions should be, you will probably be too slow in your response to be effective for the counter measure. You have to react and you have to react immediately to be effective and when you are tired that's hard to do. The best way to overcome this difficulty is to involve some degree of fatigue in your training routine.

Fatigue can take the form of physical stress or exhaustion. If your instructor asks you to run 100 yards and then perform a simple series of drills before you catch your breath, you will begin to understand the difference between gross motor skills and fine motor skills. We know from research with gunfight survivors that fine motor skills deteriorate to the point of non-existence during high stress levels. You have to train to overcome these physical deficiencies.

Fatigue can take the form of mental exhaustion. If the instructor is asking you to do a number of different fine motor skill drills in rapid succession, the brain can become taxed and confused. Each individual has to learn how to suppress the mind-numbing exhaustion and carry through to a successful conclusion of the required task. Many experts refer to these drills, which often involve clearing malfunctions of nightmarish proportions, as learning how "…to run the gun." The more you know about how to run the gun and clear malfunctions, both for revolvers and semi-autos, the better your chances are of surviving the difficulty.

Always remember, you must train hard to fight easy and hard training involves both physical and mental fatigue.

THE SPRITUAL SIDE OF ARMED SELF-DEFENSE

Most often the decision to study and train with a defensive handgun is not a conclusion that is reached flippantly or lightly. I've known many people who sought spiritual guidance before coming to their personal conclusions about training with a fighting handgun and I honestly recommend such an approach to those who have questions both for themselves and their family members.

Some individuals, either through their religious faiths or their personal backgrounds, regard the possible loss of human life as indefensible, even if their own lives were seriously threatened, and if that is their true and honest beliefs, then so be it.

But, I have yet to meet a young mother who while saying she is very uncomfortable with the thought of shooting someone, would not, when questioned further, be willing to use a gun with no second thoughts whatsoever to defend the health, safety and lives of her children. For many who have doubts on this subject it is all a question of the proximity of harm. Many, who have never experienced life-threatening danger, find it hard to understand the degree of evil that can suddenly confront them. Others can understand, because they have seen the danger and for them this issue is a no-brainer.

Mercy is always in short supply in this world and seldom is it dispensed by those who would do anyone serious physical harm during the commission of a felony.

The reason why this topic is being discussed at all in a book centered on the fighting handgun is reliability is an absolute key factor in the design and operation of any fighting handgun. The most reliable, powerful and accurate pistol in the world will do its possessor little good if that person hesitates while questioning the moral implications of their own self-defense or that of others. This is especially true when the situation demands decisive action immediately for human survival. For a fighting pistol to be effective, it must be deployed quickly and that takes commitment. Those who seek spiritual guidance and have reached their personal conclusion on this subject have made more than a beginning step toward commitment.

But, like many things in adult life, commitment is not evidenced with a simple vow. It takes action and dedication. Training is a visual and mental characteristic of commitment.

For those seeking the best training available there are a large number of firearms training academies in the United States. They come in all sizes from one-man lectures to vast far-off estates employing legions of earnest instructors. Law Enforcement has always placed a heavy emphasis on firearms training with federal agencies creating state-of-the-art facilities like the FBI Training Academy in Quantico, Virginia, the Glynco Federal Training Center in Brunswick, Georgia, and the Secret Service Training Center in Beltsville, Maryland to name only a few. State and local police agencies in every part of the United States also have their equivalent facilities, often staffed with instructors who are graduates of at least one or more of the federal training schools.

Working with static targets creates a false sense of security. What happens when the targets charge toward you at high speed? The author discovered his reaction during this phase of his training at the 'Charger' range at Thunder Ranch during one of his courses of instruction.

For private individuals, there are literally hundreds of instructors and schools who do an extremely professional job of teaching the use of a defensive pistol. My favorite is Thunder Ranch, 96747 Highway 140 East, Lakeview, Oregon 97630. Thunder Ranch is run by Clint and Heidi Smith. This husband and wife team oversees one of the best small arms training academies available anywhere and it is because Clint has been doing it for more than three decades. There is little he hasn't seen or heard on the subject.

Clint Smith, a former Indiana Sheriff's deputy and Vietnam combat veteran, is straightforward and speaks with a clarity seldom seen in a firearms trainer. His lectures are peppered with humor and laced with a simple logic that upon reflection seems so profound you will wonder why you didn't think of it first. The staff of Thunder Ranch is dedicated to teaching the fundamentals of the fighting handgun, concealed or otherwise, and their instruction is top-notch.

HANDGUNS THAT WOULDN'T BE MY FIRST CHOICE FOR A FIGHTING HANDGUN, if you know what I mean...

Once the prospective handgun owner has made a commitment, the first step is research, then training, and eventually purchase an adequate handgun. For the purposes of explanation and definition, all firearms are capable of deadly force, but some can easily be described as a poor choice for defensive use.

Clint Smith is the Director of Thunder Ranch. He is seen here explaining how to load the revolver during a class oriented toward the defensive revolver shooter. Thunder Ranch is one of the finest firearms training facilities in the world.

I am a strong proponent that anyone learning to shoot a handgun should, at the very least, own one well made .22 rimfire handgun of some description. Sadly, any firearm chambered in .22 rimfire is also a poor choice for defensive use and the problem lies directly with its lack of power. The .22 rimfire calibers include the .22 Short, the .22 Long, and the .22 Long Rifle rounds. (The .22 Winchester Magnum Rimfire is also a rimfire .22 and some consider it as a marginally effective self-defense cartridge. In some platforms, it could be, but most often it is little more than a faster .22 rimfire cartridge. There will be more about this round in the chapter on calibers.)

The beginning self-defense shooter should own at least one .22 rimfire pistol. It should be one featuring controls close to those found on his self-defense pistol. This .22/45 Ruger Standard Auto would be a good .22 pistol for someone owning a 1911 Government Model for self-defense as the Ruger pistol mimics its controls while offering the same grip angle as the 1911 pistol.

Terry Murbach is seen here with another Ruger 22/45 .22 rimfire semi-auto pistol. A good .22 rimfire pistol allows the shooter to practice more often because the ammo is less expensive and thereby allows the range time necessary to improve their skills.

The .22 Long Rifle is without question the most popular chambering among all .22 rimfires and any handgun chambered for it offers the user low recoil, a relatively low noise level, and at a far lower cost than anything seen with a centerfire handgun. The bad news is these same attributes also are indicative of relatively low power levels. Few things in life come without strings attached.

Ideally, the .22 rimfire pistol should mimic or closely copy the operating controls of the user's self-defense pistol. Many experts feel this helps train the subconscious to learn a series of somewhat complicated fine motor skills without countermanding and confusing requirements for two or more different handgun or action types. For instance if your self-

A conversion kit manufactured by Jonathon Arthur Ciener allows the shooter to convert his .45 caliber 1911 pistol to .22 Long Rifle caliber. There are a number of advantages to this but the main one is it allows the shooter to shoot more for less money.

defense handgun preference should prove to be a single-action auto-loading pistol like the 1911A1 pistol or the Browning High Power, then it only makes sense to choose as your .22 rimfire pistol the Ruger Standard Auto in .22 Long Rifle as the controls for each are pretty much the same. Ruger even offers a polymer-gripped version that mimics the grip angle and magazine release of the Model 1911 which is called the Ruger 22/45 Standard Auto pistol. If you choose a Glock pistol as your self-defense pistol, then the recommendation would be to purchase a Ciener .22 Long Rifle conversion kit to supplement your centerfire training. Revolver shooters can easily find a .22 rimfire equivalent to their favorite defensive revolver as both Smith & Wesson and Ruger have made them for years. Colt used to, but they haven't produced their Diamondback revolvers in .22 rimfire for decades now.

The big thing to understand about .22 rimfire handguns is they are not meant to be used as a fighting handgun. Lacking a suitable alternative, however, they would work for defense. Mark Moritz so wisely identified in the First Rule of Gunfighting, you must have a gun of some kind and a .22 rimfire meets that requirement. The biggest advantage of a .22 rimfire handgun that matches the operating controls of your centerfire self-dense handgun is the ability to train informally and at relatively low cost (so you can practice more often) when compared to a centerfire pistol.

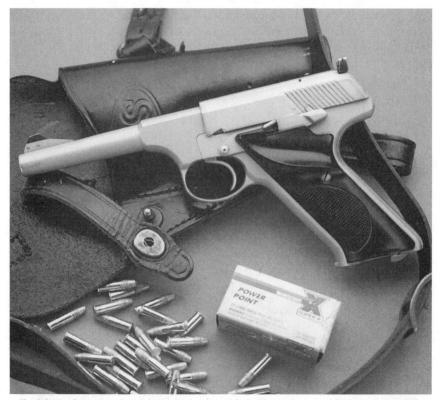

The Colt Woodsman is no longer in production from Colt, but it remains one of the best .22 Long Rifle semi-auto pistols ever produced. It is an excellent companion pistol for anyone selecting the 1911 Government Model or Browning High Power as a self-defense pistol because of its single-action design.

THE EXOTICS

There are a large number of exotic handguns available and for the life of me I have a hard time explaining why some of them exist. To the best of my knowledge there really is no such thing as an "assault pistol" in military small arms terminology.

However, as someone who enjoys and uses firearms on a daily basis I also resent the implication that guns commonly referred to as "assault pistols" by the media represent a viable threat. Not only are they ugly (perhaps their greatest attribute), but under test range scrutiny they accomplish little. In rifles, the .223 Remington chambering or the military equivalent 5.56x45mm is an excellent cartridge. When fired from a shorter pistol-length barrel, however, the exaggerated muzzle blast and flash from this rifle cartridge is good only for ridiculous Hollywood films and that, I believe, is the source of much of the media-induced hysteria surrounding these devices.

The best example of this would have to be the firearm carried by William Dafoe's character 'Clark' in the film *Clear And Present Danger*. The best way to describe this abortion is to say simply it is a pistol made from an AR-15, but if you look closely the gun has absolutely no sights (the Picatinny rail on top of the upper receiver does NOT qualify as a sighting system), obviously no stock and the whole contraption is cinched tight and close to his load-bearing harness. In the movies firearms always operate far more efficiently in the hands of celluloid heroes than they do in real life. The accuracy of the film villains is accordingly always less than what one would expect on any modern firing range.

There really is no such thing as an "Assault Pistol". At least not by commonly used military small arms definitions. The author feels pistols like this one which is based on an AR-15 style action often prove inaccurate and useless for self-defense purposes.

THE SINGLE-SHOT

Another group of exotic handguns that are excellent for their design purposes, but extremely poor choices for self-defense or fighting, are the centerfire single-shot pistols. The two most popular examples are the break-open Thompson Contender and the bolt-action Remington XP-100. Remington no longer offers the XP-100, but other manufacturers like Savage offer something very similar. In essence, they resemble cut-down rifles. All of these guns fill a niche almost perfectly.

That niche is hunting big game, in some cases dangerous big game. J.D. Jones of SSK Industries is a good friend and he has used Thompson Contenders chambered in calibers of his own design to hunt big game all across Africa, Australia, North and South America. These guns in many of his proprietary cartridges are capable of unbelievable accuracy and, astoundingly enough, unbelievable power.

J.D. relates he has stopped charging African elephants at a distance of 18 feet with a single shot from his .375 JDJ Thompson Contender. He's taken Cape Buffalo, hippos and a vast array of big game with Contender single-shot hunting pistols.

The first reaction among some would be that these acts are nothing more than stunts, but what these critics fail to realize is hunting with a big powerful handgun containing only one bullet is no different than hunting big game with archery equipment. It is a legitimate activity when performed by experts. Someone with the skill level and expertise of J.D. Jones enjoys the challenge of hunting with a single-shot firearm. The fact that the gun is also a handgun only makes the reward, both physical and emotional, when the reward is achieved that much sweeter.

Savage Arms Company builds the 'Striker' which is a bolt-action handgun for use by handgun hunters. This Savage handgun is accurate to longer ranges than most handguns, but it would be a poor choice for use in a self-defense situation.

THE SUPER HEAVY REVOLVERS

There are also some extremely heavy revolvers built for cartridges that are far more powerful than the brutish .44 Magnum. Until recently they were almost exclusively single-action revolvers, but that has now changed as both Smith & Wesson, Sturm, Ruger & Co. and Taurus are offering very large double-action revolvers in calibers like the .500 Magnum or the .480 Ruger. Even though these handguns feature double-action trigger mechanisms, they still are not defensive handguns, except possibly from the threat of a Tyrannosaurus Rex.

This big single-action revolver was formerly manufactured by Century Manufacturing. It is a powerful handgun because it is chambered the for .50-110 black powder cartridge.

Yes, a single-action revolver in .50-110 caliber does KICK!

The Ruger Redhawk in .480 Ruger caliber is definitely not built for concealed carry. It is powerful and the revolver is built to take abuse. It offers more power and penetration than most shooters will ever need or be able to use effectively.

The Freedom Arms .454 Casull is a single-action design and a masterpiece of construction and craftsmanship. It is also a member of the Super Heavy revolver class. It will provide any owner with a measure of self-protection when in the vicinity of big, dangerous game. Provided, of course, he is enough of an expert to handle the massive recoil and overcome the tendency to flinch terribly whenever one prepares to fire the beast. The same thing can be said for any of the revolvers chambering a Super Heavy caliber whether a single-action design or a double-action gun.

THE MACHINE PISTOLS

Another category of exotic handguns would be those seldom seen, except in security, military and police circles, and they are the true machine pistols. These pistols are most often used in executive protection and dignitary security. For sure there are relatively few of them in comparison to the vast numbers of conventional handguns. Their value as defensive weapons from the perspective of accuracy and liability is questionable.

Some clarifications are necessary. For some infinitely obscure reason the Germans refer to submachine guns as machine pistols, while the rest of the world defines submachine guns as carbine-like weapons firing pistol ammunition and they are often found with folding or retractable folding stocks. The machine pistol as defined by everyone, but the Germans, is most often a modification of an existing handgun designed to provide either fully automatic firing or select fire; i.e. the gun can be pre-selected to fire semi-automatically, or full-auto.

Full-auto machine pistols fill an extremely small void in the world of police and military small arms. Like their conventional predecessors, machine pistols are easy to conceal. Their main advantage supposedly lies in the fact they are capable of full-auto fire, but this technical feature brings with it distinct disadvantages.

The Soviet-produced Stetchkin is a select-fire machine pistol. It is a blowback design and chambered for the 9x18mm cartridge. Of course in full-auto fire the extended wire stock does little to increase control and most operators, unless the target is close, miss more than they hit. PHOTO CREDIT: M.O.D. PATTERN ROOM, UNITED KINGDOM

Walt Rauch works the Glock 18 in full-auto fire. Surprisingly, for a full-auto handgun, the Glock 18 is reasonably controllable and accurate at room distances, but targets at greater distances enjoy a larger margin of safety. PHOTO CREDIT: WALT RAUCH

The disadvantages are these guns are difficult to control and aim accurately. There are exceptions and the Glock 18, a select-fire variation of the Glock 17 semi-auto pistol, seems to be one specific exception. If the targets are kept at average room length distances, the Glock 18 is easy to control and reasonably accurate.

Another possible exception to full-auto control of a machine pistol would have to be the Czech Vz 61 Skorpion. This little full-auto wonder is so small the greatest difficulty with its control is due to its overall small size. The Vz 61 Skorpion fires the 7.62x17mm round, otherwise known in this country as the .32 ACP. It weighs approximately 2.8 pounds, unloaded and the overall length of the weapon with the folding stock extended is only 20.55 inches. The Skorpion is a true machine pistol and capable of select-fire. Two magazine capacities were available for the gun, either a 10-round magazine or one holding 20 rounds. The Skorpion has virtually no recoil so it is very easy to put and keep on target, assuming of course the small size of the gun and folding stock doesn't present difficulties in mounting the gun effectively. That was my biggest problem when I worked with one. It was so small I had a hard time acquiring a good cheek weld and sight picture. It was more akin to shooting a water hose than it was a firearm because it was smooth and accurate in full-auto fire. The only difference was instead of a stream of cold water I was shooting a short stream of hot small-caliber copper jacketed lead bullets at a variety of targets. During the 1970s and 1980s the Skorpion was used extensively by a number of European terrorist organizations, the reason being very self-evident.

The Steyr TMP or Tactical Machine Pistol was an attempt to revive the machine pistol concept. The TMP during its short life employed a rotating barrel as well as a polymer frame and magazine.

Another problem concerning all the true machine pistols is the inability to conceal these firearms. These pistols, as an almost universal rule fire full-auto at high rates of speed, and therefore they empty their magazines in the blink of an eye. This mandates large-capacity magazines. The larger magazine makes it more difficult to conceal the pistol, especially during dignitary protection details. Yes, the gun can be easily hidden in a briefcase or bag, but that sort of defeats the purpose of the silly thing in the first place.

The Beretta Model 93R is a true machine pistol, but it also features a folding stock to increase its hit potential. Unfortunately, it too is difficult to conceal when you load it with a 20-round magazine, compress the folding stock and then try to hide the whole affair under a tailored sport jacket.

The Heckler & Koch MP5K was formerly considered a machine pistol by many, including many non-German firearms commentators. But, innovations have moved the MP5K out of the category of machine pistol and into the classification of small and compact submachine gun with the addition of a folding shoulder stock.

The Beretta 93R was another attempt to create a practical select-fire machine pistol. The Beretta 93R offered semi-auto and three-round burst fire, but even with the muzzle ports seen here on the bottom pistol control was difficult. PHOTO CREDIT: J.M. RAMOS

The Beretta 93R could be equipped with a shoulder stock to increase control of the gun in burst-fire but all of the additional features added to increase control of the gun only added to its already large size. **PHOTO CREDIT: J.M. RAMOS**

The Heckler & Koch MP5K was formerly considered a difficult and awkward machine pistol, but the installation of a well designed folding stock turned this ugly duckling into something of a successful swan.

The Heckler & Kock MP5K-PDW is actually the former machine pistol with a few extras. A well designed folding stock has been added to the gun as well as a slightly longer barrel complete with muzzle threads for the installation of a sound suppressor. The end result is instead of a hard-to-handle machine pistol; the user now has a perfectly adequate submachine gun that is only slightly larger than its former self.

Few select-fire versions of the CZ-75 were made, but this machine pistol used the frame-mounted safety lever as a selector and the forward-mounted vertical grip was actually a spare magazine.

The American division of HK GmbH designed and built a folding stock, as well as a corresponding shoulder holster which also carries two spare 30-round magazines on the 'off' side. Using this combination of gun and holster a protection detail specialist can easily conceal the weapon and yet bring it into play almost as quickly as one would a normal pistol. The addition of the stock to this machine pistol turns it from a machine pistol with a questionable application into a truly practical, yet concealable submachine gun.

Other entries in the machine pistol classification include the select-fire CZ-75. This is a modification of the renowned CZ-75, which will be examined later, and this example carries a spare magazine that can be employed as a front handgrip.

All of these firearms are designed for use in a gunfight. They are NOT target arms, nor would they fill any normal or conventional sporting purpose. Yet, they are not common fighting pistols because they are so seldom found in society and all of them are prohibited to the average citizen by a multitude of laws condemning the possession of machine guns or shoulder-stocked handguns.

THE RACE GUNS

The last group of exotic handguns is by and large the most controversial. These are the "IPSC race guns". IPSC stands for International Practical Shooting Confederation, and member clubs can be found worldwide.

Back in 1976 men who wanted to further the study of the defensive pistol gathered in Columbia, Missouri to undergo training from Jeff Cooper at a special seminar. Cooper is often considered the father of "The Modern Technique of the Pistol" and after the training sessions these self-defense pioneers created an organization for the development of self-defense training and tactics.

The author found the Steyr TMP to be a controllable full-auto weapon, but felt the nylon shoulder strap was a poor substitute for a well made folding stock. **PHOTO CREDIT: CHRIS POLLACK**

One of the early problems was the proper nomenclature for their new group. They were all "combat" shooters, but the term "combat" was deemed too offensive and reprehensible for the general populace and the news media, so the term "practical" was adopted. Years later, many of these same attendees would admit this was their first major mistake.

It was a term that would come to haunt the organization, but in the years immediately following it's founding, IPSC-style shooting grew by leaps and bounds. The reasons were simple. IPSC style shooting was conducted under a strict safety discipline; while at the same time offering everyone interested a chance to study and practice effective armed self-defense under supervised guidelines.

Somewhere along the line, however, the train got sidetracked by those wanting to make this discipline a recognized 'sport'.

An activity that started out with nothing more than a simple .45 pistol or .38 caliber revolver, a holster, and a couple of reloads, soon featured professional shooters wearing pastel uniforms with a plethora of advertised sponsors. In appearance, they more resembled auto racing drivers than shooters. Soon, they were using guns that addressed only one goal – winning a contest that reflected an artificial environment. It didn't happen overnight, but like all things spoiled, it came in small increments.

Eventually the 'race gun' evolved from this artificial environment and it is characterized by a muzzle compensator and a red dot sight. The 1994 ban on 'ammunition feeding devices of greater than 10-round capacity' had little effect on the race gun designers and builders as the demand remained high by the competitors for high-capacity guns due to the nature of most IPSC competition course design stages which sometimes required as many as 32 rounds to complete a single stage.

The IPSC "Race Gun" was the end result when self-defense combat shooting was trivialized into becoming a "sport." The IPSC race gun is a triumph of technology, but it wins contests only because it represents an artificial environment and not reality.

If the 'race gun' satisfied a real world need then much of this criticism would be muted, but law enforcement has no need for these contraptions because they already have something far more efficient – select-fire submachine guns and assault rifles. However, IPSC competition has raised the bar on what competitors can accomplish when given the most up-to-date technology available. There is little question the skill level of the competitors using these devices is extraordinary. Their performances at a national level

Jerry "The Burner" Barnhart has been the National IPSC Champion several times over and this is one of the guns he has used in pursuit of those championships. Granted, he is an extremely skilled and talented athlete/shooter, but how would you conceal this thing?

To prove the worldwide popularity of IPSC shooting, examine this 'target' pistol from Beretta. It was built for the European IPSC market and features a muzzle compensator, an enlarged magazine release and a number of other extras.

competition are simply surreal. These highly developed devices enable the competitors to achieve many good things in terms of increased skill level and target proficiency. Some of this technology has paid dividends for our military forces as most every soldier in Iraq or Afghanistan is using a service rifle or carbine equipped with a red dot sight. The addition of this new sighting device can be directly traced to IPSC style competition and the companies that supported it early on as they developed a product to succeed in this field of competition.

In 1996 in an attempt to rectify some of the perceived wrongs that had taken place with IPSC, Bill Wilson and a number of knowledgeable shooters formerly associated with the American division of IPSC got together at Marietta, Ohio to create the International Defensive Pistol Association or IDPA. The inaugural match of the IDPA was held the following spring at Columbia, Missouri. A number of changes were initiated to create this new 'action' oriented shooting venue and chief among was a prohibition on red dot aiming devices, compensators and any magazine holding more than 10 rounds. Unlike IPSC competition, IDPA competition is geared toward every day 'street' guns and they are classified in four separate divisions.

The four divisions of IDPA are as follows; Custom Defensive Pistol is defined as a 1911-type pistol in .45 ACP caliber, Standard Service Pistol includes many of the popular 9mm and .40 caliber service pistols like the Beretta Model 92, many of the Glock pistols, the Sig P226, P228, P229 and the P239 and the Springfield Armory XD series pistols. Enhanced Service Pistol is the class for the 1911 style handgun in calibers other than .45 like the 10mm Auto, the .38 Super or the 9x23mm as well as handguns like the Browning

Bill Wilson is one of those who complained about the direction IPSC was being driven and then he put his own money where his mouth was. He financed the creation and development of a new organization called IDPA or the International Defensive Pistol Association. He is seen here at the IDPA National Championship in 1998.

Noted firearms trainer and writer Ken Hackathorn is seen here explaining many of the reasons why he and others joined Bill Wilson in creating the new IDPA organization. It brought real guns and holsters back into the realm of competition.

High Power, or the CZ-75 when used in the 'cocked and locked' single-action mode of operation. All revolvers compete in Standard Service Revolver and may NOT have a barrel length greater than 4 inches.

To explain the ins and outs of IDPA competition would take a book as large as or larger than this one. Suffice it to say, there are problems with some of the IDPA rules – the 4-inch revolver limitation being the most obvious, but that's my personal opinion, as is the classification of a 10mm Auto 1911 pistol in Enhanced Service Pistol as being equally misguided.

Even with the deficiencies though, IDPA represents a return to 'real world' handguns instead of guns built specifically to satisfy an artificial requirement. IDPA emphasizes the competitor's use of cover and limits the firing stages to 18 rounds and relatively short engagement distances between the shooter and the target. There will certainly be many readers who enjoy IPSC competition who may take issue with this analysis, but the truth is IDPA has proven far more popular than its organizers ever envisioned in the beginning.

The trend in both IPSC and IDPA currently is moving back toward more real world handguns – handguns that can be used effectively, efficiently, and yet are reliable with the minimum of care. In short, good candidates for effective handgun defense.

CHAPTER THREE

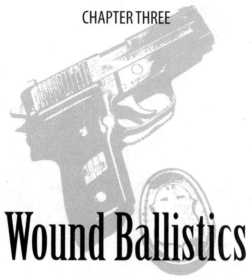

Wound Ballistics

"Bullets *crush* the tissue they strike and *stretch* the tissue around the projectile path."

This straightforward explanation of wound ballistics comes from Dr. Martin L. Fackler's introduction to the second edition of *Gunshot Injuries* by Colonel Louis A. La Garde and it explains how all small arms bullets work in living tissue.

To many, controversy enters the discussion when the effects of bullet velocity and the resulting temporary cavity, a direct result of tissue stretch, are analyzed and evaluated.

Some commentators believe the kinetic energy of pistol bullets is a valid means for gauging the effectiveness of handgun bullets. Kinetic energy is calculated with a formula that multiplies the mass of the bullet (weight in grains) times the squared velocity (in feet per second) and divided by a constant to get the result in foot-pounds of energy. The kinetic energy groupies argue that increasing kinetic energy increases "stopping power". Handgun projectiles are invariably slow when compared to the velocity of almost any centerfire rifle and carbine. Because the velocity of most rifle projectiles is exponentially higher than the average handgun-launched bullet, the increased size of the temporary cavity of the resulting wound has a marked influence on the effectiveness of the rifle-inflicted injury. However, due to their far lower velocity, handgun rounds leave a far smaller temporary cavity and therefore the temporary cavity is far less effective.

Various means have been developed to increase the effectiveness of handgun caliber projectiles, including making the bullets lighter to increase the velocity. Countless varieties of hollowpoint and frangible bullet designs have been tested. Many of these expanding jacketed hollowpoint bullet designs have proven successful because of the forced attention by the ammunition manufacturers.

Fackler, former Director of the Wound Ballistics Laboratory at the Letterman Army Institute of Research, became controversial by arguing against many of the popular and ill advised small arms wound ballistic theories promoted during the early to mid-1980s. The most condemned concept was a "computer man" which devised a Relative Incapacitation Index (RII). This theoretical solution to handgun stopping power was promoted by the National Institute of Justice. It was based on the theory of "kinetic energy deposit." Simply put it argued a handgun projectile with high kinetic energy, which dumped all its energy into the human target would be more successful than ammunition that relied on traditional performance factors like bore diameter, bullet weight and deep penetration for stopping dangerous felons.

Most of these theories centered around building ammunition with lighter bullets and expanding jacketed hollowpoints designed to work at the highest possible chamber pressures for medium bore handguns. Those who endorsed this theory for the mid-bore handgun calibers became known as the "Light and Fast" advocates. They recommended 9mm pistols or .38 caliber revolvers loaded with ammunition launching 115-grain or similar weight hollowpoint ammunition at the highest possible velocity. Many shooters have a natural tendency to accept the light and fast argument because lighter bullets recoil less and therefore are easier to shoot.

Those who held these viewpoints in disdain were known as the "Slow and Heavy" advocates. They argued in favor of heavier bullets for the medium bore diameter calibers as well as a flat recommendation for the traditional big calibers like the .45 ACP or the aged .45 Colt cartridge. These advocates wanted the biggest bore diameter possible firing the heaviest permitted bullet, but because punishing recoil is an immediate result when heavy bullets are launched at high speed, velocities are often kept low.

In a seldom seen lighter moment there are those who feel too much concern is paid to the difficulty of heavy recoil from heavy loads in handguns. During a dinner at

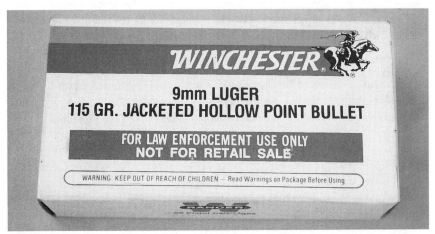

At one point in the past decade there was a strong argument over which was better in a mid-bore caliber; 'light & fast' as seen here with this law enforcement only 115-grain JHP load from Winchester or 'slow & heavy' usually found in a .45 ACP format. Noted gunwriter John Taffin once asked the author, "What's WRONG with big, heavy and FAST?"

One of the problems facing law enforcement over the years has been the non-performance of some mid-bore calibers. The answer according to some commentators can be found in the .40 and .45 caliber pistols like this HK USP pistol. PHOTO CREDIT: HK INC. USA

the Shooting Hunting and Outdoor Trade (SHOT) Show including industry writers and law enforcement trainers of forgotten vintage, I was seated next to writer John Taffin. The self-same argument broke out over the subject of light and fast versus slow and heavy. The sides were drawn almost immediately around the table as each expert put forth his own personal arguments pro or con on the subject at hand. The atmosphere grew tense as the verbal volume increased. Taffin turned to me with bewilderment in his eyes and with a question mark printed clearly in the center of his face as he leaned over and asked, "What's wrong with big, heavy and fast!?"

The pivotal event actually happened two decades ago in Miami, Florida with the tragic FBI shoot-out on April 11th, 1986. Without going into great detail, eight FBI agents engaged two heavily armed bank and armored car robbers in a hastily planned felony car stop. The result was a fight that ended with the deaths of two FBI Special Agents, two dead felons, and five out of the six surviving Special Agents seriously wounded. There is little question heroism and courage on the part of all the Special Agents saved the day and prevented the escape of these dangerous felons, but the cost was high.

The FBI SWAT Special Agent seen here is equipped with a HK MP5 submachine in 9x19mm caliber and a Smith & Wesson Model 1076 pistol in 10mm auto which is worn in a SAS-style leg holster. Since this photo was taken most of the FBI SWAT teams have been equipped with custom-grade 1911 pistols from Springfield Armory.

Too high a cost in the opinion of many and close examination of wound ballistics became the topic of the day for years and decades afterward. It is a fact that early in the gunfight two of the Special Agents struck the criminal who did the killing with what were non-survivable mortal wounds. Yet, he was still able to continue his assault on the surrounding agents, kill two and wound five of the six remaining Special Agents.

Many feel this sad event surpasses the stature and legend of the Gunfight at the OK Corral. The Dade County/Miami gunfight remains more meaningful today because it involved modern handguns and ammunition, and more shots were fired – at least 140 rounds fired at Miami versus 30 odd rounds at Tombstone. This modern day gunfight achieved immortal status because it brought into focus the issues of terminal ballistics, tactics and mindset.

This painting on the wall of a FBI training facility in New Jersey sums up the attitude of most firearms and tactical small arms law enforcement trainers everywhere. This motivation pursues the best equipment and training necessary to get the job done.

Early in the encounter, Special Agent Ron Risner opened fire and struck the prime perpetrator, Michael Platt, with a shot to the gun arm from his Smith & Wesson 9mm pistol. Risner's round fired from a distance of 42 yards severed a vital artery. Special Agent Gerry Dove, only two vehicle widths away, also struck Platt a mortal wound as Platt exited his vehicle through the front seat passenger window. After Agent Dove's bullet coursed through Platt's right arm, it entered the region of the right armpit, mushrooming as it cut a vital artery and destroyed Platt's right lung. The bullet stopped just short of the heart and Platt continued on using a Ruger Mini-14 semi-automatic .223 Rem caliber carbine to murder both Special Agent Gerry Dove and Special Agent Ben Grogan. He seriously wounded Special Agent John Hanlon, Supervisory Agent Gordon McNeill, Special Agent Edmundo Mireles, Special Agent Dick Manauzzi, and Special Agent Gil Arrantia in the ensuing gun battle.

The problem with Dove's 9mm bullet was it didn't stop Platt in his tracks. It was well placed. No one could fault Special Agent Dove's marksmanship. The bullet eventually killed Platt, but it didn't stop him SOON enough. In the time it took Platt to die (published reports estimate he had only a few minutes to live from the moment of impact on), Platt

The FBI training facility at Quantico, Virginia places a great emphasis on thorough firearms training. Here a new agent in training engages two targets, partially obscured by a no-shoot target, from behind the protective cover of the front of a vehicle.

Training to use cover is an essential part of self-defense. Students at an executive protection course run by the Heckler & Koch International Training Div. are taught how to engage multiple targets from the cover of an automobile.

fired multiple magazines of high-velocity rifle fire at the agents, flanked Dove, Grogan and Hanlon, and shot all three with fusillades of semi-auto .223 rifle fire.

It was a tragic day for American law enforcement and discussion and analysis of this event became the subject of study for those interested in effective handgun defense for decades afterward. Extreme attention was focused on bullet placement, the ammunition and the caliber of handguns used.

Experts like Dr. Fackler pointed out the primary failure of the specific round in question was its failure to penetrate to the vital organs. Dove's well-placed round failed to reach the Platt's heart.

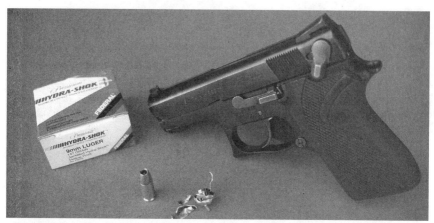

For a long time after the FBI's Dade County Shoot-Out many believed the 147-grain JHP bullet in 9x19mm caliber was the answer to their problems. This created a great demand for the 147-grain Hydra-Shok like that shown here. The Hydra-Shok bullet employed a lead 'post' in the center of its hollow cavity and this was supposed to help projectile expansion. Many discovered the post would bend as seen on the expended round in this photo and sometimes break completely off the base slug.

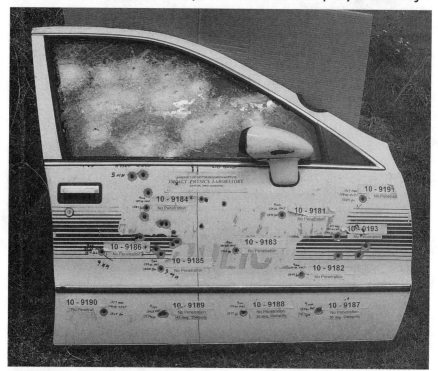

As the threat to law enforcement officers increases, some firms have developed new technology for their protection. This automobile door reinforced with Kevlar panels and bullet-resistant glass shows the result of testing with a variety of rounds and weapons often used on the street against police officers and their vehicles.

The original contract between the FBI and Smith & Wesson called for the Bureau to accept 10,000 Model 1076 pistols, but problems developed and the Bureau accepted just over 2,400 pistols before the contract was cancelled. The S&W 1076 pistol was too large for small-statured Special Agents and difficult to conceal.

The 10mm auto round has received a great deal of criticism because of the problems experienced by the FBI, but the author is one who prefers the 10mm auto cartridge for its flat trajectory and solid performance on hard-to-kill vermin. He feels it is a good round and deserves a better fate.

Granted, the discussion is centered on the difference in results that can only be counted in seconds or fractions of a second. Those seconds cost the lives of two courageous lawmen. Everyone agreed a better alternative had to be found.

The FBI went to great lengths to find a better cartridge and handgun. After much study, the Bureau selected the Smith & Wesson Model 1076 in 10mm Auto, but here a series of misadventures doomed the final result. The Federal Cartridge Company in Anoka, Minnesota initially loaded the 10mm Auto round selected by the FBI. It launched a 180-grain Sierra hollowpoint projectile at a nominal velocity of 980 feet per second (fps). This was well below the power level of the introductory 10mm Auto cartridge as loaded by NORMA. Some wags immediately christened the new FBI round the "10mm Lite" in the same fashion one characterizes low calorie beer as "Lite beer".

Whether the threat is facing executive protection specialists or the plain clothes police officer, vehicle-mounted personnel must be able to react to lethal force threats immediately and effectively. The Smith & Wesson Model 4006 in .40 S&W caliber, seen here, was first adopted by the California Highway Patrol.

Problems soon developed with the delivered Smith & Wesson auto pistols because the specification called for a trigger mechanism to fit the FBI's training protocol where the agents-in-training were taught to "prep" or stage the trigger during presentation. The Bureau was soon embroiled in controversy and accusations between it and the manufacturer (S&W) were flying as freely as bullets as the Miami shoot-out. The eventual result was the FBI wound up accepting just over 2,400 of the S&W Model 1076 10mm pistols on a contract that originally called for 10,000 pistols. At the same time the Bureau went to the Sig Model 228 and a 147-grain 9mm Federal Hydra-Shok round that featured deeper penetration.

Complicating the entire scenario during this time frame was the introduction of the .40 S&W cartridge that more or less duplicated the ballistics of the 10mm Lite round, but did so in a cartridge that could easily be chambered in pistols formerly made for the 9x19mm round. The .40 S&W round, in turn, set records for acceptance by American law enforcement agencies. In fact, the Bureau itself would eventually adopt the .40 S&W round as well as the Glock pistol for its Special Agents.

There are a number of factors at play here that more or less work against each other. One of them is the sheer physical size of the gun. The problems experienced by the FBI in the late 1980s and early 1990s in coming to grips with a better performing gun and cartridge are the same ones faced by concealed carry civilians and plain clothes law enforcement officers around the world today. Recognized powerful handgun cartridges all too often require large pistols that are heavy and difficult to conceal for small people. This last aspect is where the S&W Model 1076 failed according to the FBI Special Agents I've questioned on this subject. It was simply too large for the average female Special Agent to carry easily and conceal effectively with their normal daily office business attire.

FBI Special Agents voiced approval of the round's performance in the shootings they had witnessed or seen the official reports. Instances were related where the 10mm Auto succeeded when fire from a select-fire, but 9mm MP5 submachine gun was defeated by the thin sheet metal of a modern automobile trunk. The bad guy in this instance was neutralized because of the 10mm Auto's ability to penetrate, reach him and deliver the goods, so to speak. All of which brings us to the following question.

How do you cram sufficient power to stop a dedicated bad guy into a pistol small enough for the average adult to conceal and carry all day?

The problem is achieving a good balance between sufficient penetration of the projectile and an adequate expansion without having to resort to extremely large, hard to conceal handguns. Every expert in terminal ballistics works with gelatin because up to now it is the best media available for human tissue simulation. However, there is a problem, and that is gelatin does not have arteries or veins. This may seem like nit-picking to some, but the truth is a bullet or a piece of shrapnel to the femoral artery is so fatal, those wounded will often bleed out while they are still standing.

Added to gelatin's shortcoming, is the fact that rural law enforcement agencies often have to euthanize wild animals after collisions with motor vehicles. In our county and many of the counties surrounding my area the officers armed with 9mm pistols have discovered the 147-grain Hydra-Shok (the same load used initially by the FBI) doesn't do a very good job of putting a suffering deer out of its misery. Many have noted there is little difference

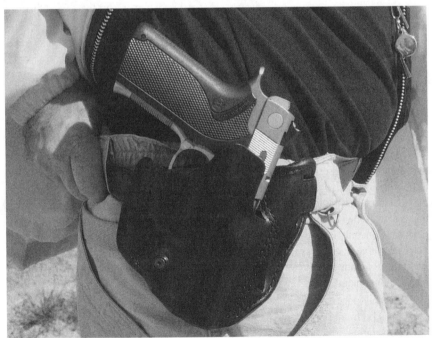

Even with all the controversy that has surrounded the FBI 10mm auto Model 1076, this veteran Special Agent was glad to be carrying his 10mm pistol along with four spare magazines. He never mentioned the extra weight of the magazines or the larger size of the pistol being a problem.

The FBI suffered a great deal of criticism for its selection of the 10mm auto cartridge, but those within the agency who had occasion to use it were pleased with the results.

between the 147-grain hollowpoint and the standard military ball round which has a horrible reputation for stopping bad guys. Some of these deputies have taken to carrying their old .357 Magnum service revolvers solely for this task or at least that's what they tell the Chief Deputy to justify the presence of a handgun they trust in the patrol car.

I've heard many criticize this method of evaluation, but I have to say I believe it is a valid, if non-scientific, comparison. A friend and retired police officer in Pennsylvania, John Lysak, used it for years to evaluate various duty loads for his department. He came to the opinion that any 9mm "+P" or "+P+" load, regardless of bullet weight, worked far better at dispatching injured deer than the standard pressure alternative.

All of this information needs to be discussed before you load your concealed carry self-defense handgun because you need to load it with the best ammunition for your particular lifestyle and situation. Understand this; except for the military and a few areas that outlaw the possession of jacketed hollowpoint ammunition, you should purchase top-of-the-line hollowpoint expanding ammo from any of the reputable ammunition manufacturers. Use the full-metal-jacket ammo only for practice but choose something that is similar in velocity and bullet weight to the round you've selected for your own self-defense. Concentrate on your practice ammo and spend more there than on your 'self-defense' ammo because practice and skill development is, to my mind at least, far more important than any dissertation on terminal ballistics from the 'light and fast' or 'slow and heavy' jelly junkies.

The only personal anecdotes I have to offer the reader at this point are all related to animals both wild and domestic. My background includes a youth spent entirely on a livestock farm and a number of years as a professional trapper. For the past 30 years I have been a farmer and had a number of part-time employments that may have added to my professional resume, but accomplished little in terms of my personal health, welfare and financial wealth.

Every expert in terminal ballistics works with gelatin because it is the best medium available for human tissue simulation. However, it is not perfect because gelatin does not have arteries or veins.

Before the FBI transitioned to the .40 caliber Glock pistol, the issue pistol was the Sig P-228 and the duty round was the 147-grain Federal Hydra-Shok round.

In my opinion, the difference between 'wild' and 'domestic' in the animal world is a "Factor of Four". The 'wild' animal can demonstrate four times the strength exhibited by the same size 'domesticated' animal. What I'm talking about here is the amount of force needed to control and contain either of the two when they are confronted and the amount of force necessary to overcome them when they fight any attempt to confine them.

There is a distinct difference between your basic domestic farm animal and the close relative who remains in the wild and that difference is the amount of "Fight" (for lack of a better word) in them when they are frightened. I realize the following is a subjective evaluation, but my experience has shown that a typical 24-pound teed-off coyote puts out about the same amount of physical resistance in terms of damage to chains, traps, snares and other capture methods as a 96-pound domestic dog. I've also seen what I felt was the same ratio and effect when dealing with errant cattle that have literally gone back to the wild.

Is it any wonder then that certain human beings can demonstrate physical strength and endurance beyond anything associated with someone their size? I believe that human beings, under certain circumstances due to either to mental instability such as delusions, or the influence of drugs or alcohol, or simply a warped sense of reality can also return to the 'wild' state of pre-historic human existence.

With that hypothesis as a preamble, I've come to the following conclusions. If you have to shoot, make sure your first shot is really good. I don't care how many you have left in the gun and how big they are, the remaining sum total won't equal the effect you achieved with the first one if your marksmanship is anywhere close to true and your caliber selection is halfway decent.

Secondly, no matter how much you research this subject and how much you work on your marksmanship there are going to be instances where everything you do in terms of body shots will fail. Your only recourse will be to 'brain' them which in a fight or a really fluid shooting situation is almost impossible to achieve.

During the 1980s and early 1990s most law enforcement departments converted from the traditional double-action six-shot revolver to high-capacity auto-loaders. Indiana Deputy Sheriff Larry Vollmer, a longtime revolver shooter, contemplates his future.

As an example let me relate a personal experience that doesn't involve bad guys or even handgun defense. I have been called upon over the years to put down wayward beef steers. Now on the face of it a beef steer is fairly innocent animal. They don't have fangs, or claws and most today don't even have horns. Even tiny teenage farm girls show them all the time at county fairs, so they must be fairly reasonable animals. This is all true, but all of the ones I've been involved with were described in every instance by the owners and the lawmen contacting me as "crazy". An animal weighing over 1,000 pounds and described as "crazy" is certainly a threat, especially if it's a black angus, it likes to stand in the middle of a blacktop road at midnight on a moon-less night and you are driving the smallest Saturn sedan General Motors manufactures.

When these ingredients meet it is a mess. Many cars today are low to the ground and a standing beef steer will almost clear the nameplate on the front of the vehicle. Upon impact the bumper takes the steer's legs out from under him and his belly clears the hood only to have everything, all 1,000 plus pounds of beefsteak, hamburger and that brown stinky stuff, land in the driver's and passengers lap. The result is there are never any front seat survivors and often there are no backseat survivors. These bovine runaways are looked upon with disapproval by just about everyone but the civil injury lawyers.

The author used this Smith & Wesson Model 657 revolver with a 5-inch barrel in .41 Magnum to drop this buck on a dead run at a distance of 70 yards with one shot. The load was Federal's 210-grain JHP and it worked quite well.

The last two I shot were killed while I was flying by in a helicopter and the gun I was using was the same gun I've used on all of them, a Remington Model 700 in 7mm Rem. Magnum caliber. I've used the 175-grain Nosler Partition bullets in the past, but on the last two the rifle was loaded with 175-grain Speer Nitrex cartridges employing the Speer Grand Slam bullet.

Now I want to state emphatically when it comes to shooting wayward 'crazy' beef steers weighing 1,000 or 1,200 pounds or more, the 7mm Rem. Magnum ain't enuff gun!

Maybe it's because I'm always the last resort. The livestock operator has already tried the cowboys, the horses and the ATVs. They don't call me until these animals are so worked up and have been run so hard that the mere sound of a pickup truck makes them gallop through the standing corn to disappear forever during the daylight hours only to reappear as a ghostly apparition in someone's windshield.

I've used this rifle because it's the same one I employed to down a bull elk in Colorado at 13,000 feet elevation with a single heart/lung shot at a distance of 275 yards. I initially found it hard to believe a domestic farm animal could do a wonderful imitation of a high velocity lead sponge, but the first two did.

The author on a pig hunting trip to Tennessee took this wild boar with a Smith & Wesson Performance Center Model 657 revolver. It was loaded with Remington 210-grain JSP loads and it took more than one round to anchor the pig. There are no guarantees in handgun ballistics.

This FBI SWAT team prepares to practice a high-risk building entry. The sniper in the foreground covers the men lined-up for the dynamic entry.

In each case, after the 'two to the body' thing (heart/lung area) produced no results, I preceded to the 'one to the head' phase to finish the task and that worked. In plain language I 'brained' them and in the case of a beef steer you are talking about hitting an object just slightly larger than a softball located behind a plate of thick bone (the horn boss). That's why I like heavy bullets in the 7mm Magnum. It's also why now instead of getting a bigger gun like something on the order of a rifle built for dangerous game in Africa, I just skipped the first part and proceed directly to the head shot.

Which brings up my closing point, no matter how good you are, no matter how much you research your ammo, when crunch time comes most everything you know may prove to be fallacy, or at the very least the exception to the million-to-one rule and you just happen to be the 'one'.

I personally have never experienced all that much success with handgun ammunition that had a velocity below 1,000 fps when my marksmanship was up to par. There are exceptions and the best example I can give is a .45 ACP handload that employed a .45 Colt cast semiwadcutter bullet weighing 255 grains. It was cast with very sharp edges on the front of the bullet (a key point I believe) and loaded to almost 800 fps in my Colt 1911 Government Model. I stopped loading this load years ago because it was extremely hard on the gun, but it was effective on feral dogs and bigger animals. Would I use it in a gunfight? Yes, but the truth is most any of the modern high-tech hollowpoints from any of the reputable manufacturers are far better than anything I can handload in terms of terminal effectiveness.

No one can always carry a powerful gun for the reasons previously discussed and the marginal guns will seldom work as needed. The point you must remember is "Have A Plan", then "Have A Back-Up Plan" because in all likelihood the first one won't work. My back-up plan even in a flying helicopter was to shoot 'em in the brain and it worked because I was aware of it before I started.

That is my 'take' on wound ballistics and what bullet you should use for self-defense.

CHAPTER FOUR

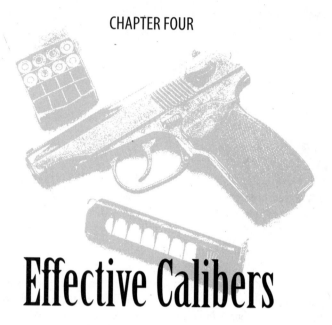

Effective Calibers

here are a multitude of cartridges and calibers that I've ignored in this chapter and the reasons are many, space considerations not being the least of them. I picked the following calibers for a simple reason. They are the ones most likely to be used in a modern gunfight involving handguns.

Gunfights, however, don't always involve handguns; the Miami Shoot-out for example and this brings out a key point. Rifles are more powerful in most any form, and they make more sense. Unfortunately, they frequently are NOT available when trouble starts and herein lays the advantage of the concealed carry fighting handgun when it comes to effective defense.

The choice of caliber therefore becomes critical in determining effectiveness and this involves more than penetration and foot-pounds of delivered energy. The paramount focus remains on the handgun's reliability and proper bullet placement by the operator. The gun regardless of caliber must work. When the gun does work, the shooter must be able to deliver the shot to the exact spot necessary to STOP the felon's actions as quickly as possible.

It is because of recoil that many small calibers have proven popular in the handguns sold and used for self-defense. Yes, they often kill, but killing, per se, is not the objective. *Stopping* the felon is the objective, and small calibers have proven to be poor stoppers.

What follows is my analysis of the more popular handgun cartridges presently available:

The Walther TPH was manufactured in Germany for 30 years and under license in the United States for 13 years. It was an extremely small pistol and although it was chambered in a .22 rimfire caliber it was often used as a deep-concealment pistol for self-defense.

Twenty-two rimfire ammunition comes in many different shapes and sizes; (from left to right) first round is a standard-velocity .22 Short, the next is a standard-velocity .22 Long, then a high-velocity .22 Short, followed by a high-velocity .22 Long, to the right of that is a standard-velocity .22 Long Rifle, then a high-velocity .22 Long Rifle hollowpoint, and the last on the right is a .22 Winchester Rimfire Magnum hollowpoint round.

The Colt Ace made before World War II was an attempt to create a .22 rimfire auto pistol with the same heft and control functions as the larger and more serious 1911 pistol in .38 Super or .45 Auto. This rare specimen is seen here in its original box along with three spare magazines. PHOTO CREDIT: WALT RAUCH

.22 Long rifle. The .22 Long Rifle round and its smaller brothers; the .22 Short and .22 Long, are the perfect cartridges for learning how to shoot a handgun. In fact, they are essential for good training, but they are terrible choices for self-defense. Having said that, firearms chambered in these calibers have probably been involved in more shootings than all the other calibers combined. The reason is simple – they're relatively inexpensive, widely available and easy to shoot moderately well. Everyone wanting to learn how to shoot a handgun should also own and practice often with a rimfire pistol, preferably one configured close to or exactly like their primary pistol. Never rely on a .22 rimfire to save your bacon in a deadly force encounter.

.22 Winchester Magnum Rimfire. I have used both Colt and Ruger rimfire revolvers with interchangeable cylinders in .22 Mag and .22 Long Rifle on a professional trap line. The cartridge works well in terms of penetration, but it is NOT a defensive cartridge, and the ammunition is too expensive for training use. This round is recommended only as a sporting cartridge with limited applications.

.25 ACP or 6.35mm Browning (6.35x15.8mm). Probably the most widely used cartridge for the untrained and non-knowledgeable person seeking a self-defense pistol. This round serves one class of self-defense shooter well, that is the person who can't afford anything better or more effective. This round is often found in lower cost guns marketed toward those on the lower rungs of our socio-economic ladder. It is an extremely inadequate choice for self-protection even when chambered in premium grade pistols like the Walther TPH or the Baby Browning. This round lacks penetration, projectile

Historically, the .25 Auto has received little respect as a self-defense cartridge, but then as Walt Rauch explains few gunshot victims have stated, "Well, he ONLY shot me with a .25!"

expansion or even velocity. It has nothing to offer except it is found in cheap, low cost pistols that only the poor can afford. I happen to believe, however, the poor should have the same rights to self-protection the rich enjoy and therefore I understand when this round is chosen out of necessity. When a .25 Auto is all you can afford it's better than the alternative, which is nothing. My friend Walt Rauch says he has never met a gunshot victim who said afterward, "Yeah, he ONLY shot me with a .25!"

.32 ACP or 7.65 Browning (7.8x17.5mm). There are some extremely small and well-designed self-defense pistols made for this older auto-pistol round. This includes the Beretta Tomcat, the Seecamp, the North American Arms Guardian and the Kel-Tec P-32. After the development of good expanding jacketed hollowpoint ammunition like Winchester's Silvertip, Federal's Hydra-Shok and Speer's Gold Dot in .32 ACP, this round has enjoyed renewed interest from the self-defense sector. Deep concealment, small pocket pistols like those mentioned are found on professionals either as back-up pistols or as the primary self-defense pistol in those instances where their attire must be minimal due to their surroundings; i.e. beaches and swimming pools, Performance, unfortunately, is as minimal as a string bikini, even with the better ammunition. However, the first rule of a gunfight is "Have A Gun" and because of their size the small .32s are there when others won't be found.

.30 Mauser and/or 7.62x25mm. This is the original "light and fast" round, even if the 'light and fast' proponents don't acknowledge it. The reason is it doesn't stop enraged felons all that well. The Russians designed a number of submachine guns around it during World War II. This round killed more Nazi bad guys than anyone else, but they hit 'em with swarms of these light bullets in full-auto fire fed by countless drum magazines. Two military surplus handguns are frequently encountered in this caliber, the Russian Tokarev and the Czech CZ-52. The ammunition most often is full-metal-jacket, corrosive and well over 30 years old. This usually means it is inexpensive for training or learning how to shoot a pistol. It is good only for defense when nothing else is available.

A Smith & Wesson .380 Sigma was used to fire a Remington .380 ACP Golden Saber round into the test gelatin block. The recovered projectiles exhibit the characteristic mushrooming of a successful design. Many consider the .380 ACP cartridge to be the lower limit of acceptable terminal ballistics for self-defense.

.380 ACP or 9mm kurz (9x17mm). The .380 ACP is described by some as being on the threshold of acceptable performance for self-defense. Formerly, its greatest virtue was the size of the pistols most often chambered for it. Due to its lower chamber pressure, these handguns operate on a pure blowback basis and therefore are often small and easy to conceal. Today however that's changed as 9mm pistols have shrunk and are now the size normally associated with a .380 size pistol. If the gun designers continue to make future .380 ACP pistols even smaller, such as Kel Tec's latest venture, this cartridge may enjoy a rebirth of popularity. For the present, though, most .380 ACP pistols offer little that can't be found in pistols of equal size, but featuring more powerful cartridges in terms of expansion and penetration. It should be mentioned there is a wide variety of expanding jacketed hollowpoint ammunition available for the .380 ACP cartridge and most of it performs quite well in view of the cartridge's limitations.

9mm MAKAROV (9x18mm). For a number of years this round was unheard of in the United States. With the demise of the Soviet style Communism a large number of Makarov pistols from former client states are being imported into the U.S. and other Western countries. Approximately equal to the .380 ACP in power level, but with a far slimmer selection of good expanding jacketed hollowpoint ammunition this round has little to recommend it. Except for one thing – Makarov pistols almost always work. The Russian-designed Makarov pistol (with good ammunition) is one of the most reliable semi-auto pistols ever built. That alone makes it worthy of consideration if one is willing to acknowledge the limited wound ballistics of this cartridge and the limited availability of good hollowpoint ammunition.

.38 SPECIAL (9x29.5mm revolver). For years this was *the* American Police cartridge. The stereotypical example being the Smith & Wesson Military & Police Model 10 revolver in a Sam Brown belt and holster. But the round's shortcomings in deadly force encounters eventually and rightly dimmed its success. The standard load for decades was a 158-grain round-nose lead bullet loaded to a nominal velocity of 860 feet per second

The Makarov pistol is a product of the former Soviet Union. It is normally found in 9x18mm caliber, a somewhat obscure chambering in the West and the United States, but the pistol itself is one of the most reliable semi-autos found anywhere.

Smith & Wesson dropped the Centennial revolver from its catalog in 1974, but reintroduced it in 1990 in response to popular demand. The Model 640 (top) was a .38 Special revolver that was rated for "+P+" high pressure loads. In 1995, a version in .357 Magnum was introduced to create an extremely powerful, yet small magnum caliber revolver.

The Old Model Ruger Super Blackhawk (top) in .44 Magnum has proven itself in the hunting fields, while the two Smith & Wesson revolvers in .38 Special caliber (below) are more often found protecting their owners on the mean streets. All three revolvers are good at what they do, but they do two entirely different things.

The introduction of the Smith & Wesson Model 19 Combat Magnum made the .357 Magnum round one of the most successful revolver cartridges in the history of American law enforcement. This medium-size, K-frame revolver was developed at the behest of Bill Jordan, and to many it remains one of the best fighting revolvers ever made. PHOTO CREDIT: SMITH & WESSON

from a 4-inch barrel. It was inadequate for everything but punching holes in paper. In the 1960s, jacketed hollowpoint ammunition was introduced first by Super Vel, then other manufacturers, greatly increasing its effectiveness. Eventually, the .357 Magnum proved more popular and the .38 Special was relegated to the need it still serves; first, as a training round for beginning revolver shooters, and second, as the round of choice for small to medium snub-nose revolvers. Recently, this round has enjoyed a rebirth of sorts because of the popularity of concealed hammer five-shot snub-nose revolvers. The FBI still issues .38 Special ammunition to those agents armed with revolvers. The duty load being the Federal Hydra-Shok 129-grain +P jacketed round. Another good load in .38 Special is the 158-grain. Semi-wadcutter lead hollow point offered by manufacturers like CCI-Speer, Federal and Winchester.

.357 MAGNUM. The .357 Magnum is actually a .38 Special round on steroids. Well, to be precise the .357 Magnum case is a tenth of an inch longer than the .38 Special case and the .357 Magnum generates a much higher chamber pressure. Otherwise, they employ the same size projectiles. After the .38 Special fell from favor as the round for uniformed police carry, the .357 Magnum picked up the slack. For years the 125-grain. jacketed hollowpoint load launched from a 4-inch revolver barrel was considered the best fight stopper in the business for law enforcement. Naturally enough, it served as the poster child for the light and fast advocates. The downside to this load was the same as with all magnum revolver rounds – excessive report and recoil. The recoil wasn't so bad, but the bark of this magnum round on an indoor firing range was sufficient to make Teddy Roosevelt's face on Mount Rushmore flinch. Yet, it was effective in shoot-outs and the Smith & Wesson Model 19 Combat Magnum was frequently seen as the epitome of the fighting handgun for law enforcement during the late 1960s and 1970s. Today, some controversy still continues over the proper bullet weight for the .357 Magnum, but ammunition with reduced velocities and sometimes heavier bullets are proving popular in all, but the smallest of the .357 Magnum revolvers. The only cautionary advice with the .357 Magnum is to avoid the 180-grain ammunition for everything but game hunting. This ammo was designed specifically for sport applications and works poorly in self-defense situations because of over-penetration.

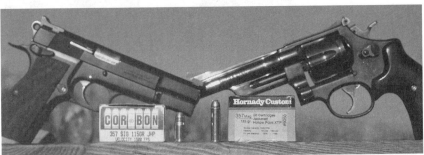

In an attempt to get the same ballistics seen from the .357 Magnum revolver like the one seen here on the right, the .357 SIG auto-pistol cartridge was introduced. The .40 S&W caliber Browning High Power seen here on the left has been rebarreled with a Bar-Sto barrel in .357 SIG. In the lighter bullet weights the .357 Sig produces equivalent velocities to the revolver, but as the projectile weight increases the .357 SIG starts to show its weakness.

9mm Parabellum, 9x19mm, 9mm NATO, 9mm Luger. Known by a wide variety of names, the 9mm Luger round is, surprisingly to many new shooters, an old round. It is older than the .45 ACP, or any of the magnum revolver rounds. It is equivalent in power to the .38 Special revolver cartridge. For years it was offered solely in a full-metal-jacket configuration (commonly called a 'ball' round) and it proved boringly dismal at stopping dangerous criminals or charging enemy infantrymen. (The military solution to

The 9mm Luger cartridge is known by many names; 9mm NATO, 9mm Parabellum, 9x19mm, but essentially it is the same round in terms of case dimensions and overall length. The Browning High Power shown here is a World War II model produced in Canada by Inglis. The Browning High Power is most often found in a 9mm chambering.

London Metropolitan Police Officer Andrew Duffey puts the 9mm Sig Model 239 through its paces. 9mm caliber pistols are chosen for police work because they offer similar ballistic performance to that found with a .38 Special revolver while at the same time possessing greater magazine capacity and a faster means of reloading.

this persistent problem was to build guns that delivered a stream of fully automatic fire, hence the introduction of the submachine gun.) Full-metal-jacket 9mm Luger ammo was even disgustingly bad at dropping varmints and feral animals when used for more benign purposes. The development of successful expanding jacketed hollowpoint ammunition increased dramatically the round's effectiveness and now instant experts loudly proclaim it is the ultimate fight-stopper. Excuse me if I fail to run and jump on board this trolley. Still, with proper ammunition the current police shooting reports are encouraging in terms of this round's increased effectiveness. Additionally, it seems to satisfy the need or the craze as the case may be, for pistols that hold a whole bunch of bullets. If you are interested in a small, easily concealable, yet high-capacity 9mm pistol, I highly recommend the Glock Model 26. However, despite this pistol's excellence, it's hard for me to forget it was a 9mm failure that ignited the wide interest in wound ballistics many years ago in the first place.

.38 SUPER (9x23SR). The popularity of the .38 Super grew out of a quirk in the rules governing ISPC competition. Jeff Cooper, the founder of IPSC, argued long and hard that shooters using heavier calibers should be rewarded with more points over those using lesser calibers, but achieving the same target score. It was a valid argument, so a power factor based on momentum was created. In this equation the bullet weight is multiplied by the projectile velocity and the total divided by 1,000 to create a minimum power factor to make "Major" caliber and score the maximum points available on the cardboard target. According to fellow Columbia Conference attendee, Jim Cirillo, Cooper hedged his bets somewhat because Cirillo at the time argued it was such a good idea bonus points should have been awarded to those who could master really heavy calibers like the .41 Magnum and the .44 Magnum. Cooper wouldn't hear of it because that scheme would have overwhelmed his beloved .45 Auto and the 1911 pistol so the bonus idea died. However, with the advent of compensators serious IPSC competitors soon discovered they could hot load the .38 Super using lighter bullets while achieving the same power factors as the fabled .45 ACP. The benefit to them was their compensators worked better due to a greater volume of gas pressure and the recoil was more manageable because the projectile weight was less, much less. There remained a small problem for the real world; the .38 Super is available in only a few expanding jacketed hollowpoint loads and the performance of the .38 Super in full-metal-jacket ammo is little better than the previously mentioned 9mm Luger. Because the round originally headspaced on the rim of the cartridge, accuracy was also substandard. That was corrected initially with custom barrels that headspace off the front of the case. (Headspace is measured differently with different case types and firearms, but it describes the fit between the cartridge case and the chamber as well as the distance between the case and the breech face of the firearm.) Now most all the manufacturers of .38 Super caliber handguns headspace off the front of the case so accuracy is much improved.

9x23mm. This is a cartridge offered by Winchester, but it was really developed by John Ricco of CP Bullets at his own expense. Basically, the 9x23mm is a .38 Super round, but in a rimless format. (The .38 Super features a 'semi-rim' making it difficult to load and feed through high-capacity, double stack magazines.) The 9x23mm offers true .357 Magnum ballistics by launching 125-grain bullets at close to 1,400 fps, but here again it comes only in what some view as a large size envelope like the Colt 1911 pistol or a custom modified SIG Mod. 220.

The 9x21mm cartridge is simply a 9x19mm round loading with a slightly longer case. It originated in Italy because their laws forbid the possession of a military round by its citizens. The 9mm NATO is a 9x19mm cartridge that is loaded to a slightly higher pressure and corresponding muzzle velocity for NATO military forces.

.357 SIG. This is another of the entrants that finds favor with those wanting an auto-pistol version of the 125-grain JHP .357 Magnum round. The Texas Department of Public Safety adopted this round late in 1996. On paper it mimics ballistics close to those of the aforementioned .357 Magnum load. The .357 SIG cartridge is nothing more than the .40 S&W case necked down to a 9mm bullet. This makes it a bottlenecked cartridge that should feed through an autoloader like perfection itself. (There are problems with overall length in some pistols, more in a moment.) The 9x22mm MFS from Hungary was essentially the same round, albeit a round developed totally separate and apart from SIG's work in the United States. Ammunition availability initially was limited, but the list of manufacturers who offer expanding jacketed hollowpoint ammunition in .357 SIG is now as large as it is for most any other law enforcement handgun caliber. The SIG Model 229 was the first pistol chambered for this round and theoretically it should be a simple task

The .357 SIG is a bottleneck cartridge that resulted when the .40 S&W case was necked down to a 9mm projectile. The goal was to create an auto-pistol equivalent to the .357 Magnum revolver cartridge. From left to right; the rounds are the Speer Lawman 125-grain FMJ, the Speer Gold Dot 125-grain hollowpoint, the Remington 125-grain JHP and the Hornady 124-grain XTP-JHP.

to equip any pistol chambered in .40 S&W with a second barrel in .357 SIG caliber. The gain? A bunch of velocity in a medium size or compact auto-pistol format. Feeding problems seem to materialize when handloading this round if careful attention is not paid to the reloaded round's overall length. A BarSto barrel in .357 SIG was installed in my personal .40 caliber Browning High Power and I discovered to my sorrow the overall length of the reload had to be kept in relatively narrow parameters for successful operation of that gun in a match. Other authorities have reported problems with split case necks in this caliber from different manufacturers so the round does require some research on the shooter's behalf.

.40 SMITH & WESSON. The success of this round is simply unheard of in the history of small arms. No other cartridge can claim the acceptance this round has enjoyed. The idea behind the .40 S&W cartridge is a beautifully simple one – build a gun with the outside dimensions of a 9mm pistol, but one offering a big bore diameter (.40″ is considered big-bore) and high-capacity magazine. Additionally, it comes with ballistic figures that many on both sides of the cartridge effectiveness argument accept. This cartridge offers a bigger bore diameter than the 9mm Luger (.354″). It offers relatively high magazine capacity for law enforcement officers, and it provides good terminal ballistics. There are, however, a couple of negatives associated with this round. The first is, it seems sensitive to pressure spikes when improperly reloaded. Some experts feel this could be the fault of incorrect and improper bullet seating depths. All shooters and reloaders should exercise caution and extreme care when reloading this round or shooting reloaded ammunition. Guns have been blown apart and one propellant manufacturer, ACCURATE ARMS, has even put a disclaimer in its reloading guide advising against the use of their products in .40 S&W pistols lacking complete support of the cartridge case when the round is chambered. (This refers to the amount of cartridge case supported and surrounded by barrel steel when the round is fully seated in the chamber.) The other negative is that accuracy has always been a random thing with pistols chambered in .40 S&W regardless of the pistol manufacturer or who made the ammunition. A big exception to this is the HK USP Compact, which I found to be unexpectedly accurate with a variety of .40 S&W ammo.

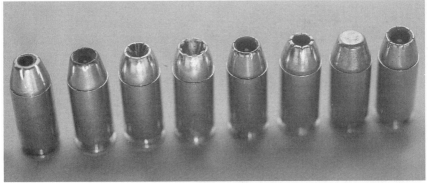

No cartridge in the history of small arms has enjoyed the sweep of success like the .40 S&W round. It enables a pistol manufacturer to package a big-bore cartridge in an envelope formerly developed for the 9mm Parabellum round. There is also an extremely wide array of jacketed hollowpoint ammunition available for the self-defense consumer.

The HK USP Compact pistol demonstrated above average accuracy for a .40 S&W caliber semi-auto handgun in the author's testing. It is a polymer-framed pistol with a double-action/single-action trigger mechanism. PHOTO CREDIT: HK INC. USA

10mm auto. This is an extremely good and bad round. Does that make sense? Well, it does if you are someone who appreciates flat shooting, inherently accurate cartridges. The bad part comes into play because this is yet another defensive round that requires a big pistol. It can only be found in pistols like the Glock Model 20, the discontinued Colt Delta Elite and the no longer offered series of Smith & Wesson autoloaders with number designations like 1006, 1066, 1076, 1086, 1046, and 1026. Smith & Wesson still makes a revolver for the 10mm round and it is the Model 610, but it is probably used more for IDPA competition than anything else and then only with .40 S&W ammo. (Like the .38

The 10mm auto cartridge is a true .40 caliber round. It was first loaded by Norma. The early 170-grain JHP loading was more powerful than later production because the factory loaded it 'down' to lessen the felt recoil and abuse on the pistols. The Winchester Silvertip hollowpoint load in 10mm auto is a popular choice for self-defense in any 10mm auto handgun.

Special/.357 Magnum relationship, the .40 S&W is essentially a shorter version of the 10mm round. You can't shoot .40 S&W ammo in a 10mm pistol, but you can in a revolver.) I've previously mentioned the history of the 10mm round with the FBI, but I have to say my favorite auto pistol is a Richard Heinie custom-built Colt Delta Elite in 10mm. A British friend, Rob Adam, used a factory stock Glock Model 20 to win the B-Class IPSC National Championship in the United Kingdom (back when they were allowed to own handguns) while competing against a full field of race gun-equipped competitors. 10mm pistols are both accurate and powerful. If you're into paper ballistics, a strong argument can be made the Glock Model 20 with 16 rounds of full-power 10mm ammo is the most powerful auto-pistol around. Why? Just add up the foot pounds of potential kinetic energy in the gun and compare it to a .44 Magnum Desert Eagle. The 10mm cartridge may be falling from popular favor, but don't be misled, it's still a fabulous round that offers much to those who appreciate flat-shooting accurate rounds in a conventional auto-pistol format.

The 10mm auto cartridge was first developed for the Bren Ten project, but that pistol proved to be a marketing failure. Colt revived the 10mm auto round with the introduction of the Delta Elite. It offered magnum revolver performance in an auto-pistol format. The gun seen here is a custom made Springfield Armory 1911 pistol in 10mm auto from Richard Heinie, one of the best custom pistolsmiths in the business. **PHOTO CREDIT: HEINIE SPECIALTY PRODUCTS**

.41 MAGNUM. It's hard for me to discuss this round objectively. I've carried a Smith & Wesson .41 Magnum revolver, almost daily, for more than 30 years. The .41 Magnum has never failed me in terms of bringing down what I was shooting on our farm. I've carried a .41 Mag when I worked briefly as a police officer, as a licensed private investigator, and as a bonded messenger and courier for several years when the firm issued only .38 Special revolvers. I still believe a good revolver chambered in an adequate power level remains a viable gunfighting tool if the shooter is equal to the task. In terms of self-defense, the old Smith & Wesson Model 58 with its fixed sights and 4- inch barrel was hard to beat

When the .41 Magnum cartridge was first introduced in 1964 it was offered in the Smith & Wesson Model 57, a deluxe model featuring a target hammer, a target trigger, a deluxe blue finish, diamond center target grips and fully adjustable rear sight. Later a Military & Police version was made available at lower cost and with fewer features. It was called the Model 58 and the lower gun in this photo is a nickel-plated Model 58 from the first production run, but with replacement grips and a Tyler T-grip adapter. The upper gun is an ivory-gripped Model 657 with a custom 5-inch barrel, also in .41 Magnum caliber.

for reliability. The Winchester 175-grain Silvertip hollowpoint offering works well inside the thorax of a whitetail and it is one of the lesser recoiling factory loads in this caliber. Because I have used a .41 Magnum revolver to take seven whitetail deer with one shot each I am convinced this round and revolver will serve me well if a deadly force threat should ever materialize.

.44 SPECIAL. This is an old round and for years ammunition companies loaded it down for safety concerns when fired in older guns. Today, there is more available in terms of factory hollowpoint ammunition, but the velocities are still relatively slow. For self-defense and law enforcement applications, the .44 Special is a round steeped in history, especially west of the Mississippi River where lawmen for decades used it to good effect. Its appeal is limited today because of the factors previously enumerated for all cartridges requiring large revolvers. Big revolvers are no longer popular even for uniformed carry, so there isn't much call for a good "four-de-four". Charter Arms makes a hideout revolver in .44 Special called the Bulldog. It is one of those "It Kills In Front and Injures Behind" kind of guns. It kicks like a mule, but it is the last word in big-bore hideout guns for truly brave souls.

.44 MAGNUM. Ah yes, the caliber used by that celluloid San Francisco police inspector "Dirty" Harry Callahan. Clint Eastwood should have been given stock in Smith & Wesson because he sold so many S&W Model 29 revolvers after the first "Dirty Harry" movie. It was hard before the film to purchase a Smith & Wesson .44 Magnum and afterwards it was close to impossible. Unfortunately, the .44 Magnum has proven successful in only limited applications as a fighting handgun. It works well if you're in an occupation where you might encounter dangerous game; i.e. mad moose, angry alligators, or grumpy grizzly bears. It also works well if you're a handgun hunter of most anything four legged. For many shooters, however, the .44 Magnum is too much weight, too much recoil, and way too much penetration. The success of the .44 Magnum as a sporting handgun cartridge is one of the reasons most firearms commentators put the .41 Magnum on the Endangered Species list. The .44 Magnum is a good cartridge with power aplenty for most situations and a 4-inch Smith & Wesson Model 29 handled properly is

The .44 Special round is often found in a low-velocity load with a lead round-nose bullet. The Winchester Silvertip hollowpoint is a big improvement over the traditional load in terms of its terminal ballistics.

The .44 Magnum has been popularized to the point of legend in Hollywood films, but for years this was the most powerful conventional handgun cartridge available. That is no longer true. The .44 Magnum 240-grain lead semi-wadcutter from Winchester (far left) is still a serious round for big game. The 300-grain jacketed soft point handload (third from the left) offers the most projectile penetration available in a conventional revolver.

still a valid concept, but like the .41 Magnum it takes a dedicated individual to master and shoot it well.

.45 ACP (11.43mm). This cartridge, for many professionals, is *IT*. There is no substitute in their minds and for good reason. It is an old cartridge and it established a track record that few will ever be able to challenge for stopping bad people in their tracks. For years the standard load was full-metal-jacket 230-grain projectile launched at an average velocity of 860 fps from the 1911 pistol. It gained legendary status for stopping enemy soldiers and proved effective in a variety of scenarios. The introduction of good expanding jacketed hollowpoint ammunition only increased the round's effectiveness. It's hard to argue against the success of the .45 ACP in serious social interaction, but it should be mentioned the Texas Department of Public Safety went from the .45 ACP to the .357 SIG and they like the smaller round much better, so that certainly raises some questions. The downside of the .45 ACP has always been the perceived recoil, but when compared

The .45 ACP is an extremely versatile round. It can be loaded to mid-range velocities for accurate and easy-recoiling target shooting or it can be loaded to the maximum with any of the modern expanding jacketed hollowpoint bullets for the best performance in a concealed carry handgun.

against a modern magnum handgun the .45 ACP is a pussycat. If it isn't, loads using lighter bullets lessen the perception to a great degree while at the same time maintaining a respectable performance against dangerous felons. Now, 185-grain hollowpoints are often used in alloy-framed .45s to lessen the felt recoil. This caliber is a serious fighting caliber and will be so for years to come. There are even small handguns like the Colt Officer's Model and similar pistols from Springfield Armory, Kimber and others that answer

The 1911 Government Model pistol for many is *the* fighting handgun. This Les Baer Premier 1911 is an extremely accurate example of a good 1911 pistol. The author added the custom laser engraved ivory grip panels and marvels at this pistol's accuracy and reliability.

Not all .45 Automatics are 1911 clones of the Government Model. Smith & Wesson has manufactured over the years a number of different .45 Auto pistols. This S&W Model 457 was a reduced-size .45 auto featuring a 7+1 ammunition capacity.

The 200-grain Speer JHP .45 ACP cartridge, shown on the left, earned accolades for its terminal performance in gunfights. It was known as the 'Flying Ashtray' and it worked quite well. It has been replaced by an even better-performing Speer Gold Dot load. The Winchester load on the right has always been a solid performer for those carrying a .45 ACP pistol for self-defense.

The .45 ACP round on the left is a 'match' round in that it was designed solely for target use and not a self-defense application. The full metal jacket (FMJ) round on the right is the standard 230-grain 'ball' round for the .45 ACP from Federal. It is often referred to as "hardball".

the need for reduced size. Bear in mind that reduced size also means reduced muzzle velocities because of the shorter barrel lengths. The .45 ACP is an accurate cartridge and powerful. Just saying the words, "Forty-five Auto" often conjures up the image of a fighting handgun to many, and for good reason. As long as smokeless powder is used to propel projectiles in defensive situations, the .45 ACP will remain an effective problem-solver.

.45 GAP The acronym stands for 'Glock Automatic Pistol'. This is an extremely new cartridge and it is the result of one manufacturer's attempt to solve the size versus power dilemma. Prior to the introduction of the .45 GAP powerful pistols were by nature large. The .45 GAP cartridge duplicates much of the ballistic performance found with the .45 ACP round. It does so in a round that has a shorter overall length. This shorter length makes it easy to make a pistol with a smaller grip circumference and an overall smaller pistol. The .45 GAP operates at the same chamber pressure as the .45 ACP +P load. Originally loaded by the ATK companies (Federal Cartridge Company and CCI-Speer) with either 185-grain or 200-grain bullets, Winchester just recently introduced their own .45 GAP ammo that features 230-grain bullet weights. This round is so new it literally has no track record. Yet, it is reasonable to expect the Glock company to introduce a number of smaller size pistols that will be built specifically for this cartridge. As it is the round accomplishes much for those who want a Glock in .45 caliber but are handicapped by small hands or a short trigger reach because the Glock Model 37 (the pistol chambered for the .45 GAP) has a frame the same size as their easy to manage Glock Model 17. The .45 GAP is sure to be a law enforcement and civilian self-defense round of the future.

The .45 Colt cartridge as originally loaded used black powder to launch a 255-grain round-nose lead bullet. Today, the propellant is smokeless powder, but the velocity numbers are basically the same except for the Winchester Silvertip offering. It is faster because of the lighter weight of the Silvertip hollowpoint.

.45 COLT (11.43x32.1mm Revolver). This really is an old cartridge. Introduced in 1873, it served for a number of years in the Indian wars of the American West as well as performing its share of duty taming various rowdy cow towns. Back when all handgun cartridges employed black powder it established its credentials early on by putting a premature end to any gunfight. Originally loaded to launch a 255-grain lead round nose slug at a nominal velocity of 855 fps, the introduction of smokeless powder did little to change its performance. It is NOT a magnum cartridge in terms of its trajectory or terminal ballistics on big game. It is an effective gunfighting round, but again because it is a large round it takes a large revolver to shoot it. Many argue against this round because they feel if you're going to have to carry a large pistol you might as well carry a .44 Magnum or even a .41 Magnum. Both of those rounds offer more in terms of downrange ballistics and tissue penetration, but the .45 Colt survives. It even flourishes where the .41 Magnum dims, the major reason has to be part nostalgia combined with a love for big-bore, heavy bullets. A gunsmithing instructor once told me that a 300-grain cast lead .45 Colt bullet with a heavy charge of powder behind it would take down any misbehaving NFL linebacker in the business. While we live in the age of benevolent enlightenment and his statement was obviously politically incorrect, personal observation has yet to indicate he was even faintly wrong.

So, in summary it can be argued the most effective handgun is not always the most powerful one. Rather, it is the one the shooter can use to its best effect because of a combination of gun's reliability, the recoil level and accuracy of the cartridge and the shooter's own skill at marksmanship.

CHAPTER FIVE

Service Revolvers

U ntil the mid-1980s revolvers dominated American law enforcement. For years the semi-automatic pistol was considered too ammunition sensitive to be sufficiently reliable for service as a law enforcement sidearm. The irony surrounding the most successful police handgun of all time, the swing-out cylinder, six-shot, double-action revolver, is it was introduced at approximately the same time as the first semi-automatic pistol. The fact the revolver was preferred for many decades over the semi-auto design can be traced directly to the question of reliability.

It took the invention of smokeless powder to make semi-automatic pistol designs feasible. Black powder produces too much fouling for any of the early semi-auto pistols to function properly and little has changed in the 100 years since the introduction of both smokeless powder and semi-auto handguns. Any new technology goes through a natural process of improvement. Even though smokeless powder was far more forgiving in terms of keeping the firearm clean, the early smokeless powder raised its own concerns about reliability. Law enforcement administrators took it as gospel the swing-out cylinder, double-action revolver was more reliable because a second shot, should the first shot be a misfire, was only a full trigger pull away.

For decades this was the mantra. The double-action revolver was more reliable because a second trigger-pull would rotate the cylinder and present a fresh cartridge to the firing pin. (Assuming of course, there were remaining cartridges still in the cylinder.) This simple technology enabled anyone equipped with a double-action revolver to keep firing and not be saddled with a malfunctioning sidearm.

Massad Ayoob, well known firearms and police writer, examines a seven-shot Taurus .357 Magnum revolver at a past SHOT Show. Many manufacturers now offer revolvers with more than six rounds.

The really amazing thing about this whole thought process is that it persevered in American law enforcement for so many decades after the introduction of the semi-auto pistol.

Some of this perseverance can be traced to the natural human tendency to resist change and stay with the familiar. Another aspect of it has to be the admiration by many who work with firearms on a daily basis for a finely crafted, well put-together blue steel revolver. Both Colt and Smith & Wesson manufactured some wonderful revolvers between the 1920s and the late 1960s. The amount of hand-fitting required to assemble a revolver before the war was reduced after World War II by both companies and some collectors feel the overall quality of the later guns exhibit this lack of attention. But the guns, up and until the early 1970s, still retained beautifully deep blue finishes on their carbon steel parts and for many years the wood grips were still hand-checkered. The mere possession of such a firearm granted the owner a feeling of pride and accomplishment. Despite what anyone will say about progress, few in law enforcement will acknowledge the same feelings today about guns made from black plastic and unpolished steel.

The Model 325 from Smith & Wesson is a recent introduction in .45 ACP caliber. It features a lightweight frame and a short 2-inch barrel. It is similar in nature to many of the cut down 1917 revolvers that were carried prior to World War II by those who routinely traveled in dark places.

A Plastic Revolver????? Yes, the Russians had this prototype on display in Europe in 2001. It was a break-open design and chambered for the .357 Magnum cartridge. Surprisingly, the author found it well balanced and interesting because it utilized a modular trigger system within the polymer grip and frame.

Many beginning shooters in the 21st Century have a hard time relating to revolvers. To them the revolver is an antiquated design offering low capacity, five or six shots, when compared to a minimum of eight rounds if a .45ACP, or as many as 16 cartridges if a 9mm. Additionally, the revolver is not an easy handgun to learn to shoot well because all too often the beginning shooter will grip the gun low, leaving the barrel axis well above the center of their arm. This helps exaggerate the recoil of the firearm and lessens control. Unlike the polymer-framed semi-auto alternative, which cushions to a small degree the felt recoil of the gun due to the flexing of the plastic frame as well as having a grip shape that forces the shooter to grip it higher.

The author's first magnum caliber revolver was this .357 Magnum Smith & Wesson Model 27 with a 6-inch barrel. He purchased it new in 1968 for the princely sum of $143 and change. Although it still maintains a good appearance he says the gun is 'tired'.

Yet despite all its shortcomings and the perceived misconceptions about the inefficiencies of a revolver, they still remain one of the more reliable handgun designs ever created.

REVOLVER EFFICIENCY and THE QUESTION ABOUT THAT GAP?

The classic swing-out cylinder double-action revolver design consists of a frame, a set of grips on the bottom portion of the frame, a barrel, a cylinder that rotates on a center pin mounted to a crane or yoke, a cylinder release which depending upon the manufacturer must be activated either through a push or a pull, a trigger and corresponding internal trigger mechanism. The trigger mechanism through action of the trigger will rotate the cylinder because of the action of the 'hand' against the ratchets on the back of the cylinder until the 'bolt' locks against the cylinder notch to enforce alignment between the chamber and the barrel. The rotation of the cylinder also presents the next firing chamber to the firing pin, which in turn will be struck by a blow from the hammer. The hammer is cocked and then released by the trigger pull. The hammer may be visible or it may be concealed and the firing pin may be frame-mounted or found on the front face of the hammer. Once the hammer falls, the firing pin makes contact with the cartridge primer and the weapon fires. When the revolver is fired single-action, the thumb is used to pull the hammer back until it is 'cocked'. Pressure on the trigger fires the gun.

Revolver cylinders commonly used to hold only five or six cartridges, but depending upon frame size and manufacturer it can hold as many as eight .357 Magnum rounds or 10 .22 Long Rifle rounds. The revolver receives its name due to the revolution of the cylinder and they are often called 'round guns' because of the shape of the cylinder or sometimes 'wheelguns'.

The Model 686 Plus was the first seven-shot .357 Magnum revolver produced by Smith & Wesson. Computer controlled manufacturing equipment provides for the design and machining of parts that formerly was extremely difficult, if not impossible.

Due to its design a gap is necessary between the cylinder and the barrel. The bullet must literally jump this gap to enter the barrel. The back of the barrel has a somewhat funnel shaped feature called the 'forcing cone' to help 'true' up the bullet before it engages the rifling and begins its acceleration down the barrel toward the muzzle.

Even though this barrel/cylinder gap is easily measurable with a common automobile feeler gauge, the gas pressure within the chamber and barrel remain sufficiently high to generate significant projectile velocities. This seems to be a strange way of doing things to the MTV Generation, but the fact is it worked in the 1850s with black powder guns and it works equally today in the 21st century with modern ammunition. Technically speaking, there is a small loss of velocity. Because of this gap, there is a noticeable flash from it as well when the revolver is fired in low-light conditions, but for all practical purposes the cylinder gap velocity loss is inconsequential.

While not as true today as it once was, revolvers as a general rule have been available in far more powerful chamberings than traditional auto-loaders. All of the magnum handgun cartridges, including the latest to be introduced: the Smith & Wesson .500 Magnum, have all been originally developed for revolvers.

The .357 Magnum was introduced in 1935 at the behest of firearms writer Phil Sharpe. Smith & Wesson was the first to offer a revolver in this chambering. It was originally intended to be a custom order type of thing on their largest frame (at the time) the N-frame revolver. This custom order arrangement was described as a "Registered Magnum". The term back then had no connotations of an over-intrusive government, Janet Reno or even Bill Schumer, but merely reflected the fact the gun was so special the gun and original owner were "registered" with the company because it was such an exclusive deal. The management of S&W was still reluctant to mass-produce the .357 Magnum revolver because they felt there would be little demand for such a powerful handgun. The reader

The author was able to locate a used Smith & Wesson Model 27 as well as a used 3-1/2-inch barrel. He returned this gun to the factory and they installed the 3-1/2-inch barrel, put on a gold bead front sight as well as tune the trigger action. He says it is a favorite gun for just plinking and making empty brass.

is reminded this was during the Depression, so money was most certainly an issue in everything that was done. The S&W management was wrong. The .357 Magnum Smith & Wesson became extremely popular for police officers and sportsmen and remains one of the most successful centerfire revolver cartridges of all time. General George Patton carried an ivory-stocked Smith & Wesson registered .357 Magnum on the left side of his General Officer's belt during the campaign to defeat Hitler and Nazi Germany. On the right side he carried his engraved nickel-plated ivory handled Colt Single Action Army revolver. A number of large city police departments ordered and received registered .357 Magnum revolvers, but according to Registered Magnum collector Dick Burg most of these departments did not furnish the sidearm to the officer. The individual officer had to purchase the service revolver out of his own private funds and in the 1930s that would have represented a significant portion of an officer's pay. However, it is known that Kansas City, Missouri, St. Joseph, Missouri, Indianapolis, Indiana, Cincinnati, Ohio and Washington, D.C. police departments all ordered registered magnums from Smith & Wesson prior to World War Two.

Smith & Wesson was also the first to chamber a revolver, again another N-frame, in .44 Magnum at the insistence of legendary gunwriter Elmer Keith. This revolver would eventually become known as the Model 29. Sturm, Ruger & Co., at the time an upstart of a gun manufacturer when compared to Smith & Wesson, scored a great coup by discovering the development of the cartridge and soon after the S&W introduction Ruger announced and demonstrated their own version which was the Ruger Blackhawk single-action revolver. (Collectors have labeled these first Ruger Blackhawk .44 Magnums the 'flattop' versions.) Both the Ruger Blackhawk revolver and later the Super Blackhawk revolver together with the Smith & Wesson Model 29 went on to become the favored choice of sportsmen and outdoor guides. In fact, a good argument can be made it was the

The first Smith & Wesson .44 Magnum revolvers came in a dark box, some collectors claim they're blue while others feel they are black. The author believes his is black, but the gun, despite its age, is accurate and well balanced. This example although not in 'mint' condition is a wonderful example of how Smith & Wesson used to make revolvers.

The Colt Anaconda was Colt's first .44 Magnum revolver and it was introduced 25 years after the cartridge was first unveiled. The Anaconda is a reliable revolver.

introduction of the .44 Magnum revolver cartridge that helped develop the fairly recent concept of hunting whitetail deer with a handgun.

The .41 Magnum followed in 1964. It was created at the behest of gunwriters like Bill Jordan, Elmer Keith and Skeeter Skelton. Their goal was to equip America's law enforcement officers with a better, more efficient revolver cartridge than the common .38 Special in use at the time. While the .41 Magnum cartridge is appreciated by many, it failed to achieve this initial goal. The guns, the Smith & Wesson Model 57 and Model 58, were too heavy for the majority of officers. All too often the police departments received the ammunition intended for sport hunting and not police use. The result was for the average officer too much gun and too much recoil, together with too much penetration. But when it did work, it worked as designed because the late Tom Ferguson told me the city of San Antonio, Texas was one of the first to adopt the Smith & Wesson Model 58 when he was an officer

Originally, this Smith & Wesson Model 29-2 was equipped with a 4-inch barrel, but for a short period of time the factory had a small supply of 5-inch carbon steel barrels. The author feels the 5-inch barrel length is better than either the 4- or the 6-inch lengths the factory offered with their N-frame revolvers for so many years. It carries well in a holster and offers a good sight radius for distance shooting.

The Taurus Titanium Tracker in .41 Magnum is a five-shot, medium-frame double-action revolver. The author was somewhat disappointed in the feel of the double-action trigger, but liked the grips and the overall balance of this powerful revolver.

The author admits to a sentimental affection for the .41 Magnum cartridge and its corresponding revolvers. This is a favorite of his. It is a Smith & Wesson Model 657 with a custom 5-inch barrel, a McGivern gold bead front sight and custom made ivory grips that have his logo scrimshawed on the right side.

This Smith & Wesson Model 57 with a custom made five inch barrel had to be totally rebuilt due to excessive use by the author. It cost more to rebuild than it would have for a new one, but the author continues to use this .41 Magnum on a daily basis.

with that department. In the first year they had 12 shootings involving the .41 Magnum caliber service revolver. All 12 were what would be classified as "one-shot stops" he said with a big smile on his face. Eleven hits were recorded on 11 of the criminals and the other involved an officer unintentionally discharging his .41 Mag. The perpetrator surrendered immediately, even though he was untouched by gunfire. The sound of the big magnum discharging convinced him of the error of his ways. Ferguson really liked the .41 Magnum and felt the cartridge and corresponding police revolvers were mishandled during the introductory phase by both Smith & Wesson and the ammunition companies.

Tom Ferguson wasn't the only law officer who used a .41 Magnum. Buford Pusser of *Walking Tall* fame and McNairy County, Tennessee Sheriff used one on February 1, 1966 to save his own life. An intoxicated Louise Hathcock tried to kill him with a Smith

& Wesson Airweight .38 Special revolver (serial number 44206). Pusser had two warrants for Hathcock's arrest, one for illegal possession of whiskey in a dry county and the other for theft. Hathcock operated the Shamrock Motel and she specialized in robbing her out-of-town guests. Initially resisting arrest, Hathcock told Pusser she had something to tell him in confidence and asked him to step into her private quarters behind the motel's office. Upon entering the office she drew the .38 and opened fire at a distance of 2 to 3 feet, missing the young Sheriff. Pusser jumped back and fell sideways on the bed. She then approached him and took aim directly at Pusser's head. Her revolver malfunctioned on the next round. By now, Pusser was able to draw his nickel-plated .41 Magnum Smith & Wesson from his duty holster and he fired his first shot at Hathcock. It struck her high toward the center of her upper left shoulder. (An IDPA competitor would classify this as a 'C' hit.) Pusser continued to work the trigger and his second round entered her left side and exited under her right breast. (an 'A/B/ hit.) Mortally wounded Hathcock struggled to fire her revolver one more time after she fell to the floor, but Pusser shot her just under the left side of her jaw with the bullet exiting the top back of her head. (another 'A' hit.) That ended the exchange, which took place at a distance of 7 feet according to the deputies outside the room. Pusser's revolver was a Smith & Wesson Model 57. It was carried in a black basket-weave cross draw holster that was made for a 4-inch Colt Python revolver.

All of these powerful handgun rounds were first pioneered in revolvers and the barrel/cylinder gap did little to hinder their efficiencies, their power or the resulting accuracy.

SOME HISTORY ON THE DOUBLE-ACTION REVOLVER

Early authorities when first introduced to double-action shooting described the process as "trigger cocking." By that they meant the hammer was cocked through action of the trigger, which is an accurate description even today, but most describe it simply as "double-action shooting".

Some have credited Joseph Rider in 1859 with invention of the double-action revolver. Rider was an employee of Remington and invented the Remington Rolling Block rifle action. An Englishman, Robert Adams, had already developed a trigger-cocking percussion revolver and was marketing it by 1851. The Adams revolver had a .50 caliber bore and a five-shot cylinder. It proved to be a strong, early rival of Colt, at least in England and Europe. Unfortunately, the Adams revolver was what would be described today as a 'double-action-only' or DAO. It had no single-action capability and therefore drew much criticism in terms of its poor target accuracy. It was faster in instinctive or reactive shooting, but it was difficult for many shooters to maintain a steady hold and good sight picture while pulling the heavy Adams trigger through its long trigger pull.

This only demonstrates that few things are new. Prior to the transition to semi-auto pistols, many large metropolitan police departments had all their service revolvers altered to DAO status. The fear was the officer would unconsciously or deliberately cock the revolver while holding a suspect at gunpoint and then be startled into inadvertently firing the revolver by a sudden movement from the suspect or a bystander. The fact remains however, even with semi-auto designs, DAO handguns are more difficult to shoot accurately and little has changed since the original complaints were voiced against the Adams revolver before the American Civil War.

Unlike their revolvers, Smith & Wesson's DAO auto-pistols have no second strike capability. If the round does not fire with the double-action trigger pull, the slide has to be racked to chamber a fresh round and recock the mechanism.

The S&W Model 57-2 shown at the top is a custom revolver that is one of an identical pair of revolvers. They were made for the author and the British gunwriter Rob Adam. The American flag is on the right side of each barrel of the two while the left side shows the Union Jack. Unfortunately, Adam no longer can possess his twin to this revolver because the British government outlawed all handguns and forced him to get rid of it. The bottom revolver is a S&W Model 24-3 in .44 Special featuring a 3-inch barrel and round-butt frame. There are a number of shooters and collectors who appreciate a well made .44 Special revolver and many feel this particular revolver is one of the finer examples.

Double-action revolvers enjoyed limited success prior to the turn of the 20th century because Colt and Smith & Wesson introduced various primitive double-action models in hopes of military and civilian sales. Difficulties arose soon because many of the earlier designs just were not durable enough for rough service on the frontier or in the hands of a military trooper. It wasn't until the military adopted the Colt Model 1894 in .38 caliber that double-action, swing-out cylinder revolvers made a serious impact on the world of fighting handguns. Unfortunately, their impact soon proved to be more of a shallow splash for a number of reasons, not the least of which was the ammunition's proven ineffectiveness in the Philippine campaigns of the Spanish-American War.

The Colt 1894 .38 caliber revolver was the first of a series of revolvers that underwent continual upgrade because of design deficiencies. Modern shooters should know Colt double-action revolvers all have cylinders that rotate clockwise when viewed from the rear. One of the early problems with the first Colt .38 was the cylinder rotated counter-clockwise and was on occasion *self-opening*. While some might think that an advantage, the serviceman who had this happen to him during a squabble with angry natives in the Philippines, didn't find it a particularly endearing trait. He desperately needed to fire the remaining rounds in the cylinder to guarantee, or at least help with his own survival. Sadly, the performance of the .38 Long Colt cartridge against the Moros during the action in the Philippines did little to maintain any kind of a guarantee. The Moros were tough, dedicated opponents and damned hard to stop, especially after they ingested drugs in preparation for a coming battle. There were many documented instances where American military personnel armed with the .38 Colt emptied their revolvers into charging Moros to no effect. They suffered the indignity of having the Moro warrior kill them with a crude native made blade.

There have been revolvers made for the 9x19mm cartridge and they worked without the need for 'moon' clips. This Model 547 from Smith & Wesson was built on the K-frame and featured a six-shot cylinder. The spent brass was ejected through action of six individual spring ejectors.

The failure of the .38 Colt revolver remains with those who study these things and makes it hard for many students of small arms to accept any medium-bore military pistol as an adequate means of self-defense for military personnel. History has a tendency to repeat itself and more than a few are wondering if that isn't what is happening today in Iraq and Afghanistan with the dismal performance of the 9mm M9 service pistol. The ballistic performance of the 9x19mm military full-metal-jacket round when compared to the 148-grain Long Colt of 100 years ago is not that much different. Is it any wonder the Marine Corps has returned to the .45 ACP for some applications?

In 1899 Smith & Wesson introduced their Model 1899 Hand Ejector in .38 S&W Special caliber. It wasn't long before this revolver which evolved into the legendary Smith & Wesson Model 10 Military & Police revolver became synonymous with the term "police revolver". It also was the bread and butter product for Smith & Wesson for many years.

During World War I, revolvers played an important role for the men fighting in the trenches. Trench warfare was a miserable, dirty and deadly experience. Previous to the 'Great War' military movement was achieved through breakthroughs brought on by cavalry troops charging against the weak points in the opposition line. The belt-fed machine gun put a stop to the cavalry charge in an earnest and lethally efficient manner. Several technologies, like the airplane, poison gas and the machine gun were revolutionary. They were often misapplied and this led to a stalemate condition resulting in lines of opposing trenches stretching from Switzerland all the way north to the French/Belgium seashore. Neither side could overcome the opponent's use of the same technology. Men armed with long rifles soon found that short, handy, powerful and reliable handguns were a decided advantage in the muddy trenches when defending against raiders who surreptitiously crossed No Man's Land.

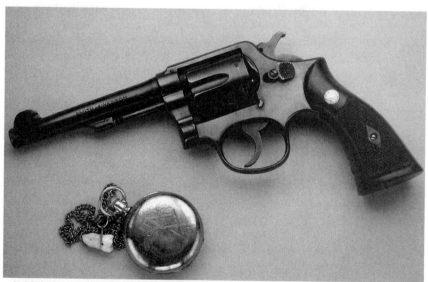

Smith & Wesson established their reputation with what became known as the Model 10 Military & Police revolver in .38 Special caliber. The example seen here was produced shortly after World War II ended and as such it was known simply as the Military & Police revolver.

The series of revolvers from Smith & Wesson known as Mountain Revolvers all share some common characteristics, if not common calibers. They feature thin 1950s-style barrels, the front edges of the cylinder are well-rounded and they have round-butt frames. This S&W Mountain Gun is chambered for the .45 Colt cartridge.

The United States entered the war in 1917 and was totally unprepared for the conflict. Among the many shortcomings was a shortage of effective handguns. In 1911 the United States Army adopted the John Browning-designed and Colt-manufactured Model 1911 semi-automatic pistol in .45 ACP. The 1911 pistol would go on to become the quintessential American fighting handgun, but in 1917 there weren't enough of them to arm the Doughboys fighting in France. The alternative was a revolver chambered in the same cartridge as the Colt semi-auto and both Colt and Smith & Wesson built them.

They were large revolvers. The Colt model was the New Service, and the Smith & Wesson was the Model 1917 and built on the N-frame. These same revolvers would later serve American law enforcement during the Great Depression. They were big-bore, serious fighting revolvers and they were cheap when money was scarce because the government declared them war surplus. Prior to America's entry into World War I, Smith & Wesson had already been building many revolvers for use as fighting handguns in the Great War. The British recognizing the difficulties of fighting in the confined space of the trenches ordered a number of Smith & Wesson's New Century revolvers, or what many recognize today as the 'Triple Lock', chambered for the .455 British revolver service cartridge. The Triple Lock was not a gun to use in the muddy trenches of the Somme or on the Belgium frontier. For one thing the Smith & Wesson New Century was a testament to close tolerances and hand-fitting, these close tolerances together with the underlug shroud which protected the ejector rod became repositories of mud and embedded dirt. Too much dirt and mud and the gun didn't work as it should. In the filthy environment of the trenches it was not the easiest pistol to take apart and clean. The experience gained with the New Century

The S&W Model 625 Mountain Gun in .45 Colt was manufactured for a limited run. It is appreciated by those who like shooting big heavy bullets at moderate velocities. The Mountain Gun concept has proven popular because it provides the outdoor enthusiast with a lightweight, but powerful 'trail' gun.

and the British before 1917 was certainly reflected in the design of the revolver Smith & Wesson manufactured for the American soldier with the Model 1917. The ejector rod shroud was noticeably missing and many experts feel this was to help keep the gun clean and functioning in an absolutely detestable environment.

Prior to the attack on Pearl Harbor, the British approached Smith & Wesson in a quest for small arms as they were once again at war with the German people and a fanatical leadership. Only this time they didn't want a fighting handgun, but a carbine, to be specific a 9mm carbine. Unfortunately, someone got it wrong and the whole project came to nothing after all the upfront money had been spent. The Brits could have easily forced Smith & Wesson into bankruptcy and oblivion. A forward-thinking manager at the company talked the British War Office into accepting an equivalent amount of Smith & Wesson revolvers, chambered for the .38 S&W cartridge featuring a 200-grain bullet, and called appropriately enough the .38/200 British service cartridge. (Note: it was NOT based on the .38 Special case and the two do not interchange.) The deal worked and the company was saved while the British armed forces were provided with over 500,000 of the British Service revolvers based on the mid-size .38 Military & Police Hand Ejector with either 4-, 5- or 6-inch barrel lengths. Later after the United States declared war on Japan and Germany, Smith & Wesson would start producing the same revolver for American military forces but the "Victory" model as it was called was chambered for the .38 S&W Special cartridge.

POLICE REVOLVERS

All during the 1920s, the 1930s and the 1940s Colt dominated the law enforcement market in terms of numbers sold and carried by the average American peace officer. A very popular model was the Colt Police Positive and it was a somewhat smallish medium frame double-action revolver that featured Colt's distinctive trigger mechanism. All of the locking for the cylinder was at the rear and involved not only the cylinder pin but the hand as well. The ejector rod on the front of the cylinder was left 'free' and did not engage a locking latch like that seen on the rival Smith & Wesson product. Be that as it may, Colt double-action revolvers were used by many of the top shooters during this time to win slow-fire and rapid-fire bull's-eye shooting championships. Colt stopped manufacture of their massive New Service revolver in 1942. It marketed no big-bore caliber service revolvers to law enforcement until the Colt Trooper and the Colt .357 Mag double-action revolvers were introduced in 1953. What many view as the ultimate Colt double-action revolver was introduced in 1955 and that was the Colt Python. The Colt Python remains in the eyes of many as the finest double-action revolver ever produced by the Colt Firearms Company if not one of the finest double-action revolvers ever made by anyone anywhere.

During the 1950s and 1960s, Smith & Wesson gained a dominant position in law enforcement sales. First it was their medium frame revolvers in .38 Special that earned acclaim. The Smith & Wesson revolver with a fully adjustable rear sight was a feature highly sought after by all shooters, not just law enforcement. Fully adjustable rear sights are considered common today, but for many years following World War II that was not the case in the handgun marketplace.

By far the most successful revolver for Smith & Wesson in the police market was the fabulous Model 19, or the .357 Combat Magnum. Smith & Wesson helped develop this cartridge and by the late 1960s it was becoming the universal police cartridge. The reason

To many the Colt Python is among the best, if not the best, double-action revolvers ever made. This example in the author's collection is an Ultimate Stainless model and features custom-made grips from the late proprietor of Bear Hug Grips.

was simple. It was the Model 19 built on the medium size K-frame and not the previous large and heavy N-frame. Police officers and others who packed a gun for long hours on a daily basis appreciated the weight savings while at the same time having the same amount of power available to deal with whatever criminal problem materialized.

The original .357 Magnum became known after 1957 as the Model 27. It was large and heavy. There was a budget-minded version called the Model 28 that featured less polish and no checkering on the top strap of the frame and barrel. It proved popular with law officers on a limited budget who were forced to purchase their own sidearms, but it was just as large and just as heavy. The one good benefit to these heavy guns was their ability to dampen the felt recoil from robust .357 Magnum loads. The Model 19 was not meant to consume a constant diet of full-power .357 Magnum ammunition and few were the men who would attempt to do so. The S&W Combat Magnum was designed at a time when police officers would practice and qualify with the lesser recoil of mild .38 Special ammunition and then load the gun with.357 Magnum loads as they went back to patrol duty. Jeff Cooper was the main critic of this procedure as he rightly stated that officer's not experienced with their duty round would not shoot it well during gunfights. The Smith & Wesson Model 19, however, didn't hold up over an extended period of time when fed a continuous diet of high-pressure .357 Magnum loads.

The .357 Combat Magnum was the brainchild of U.S. Border Patrolman Bill Jordan. He was also the fastest gun around during his service days. He wrote a book about gunfighting entitled *No Second Place Winner,* which more or less sums up the whole concept in one phrase. He knew what peace officers needed and he alone got Smith &

The Smith & Wesson Model 696 is no longer in the catalog. Not that it's gone, different areas of the country are seeing these L-frame revolvers sell for a premium because of their .44 Special chambering. These five-shot .44 Special revolvers work well in a self-defense application and those who appreciate big-bore revolvers prefer them.

At least one Smith & Wesson Model 19 was used to protect the President of the United States. This Model 19 Combat Magnum is Walt Rauch's service revolver from his days at the United States Secret Service. Super Vel was the first handgun ammunition to feature an expanding jacketed hollowpoint that actually worked as advertised. **PHOTO CREDIT: JOSH MARKOWITZ**

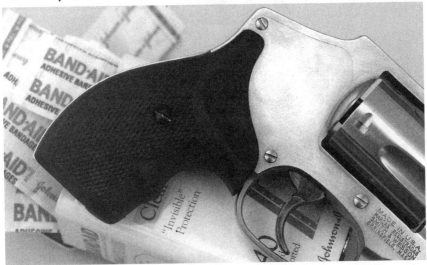

The Uncle Mike's Boot Grip which comes standard on many of the Smith & Wesson .357 Magnum J-frame revolvers is great for concealment, but poor in terms of managing the felt recoil.

Wesson to build the Model 19. It became synonymous with a fightin' revolver during the 1970s. Everyone who carried a gun had to have one and I've owned several.

Smith & Wesson came out with the L-frame revolver in 1980 to correct the durability problem encountered from constant use of the full-power .357 Magnum ammunition. It was a revolver built with a grip identical in size to the previous K-frame. It has proven extremely popular over the past two decades and can still be found in the holsters of those who refuse to jump on the auto-pistol bandwagon.

Colt was one of the last revolver manufacturers to build a .44 Magnum, and in 1990 it finally appeared. It was the Anaconda. They are strong, well-built revolvers even if they lack the fit and finish of the wonderful Python revolver. Initially the Anaconda had some accuracy problems with the barrels. That was corrected soon after introduction and today they remain a good deal for anyone interested in a .44 Magnum double-action revolver.

Sturm, Ruger & Co. as all this was going on was not sitting idly by and waiting for business. Ruger introduced a number of well-designed, innovative, double-action revolvers that earned accolades for their strength and accuracy. The Ruger GP-100 was Ruger's answer to the Smith & Wesson L-frame and it was introduced in 1986. The real winner in Ruger's portfolio was the Redhawk, a double-action revolver that is built like a Mack truck. Until the advent of the recently introduced Smith & Wesson X-frame, the Redhawk was acknowledged as the strongest and toughest double-action revolver ever built. The surprising fact is it is about the same size as the long discontinued Colt New Service, so while large it is still a 'hand' gun and not something that requires wheels.

Taurus International entered the .44 Magnum sweepstakes in 1994. These made-in-Brazil revolvers have an apparent similarity to the products made in Springfield, Mass.

The GP-100 was Ruger's answer to the Smith & Wesson L-frame revolvers as seen in the Model 586 and 686. Despite the advertising war at the time between Ruger and Smith & Wesson, the GP-100 is a strong, well made and accurate .357 Magnum revolver. PHOTO CREDIT: STURM, RUGER & CO.

They are not the same, but they do have a similar balance, which is a good thing. At one time Taurus had a custom shop and one of the products from their custom shop was a short-barreled .44 Magnum with the Schumann venture barrel porting system. Elmer Keith once told me he didn't like little holes being drilled in his gun barrels and for the most part I agree with Elmer, but I have to say the Schumann system worked exceedingly well at taming the felt recoil from the short Taurus .44 Magnum.

The Ruger Redhawk is built like a Mack truck. It is strong and capable of withstanding rough use and punishment. This model however is chambered in .45 Colt caliber so it can enjoy a rather leisurely life.

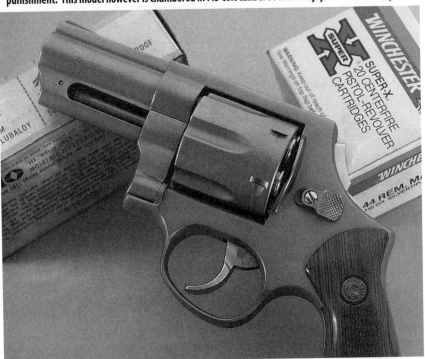

Taurus revolvers are made in Brazil. This .44 Magnum Taurus has a feel and balance to it that is similar to the Smith & Wesson Model 29, but these revolvers are different internally from the S&W product.

Taurus also produces a five-shot .41 Magnum snub-nose and a version with a longer barrel called the "Tracker." If you are used to the smoothness of a good S&W, then you probably won't be satisfied with the factory trigger found on most Taurus products. One thing about these smaller Taurus big-bore magnums is the exclusive Taurus 'Ribber' grip. I generally don't care for synthetic grips, but this one is good and it really works at taming felt recoil. This makes it easy to recommend.

Currently, the magnum caliber revolvers are most often used in the hunting fields and are seldom found in police cruisers or inspected during roll calls. There are those who feel the sun has finally set on the fighting revolver, but there are a few who don't quite agree. Clint Smith of Thunder Ranch has a class just for revolver shooters. It was my great pleasure to attend one. What follows are my impressions of that class.

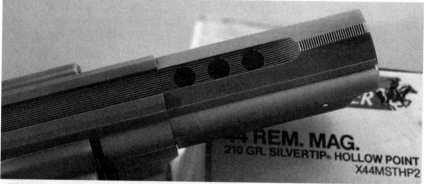

When Taurus operated a custom shop they produced these .44 Magnum revolvers that offered the Schuemann Venturi porting system. The system worked quite well in taming the felt recoil of the short-barreled .44 Magnum Taurus.

This Taurus custom .44 Magnum proved accurate and because of the porting it was tamed to a controllable level.

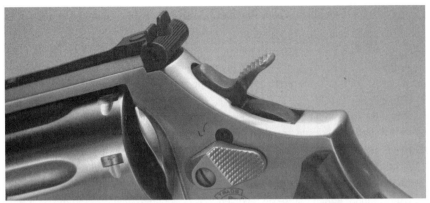

For years double-action revolvers were made without manual safeties. While the key-operated internal trigger lock does not actually function in the same way as the manual safety does on an auto-pistol, the internal trigger lock is a 'safety' device the modern consumer of new Smith & Wesson revolvers must accept.

The best feature on many of the Taurus double-action revolvers in the opinion of the author is the patented Taurus 'Ribber' synthetic grip. This is one grip that helps cushion and dampen the felt recoil from hard-recoiling, powerful revolvers.

EFFECTIVE DEFENSE WITH A REVOLVER

"The great thing about these guns is you only have to do one thing to make them work," Clint Smith said as he began pulling seven concealed revolvers, of all sizes, from under his vest, out of his shirt and from inside his jeans. The simplicity of the revolver is the strongest advantage offered to anyone seeking a reliable self-defense tool.

To operate a revolver all one has to do is pull the trigger. There are no manual safeties (well, at least there aren't any on the ones made before the last couple of years). There are no slide releases to operate and there aren't any decocking levers to get confused over. Revolvers are simple machines.

The WEAK point of the revolver in Smith's estimation is you more or less have to disassemble the gun in order to reload it.

The Thunder Ranch course on revolvers was designed to help develop the skills that only a couple decades ago were routinely being taught at police academies and firing ranges all across America. With so much attention being paid to autoloaders over the past two decades the proper manipulation of the combat revolver in a fight is slowly being forgotten to the point of obscurity and benign neglect.

"Probably more pistol fights have been won by revolvers than auto-pistols," was the next statement from Smith as he explained the reason why revolvers are still workable defense tools.

What are the two most important factors facing anyone concerned with being in a gunfight?

What will the threat look like? And what will it take to win the fight?

The answer to the first one is: no one can tell you what the threat will look like. For women, the statistical chances are great their attacker will be a man of some description, but beyond that there is precious little useful information. For men, they carry with them years of baggage and prejudice that colors, or in many cases, blinds their awareness.

The Smith & Wesson Model 610 is a 10mm revolver, but it is winning hearts on the IDPA competition circuit in the Standard Service Revolver category. Only no one is shooting 10mm ammo in them. They are filling their full-moon clips with .40 S&W ammo because it offers less recoil and the case is shorter so they eject from the gun quicker and easier.

The answer to the second question is: no one knows exactly what it will take to win the fight because no one can predict with any certainty who will be the attacker.

With that base assumption and open-ended question as the pretext, Smith then elaborated on the three goals of the Thunder Ranch Revolver course of instruction; 1.) to teach marksmanship with the revolver, 2.) to improve the shooter's physical manipulation and mechanical skills with a revolver, and 3.) to establish and promote the student's mental conditioning.

"Repetition is the mother of skill" Smith said as he explained how the course of instruction and the resulting drills would involve what would seem to be mind-numbing repetition of the same basic operations. "A revolver is a thinking person's gun. You have to *think* to fight with this thing," Smith said as he held up a Smith & Wesson Model 19 Combat Magnum with a 4-inch barrel.

To explain in a step-by-step process, you have to keep the revolver "gassed up" (to use his words) and that means you have to open the cylinder and remove it from within the frame, but yes it is attached to the crane. The shooter then must manually remove the fired case or cases (whatever the situation) from the respective chambers in the cylinder, and then reload the individual chambers before replacing the cylinder back within the frame of the revolver. Most often this entire process occurs while under great duress and these movements require fine motor skills which on an auto-pistol require only gross motor skills.

Following this explanation, the main emphasis on the first day was learning how to keep the guns "gassed up" and it was a process that did NOT involve working with speedloaders. Smith had each revolver shooter fill a strong side pocket with plenty of loose ammunition. They were then instructed to load ONLY one round in the cylinder. The key part in the next

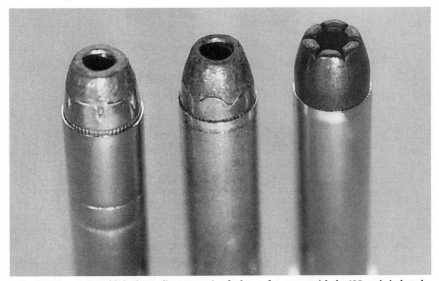

The .357 Magnum established a sterling reputation for law enforcement with the 125-grain jacketed hollowpoint round (left), the 158-grain jacketed hollowpoint (center) worked well, but many feared it over-penetrated, while the 180-grain Black Talon (right) and equivalent .357 Magnum loads were designed solely for hunting purposes.

step of the drill was remembering which way the cylinder rotated. Why? Because you want to close the cylinder and place it back in the frame in such a way the single loaded chamber in your five-, six-, seven- or eight-shot revolver is the next one to fire. Smith & Wesson revolvers rotate counter-clockwise. Colt double-action revolvers rotate clockwise. This is vitally important to know and understand because you want the freshly fired case at the top of the cylinder when you open and remove the cylinder from the gun.

While we were learning all these vital revolver manipulation skills, Smith was also reminding everyone to keep the gun 'high' relative to your field of vision. You must maintain visual contact with your adversary and the gun. During the reload, it should be in the lower portion of your vision as you watch your opponent, but high in relation to your body. None of the shooters in training at Thunder Ranch during my visit were allowed to lower their revolvers down to the level of their belt buckle. This is a technique often used in competition because it is fast due to the short distance between the speedloader carrier and the revolver at this level.

We were also reminded, "The proper way to use a double-action revolver is to fire it only with a double-action trigger pull and this reflects the opinion of the management of Thunder Ranch." To put a finer touch on it, the double-action trigger pull should be one continuous rearward stroke pulled completely through, then the trigger finger should move forward smoothly so the mechanism can reset.

The Smith & Wesson Model 686 PLUS is a seven-shooter. The trigger action is noticeably different than the traditional six-shot version.

▶ The Smith & Wesson Centennial in .357 Magnum caliber is a combination of maximum power in a minimal package. It is a triumph of technology, but the author questions its application if the average shooter has trouble managing the felt recoil.

You don't use up a lot of ammo when you are doing one round drills with a sixgun. You do learn the importance of positioning the cylinder in such a way that the single round in it is the first chamber presented to the firing pin on the subsequent trigger pull. You also learn that once you get the movements down, you can really reload a revolver rather rapidly with nothing more than a few spare rounds in a strong side pocket.

Two-round drills were the next order of business and the routine was as before; keep the gun high during the reload. Remember which way the cylinder rotated and position the fresh rounds to be the next fired and use only a double-action trigger pull when you fired. This was followed by a repeat of the two-round reloading sequence. The truth is after an hour or so of these drills my attitudes toward speedloaders changed.

Speedloaders are nice if you have an empty gun, but they add nothing if you have to fire two, seek cover and then ponder the reload. Do you throw away four good rounds to replace the two you've fired? Not with this technique and not only that if you practice it for just an hour or two it becomes natural, smooth and speedy.

Three-round drills were next. Here you start to use more time to replace and replenish the rounds in the cylinder. With the one-and two-round drills the shooter was advised not to dump the entire cylinder but to push the end of the ejector rod in about a half an inch and that would raise the fired cases above the non-fired cases in the cylinder when the muzzle was pointed or angled down. It was easy with one or two fired cases to pluck these cases out of the cylinder in one smooth motion, but grabbing three spent cases became a little more difficult. It was not impossible, just more difficult.

The hardest thing I had to learn was after firing four or five rounds was to dump the entire cylinder for a six-round speedloader reload. Throwing away good rounds is a tough decision for the revolver shooter in a fight. It raises the question, which is more important; the speed of the reload, or the total number of rounds you will need to win the fight? A partial solution is to carry as much spare ammunition as possible and this training has influenced my thinking since the class.

I find I combine at least one speedloader with a number of loose rounds for spare ammo. Since I normally use a six-shot revolver, I carry my loose rounds in multiples of seven. Why? Because if during the reload I drop one round (the complications of a gross motor skill ability doing a fine motor skill requirement) I can still load the cylinder with six rounds if need be.

Many semi-auto shooters will ridicule these techniques and revolvers in general. Clint Smith brought out a great point when he reminded everyone at the end of the class that you don't know where you will be when the threat materializes, nor do you know what it will look like. Also, you have no idea what it will take to win the fight. It could be if you are normally a semi-auto shooter that your only choice of self-defense will be a revolver someone else brought to the fight. Anyone interested in armed self-defense should know how to fight effectively with a revolver. I don't always carry a revolver for self-defense, but after taking the Thunder Ranch revolver course I don't feel undergunned or at a disadvantage when I do.

CHAPTER SIX

The 9mm Pistols

D espite the controversy surrounding the effectiveness of the 9mm cartridge, there are many popular pistols chambered for this round. Because the round is the most widely chambered military pistol cartridge in the world today these pistols form a class unto themselves.

The German Luger is a single-action semi-auto pistol. It was a revelation at its introduction because it proved the concept of a self-loading semi-automatic pistol as practical and reliable.

This European produced Luger in 9mm caliber is not a relic of the World War I, but rather a relatively recent reproduction of the original Luger pistol. Many commentators feel the Luger pistol was the first truly successful semi-auto pistol for military applications and as such it has its share of fans found worldwide.

What is commonly referred to as a "9mm" or simply "Nine" is one single cartridge that is known by several names: 9mm Luger, 9mm Parabellum and 9x19mm. There are pretenders, however, and one should never confuse the .380 ACP (9x17mm) with the Parabellum cartridge, nor should the 9mm Makarov (9x18mm) round be considered in the same class as the 9mm Luger round. Both the .380 ACP and the 9mm Makarov rounds are relatively low-pressure rounds designed to be used in blow-back action pistols. The 9mm Luger is a higher-pressure cartridge requiring, in most handguns, a locked-breech mechanism.

The 9mm Luger originated with the Luger pistol in 1902. The toggle-action Luger pistol was first introduced with a .30 caliber, bottlenecked cartridge, called appropriately enough, the 7.65mm Parabellum, but it was a non-performer for fighting. In an effort to increase effectiveness, the cartridge case was 'blown out' with the shoulder removed, eliminating the bottleneck. The 9mm is not a straight-walled case like many revolver cartridges. It is one featuring a slight taper as the case mouth has a slightly smaller diameter than the area in front of the extractor groove surrounding the base.

It was named the 9mm Parabellum. Although the pistol was known in America as the Luger, this handgun was called the *Parabellum* by everyone else in the world. The German manufacturer, DWM, coined this name. The word "Parabellum" is derived from the Latin phrase *Si Vis Pacem Para Bellum* or "If you want Peace, Prepare for War". It naturally followed this new cartridge would be commonly referred to as the 9mm Parabellum.

◀ The German Luger was the first fighting pistol to be chambered for the most successful centerfire auto-pistol cartridge of all time, the 9mm Luger. The Luger seen here was manufactured in the United States out of modern materials like stainless steel for those who appreciate this legendary pistol.

It is also known as the 9x19mm round because the empty case length is 19mm. The bullet diameter is 9mm (.354"), but another more modern term for it is 9mm NATO because the North Atlantic Treaty Organization (NATO) adopted it as the standard service pistol round. (It should be noted NATO military organizations load the 9mm service pistol ammo to a specification requiring higher chamber pressures and resulting increased velocities over those found with commercial 9mm Luger specifications.)

To increase the available firepower of the Luger pistol when used in trench warfare of World War I, the Luger was equipped with a 'snail' drum magazine which gave the pistol a far higher ammunition capacity over its single-column original. The drum magazine required the use of a loading tool (seen at the right) and other extras to fill it to full capacity.

9mm Parabellum ammunition can come in almost any bullet shape. Military ammunition is usually either a 'ball' or full metal jacketed round, but it can also have a small flat point with a tapered cone profile. When the bullet tip is painted black, it usually indicates either high-pressure ammo, or armor piercing ammunition, depending of course upon the specific manufacturer. Hollowpoint ammunition is pretty much self-explanatory and in the United States widely available.

▶ The Browning High Power was the first high-capacity 9mm pistol. The example shown here is the 4th such pistol from a run of 100 guns that were custom built by pistolsmith Wayne Novak.

The next important pistol in the life of the 9mm Parabellum cartridge was the Browning High Power. Called the P-35 or the Model 1935, Grand Pruissance, Fabrique Nationale, the manufacturer, produced John Browning's last design. Browning died on November 26, 1926, but a little over three years prior to his death he filed for patents covering certain design details for the pistol, which was introduced nine years after his death. However, the *real* father of the pistol that would become known the world over as the Browning High Power was Dieudonne J. Saive. Saive was the genius who would solve the puzzle of stuffing 13 rounds of 9mm Parabellum ammunition into a single, but small detachable box magazine, and he was still able to keep the overall dimensions of the grip containing this box magazine comfortable for a majority of pistol shooters.

It was a triumph of design. The Depression was on and money was tight, so it took FN several years to find the capital necessary for the new pistol. FN was, of course, extremely concerned about slow sales. They actively promoted the idea that it was John Browning's last pistol and the subterfuge worked. Even to this day some small arms commentators believe it was John Browning's last work when a review of the historical record will easily prove otherwise.

The Beretta Model 92F became the M9 and M10 service pistol after acceptance as the service pistol of the United States military forces in 1985 and subsequent years. It serves now with our forces in Iraq and Afghanistan.

The Gunsite Gunsmithy produced an excellent example of a fighting pistol in .45 ACP.

▲ Nothing is as beautiful as an engraved Colt with ivory grips. Originally, the beauty of this gun was in its dependability and reliable operation.

Introduced in 1873, the Colt Single Action Army revolver became the sidearm of the U.S. Cavalry and the choice of thousands who settled in the American West.

▲ The 10mm auto cartridge was first developed for the Bren Ten project, but that pistol proved to be a marketing failure. The gun seen here is a custom Springfield Armory 1911 pistol in 10mm auto from Richard Heinie, PHOTO CREDIT: HEINIE SPECIALTY PRODUCTS

▲ This 10mm auto Colt built by custom pistolsmith Richard Heinie has been used by the author for more than a decade. It has seen extensive use in a variety of applications and performs beautifully. PHOTO CREDIT: HEINIE SPECIALTY PRODUCTS

The S&W Model 640 (top) is a .38 Special revolver rated for "+P+" loads. In 1995, a version in .357 Magnum was introduced to create an extremely powerful, yet small magnum caliber revolver.

The introduction of the Smith & Wesson Model 19 Combat Magnum made the .357 Magnum round one of the most successful revolver cartridges in the history of American law enforcement. PHOTO CREDIT: SMITH & WESSON

◄ The Smith & Wesson Centennial in .357 Magnum is a combination of maximum power in a minimal package. It is a triumph of technology, but the average shooter will have trouble managing the felt recoil.

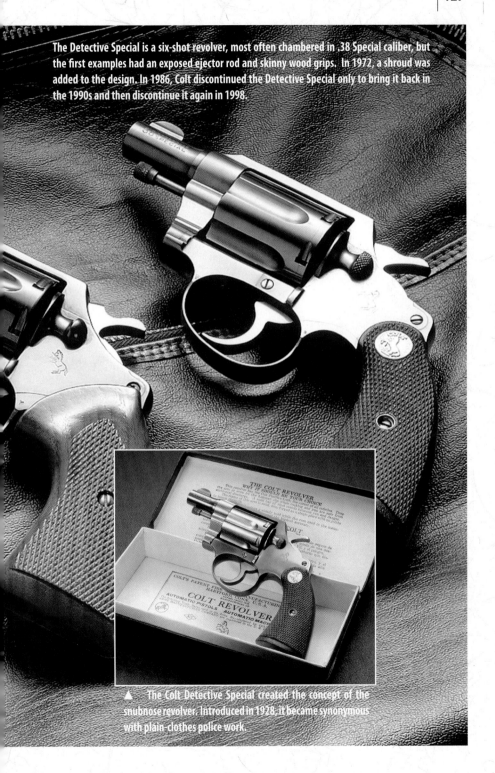

The Detective Special is a six-shot revolver, most often chambered in .38 Special caliber, but the first examples had an exposed ejector rod and skinny wood grips. In 1972, a shroud was added to the design. In 1986, Colt discontinued the Detective Special only to bring it back in the 1990s and then discontinue it again in 1998.

▲ The Colt Detective Special created the concept of the snubnose revolver. Introduced in 1928, it became synonymous with plain-clothes police work.

The CZ-75 is one of the most successful 9mm pistol designs seen since the close of World War II. The great irony is it was designed under a Communist regime that failed to protect this design with a 'capitalist' international patent. It has been copied extensively.

▲ The German Luger was the first fighting pistol chambered for the 9mm cartridge. The Luger seen here was manufactured in the United States for those who appreciate this legendary pistol.

▲ The Glock has revolutionized the world of handguns. Many feel it is a pure fighting pistol. The mid-size Glock Model 19 shown here initially came with a 15+1 magazine capacity.

▲ SIG 'Classic' pistols have proven popular with many different law enforcement agencies. The SIG Model 228 (left) was once the issued pistol for the FBI. The SIG Model 229 (center) is a .40 caliber version of the SIG 228. The SIG Model 226 (right) was the close competitor to the Beretta in the U.S. military trials of the 1980s.

► This "Thunder Ranch Special" 1911 Government Model from Wilson's Gun Shop, Inc. is a special tribute to Thunder Ranch and effective handgun defense.

▲ The HK USP pistol was a direct response by HK to the demands of the American market. The HK USP was one of the first pistols to come with an accessory rail for the mounting of a tactical lamp.

◄ This custom P-12 from Richard Heinie sports fine-line checkering on the grip, a squared off triggerguard, Heinie's own rear sight and a number of other custom features.

▶ The GP-100 was Ruger's answer to the Smith & Wesson L-frame revolvers as seen in the Model 586 and 686. The GP-100 is a strong, well made and accurate revolver. PHOTO CREDIT: STURM, RUGER & CO.

For years the caliber selection in any Browning High Power was mostly 9mm Parabellum with an occasion small run of .30 Luger thrown in specific European markets. The addition of the .40 S&W Browning High Power (seen here on the left) raised the power level of this popular pistol.

▲ The Smith & Wesson Centennial, the Model 40 (top left) featured a grip safety sticking out the back of the grip. The Model 42 (top right) was the same revolver featuring an alloy frame and lighter weight. The revolver on the lower right is a custom Model 640 from the Smith & Wesson Performance Center while the Model 642 at the lower left is an alloy-frame with a stainless steel barrel and cylinder.

▶ At least one Smith & Wesson Model 19 was used to protect the President of the United States. This Model 19 Combat Magnum is Walt Rauch's service revolver from his days at the United States Secret Service. PHOTO CREDIT: JOSH MARKOWITZ

Effective Handgun Defense can be achieved with an easy to conceal, easy to shoot 9x19mm handgun like the Walther P99C AS shown here at top, or the engraved Smith & Wesson Model 57 in .41 Magnum. The author prefers the power of the revolver, but acknowledges the advantages offered by a small lightweight polymer semi-auto for concealed carry self-defense.

◄ The author commissioned engraver John Peace to engrave with full coverage this 'S' prefix Model 57, .41 Magnum Smith & Wesson revolver with a four-inch barrel to honor his daughter, Valerie Victoria, who was tragically killed in an automobile accident when she was 17 years old. He did this to create a family heirloom that would preserve both her memory and his love for revolvers of this type.

Because the author believes a companion handgun in .22 rimfire to the one owned in a serious caliber is an absolute necessity, he had John Peace engrave this Smith & Wesson Model 18 with a four-inch barrel. It honors his son and carries scenes of his childhood. Both the .41 Magnum revolver and this .22 rimfire revolver are fitted with elephant ivory grips and depict images and sayings within the engraving that are important to members of his family.

▲ The Walther TPH is an extremely small pistol and although it is chambered in a .22 rimfire caliber it is often used as a deep-concealment pistol for self-defense.

▲▲ Colt Firearms celebrated the 20th Anniversary of the founding of the International Practical Shooting Confederation (IPSC) with a series of commemorative pistols. The "DVC" seen engraved on the slide stands for; Diligentia, Vis, Celeritas. Translated from Latin they are Accuracy, Power, Speed.

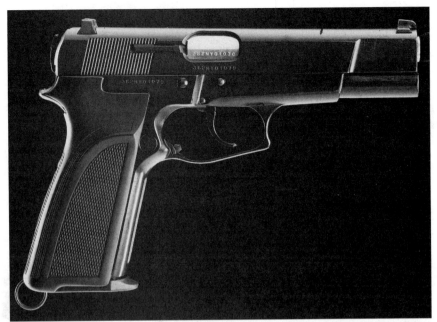

FN, the manufacturer of the Browning High Power, developed the BDAO as a replacement pistol for police and military forces wanting a double-action-only semi-auto pistol. It maintains the same lines and overall shape as the Browning High Power, but the internal mechanism is completely different.
PHOTO CREDIT: FN HERSTAL

The Walther P-38 was the first successful double-action/single-action 9mm semi-auto pistol in the history of small arms. The method used to lock the barrel and its trigger operation is very similar to that found on the current Beretta Model 92.

The Browning P-35 was a big success. It was used by both sides in World War II and it is probably *the* most frequently encountered 9mm pistol in the world today where armed men are found. It is still being manufactured, but it was the concept and execution of the high-capacity handgun magazine that made the Browning High Power such a landmark among 9mm pistols.

The next step in the progression of 9mm pistol designs was seen three years after the introduction of the Browning High Power and that was the Walther P-38.

The Luger remained Germany's service pistol after World War I, but the Treaty of Versailles forbade the manufacture of 9mm service pistols by German or Austrian arms manufacturers. Sometime in the 1930s the German military began secret research on a replacement pistol for the fabled Luger as they started to covertly rebuild their military forces. The problem with the Luger was it required extensive machine time. This was a precious commodity in a country rearming for war under Adolf Hitler. During the war that followed the problem was exacerbated by daylight raids from the American 8th Air Force and nighttime bombardments by the Royal Air Force Bomber Command.

The Walther P-38, even though it had more parts (58) than the Luger (54), was designed for mass production. By contrast, the Luger pistol required 778 separate operations for manufacture, of which 136 needed to be performed by hand. But, the really important feature of the Walther P-38 had to do with its method of operation. It was the first double-action semi-automatic pistol to be offered in 9mm Parabellum.

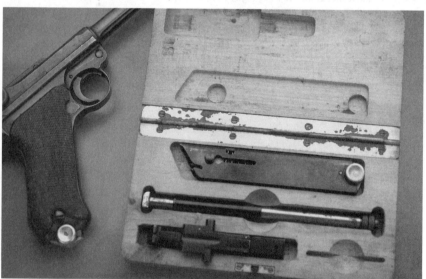

To aid in training a new shooter with the Luger pistol, the factory manufactured this .22 caliber rimfire conversion kit. The kit is shown here in its original wood packaging and used common .22 Long Rifle cartridges to operate.

▶ **Following the interest in polymer-framed handguns, Sturm, Ruger & Co. introduced their own series of polymer-framed pistols. Ruger pistols are known for their rugged dependability and the polymer models are no exception to the rule.**

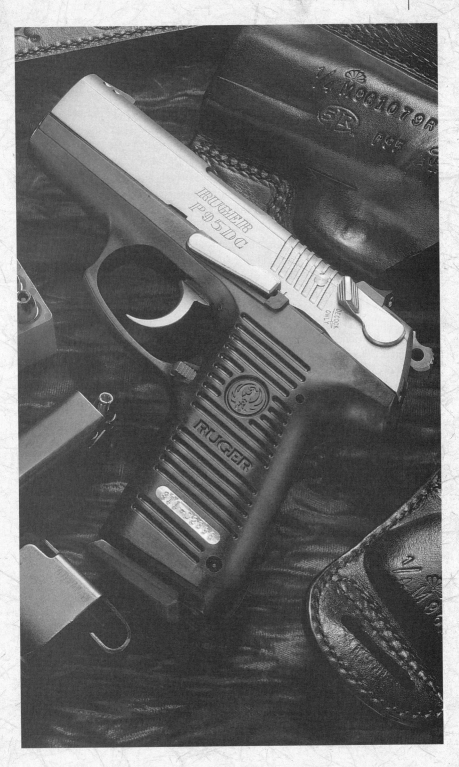

The previous Walther Model PP proved a double-action semi-auto pistol could be reliable. Introduced in 1929, the Walther PP was a blowback pistol. Yet, the 9mm Parabellum cartridge required a locked breech design. Unlike the Browning-designed pistols, which employ a dropping barrel to unlock the barrel from the slide, the Walther P-38 used a 'dropping block' which was located under the barrel to lock its action. The Walther P-38 could be cocked like a single-action semi-auto and fired accordingly. It could also be fired quickly and solely through constant pressure against the trigger, starting with the hammer in the 'down' position.

It is this feature that many of the military and police 9mm pistols presently available have copied. Of course, the argument continues as to whether the double-action capability of a semi-auto pistol is really needed. One of the most often repeated critical comments came from Jeff Cooper. He described the double-action semi-auto pistol as being the solution to a problem that didn't exist.

Cooper is a dyed-in-the-wool single-action auto advocate and his reasons are sound. There exists today a number of police administrators and others in both police and military circles who demand the first shot be operated by means of a long double-action trigger pull. The concern lies with what used to be described as "accidental discharges" (AD), but more often now are classified as "negligent discharges" (ND). The argument is a long double-action trigger pull is safer because there is less chance of the gun firing unintentionally. Concern is often expressed over the ease by which a single-action auto can be fired. Some feel it *is too easy* to fire a single-action handgun and this leads to the negligent discharge.

The truth is proper training eliminates many of these concerns and anyone handling a handgun should understand any time a finger is inside the trigger guard, the pistol is ready to be fired. Another difficulty is some authorities who are critical of single-action autos are also the ones most reluctant to spend the money necessary for really extensive

Corrosion resistance is important because humid climates can damage internal mechanisms and render any pistol carried close less than mechanically perfect or reliable. For this reason, the stainless steel version of the Beretta Model 92 has proven popular among law enforcement professionals.

firearms training. Good training will correct many shortcomings. Two rules all good firearms trainers and knowledgeable firearms safety instructors emphasize is: Never Point Any Firearm At Anything You Are Not Willing To Destroy; and NEVER Put Your Finger On The Trigger UNTIL Your Sights Are Aligned On The Target. These two commandments are inclusive and work on all types of safety mechanisms or methods of mechanical operation, and if followed faithfully they eliminate negligent discharges.

LOCATION OF THE SAFETY ON A 9MM PISTOL

One of the complaints concerning the Walther P-38 was it had the mechanical safety located on the slide and it worked in the opposite direction of the safety lever found on the 1911 Government Model pistol. Most American shooters, and those from other countries trained on the 1911 pistol, found this to be more than inconvenient because once trained to push the frame mounted safety "down", it was almost impossible to instinctively push the same slide-mounted lever "up" in an immediate reaction drill.

This problem continues yet to this day in auto-pistol design. Invariably slide-mounted safety levers are usually pushed forward or "up" to fire, while most all frame-mounted safety levers must move down to fire the gun. After years of intensive study and practice, I have to agree with those who prefer the 1911 style of operation as I have found it is extremely difficult to relearn the 'push up' method of manual safety operation on any slide-mounted safety. Of course, the counter argument is if you learned on the slide-mounted safety in the first place, it wouldn't be so difficult. Interviews with beginning IPSC and IDPA shooters cast this claim in a very weak light. They all report it is easier to operate the 1911 style frame-mounted safety than the upward-swinging slide-mounted safety.

The Browning High Power is often chosen for custom projects by talented gunsmiths. The sights have been replaced with Novak Lo-Mount rear sight and a dovetail front sight, both featuring tritium glow-in-the-dark inserts. The surface finish on the top of the slide has been stippled to reduce glare and grip area has been stippled as well to increase the user's purchase.

The reason this is such a point of contention among authorities is law enforcement officers, and certainly military personnel, are required to carry their sidearms with the safeties engaged. In a reactive scenario, speed is essential, and operation of the safety mechanism is a key factor in the speed of deployment for the defensive pistol.

The test of any self-defense pistol is its accuracy and reliability. This small Swiss-made Sphinx 'hide-out' pistol was both, but it was manufactured before the period where the firm was owned by a non-Swiss firm who lowered the standards initially established with the Sphinx. Today, the firm has returned to Swiss ownership and a return to far higher standards of manufacturing.

The CZ-75 pistol is one of the most successful 9mm pistol designs seen since the close of World War II. The great irony is it was designed under a Communist regime which failed to protect this design with a 'capitalist' international patent. It has been copied extensively and the CZ-75 in any of its mutated forms remains one of the better fighting 9mm pistols of the last 30 years.

The Swiss manufactured Sphinx pistol was a design lifted from the CZ-75, but it was an extremely high-quality pistol, better in many ways than the original, due to the Swiss proclivity for superb quality in manufactured goods. The pistol shown here was the Sphinx "MASTER", a superb and super-accurate competition pistol.

The .380 ACP cartridge is not as powerful as any 9mm Luger round as this photo demonstrates. Any two of these bullet strikes from a 9mm Luger pistol would have neutralized this Skipper target and dropped it to the ground. The .380 Sphinx failed to do that with an entire magazine of ammunition.

One solution to this quandary was developed behind the Iron Curtain during the glory days of the Evil Empire. The CZ-75 is a design that many have copied and for a very excellent reason, it's a great pistol. CZ is located today in the Czech Republic, but during the Cold War, Czechoslovakia was part of the Warsaw Pact and thoroughly communist in its political outlook. All communist countries followed the Soviet example and adopted arms and calibers of Russian origin. The CZ-75 was the first 9mm semi-auto pistol developed expressly for sale to the West and it offered a new idea in auto-pistol manual safety designs; it was a dual mode design. It could be carried in the conventional double-action/single-action mode of operation, or it could be carried 'cocked and locked' like the legendary 1911 pistol.

The safety was mounted on the frame and the CZ-75 was hammer fired. The CZ-75 could be carried with the hammer down over a loaded chamber and then fired through application of a long double-action trigger pull, or it could be carried and holstered with the hammer cocked and the manual safety engaged. The irony is due to politics the Czechs could not market their pistols in the United States and because CZ failed to secure world patent protection for their design the Tanfoglio firm of Italy copied it. Tanfoglio built a good business marketing the pistol to the West and the design is so solid that two shooters, American Doug Koenig and Frenchman Eric Grauffel, have won the hard fought IPSC World Championship using pistols based on this design. This is a tremendous endorsement for any handgun design because all other World Champions have used pistols based on the John Browning 1911 format. The CZ-75 has been upgraded to a variant called the CZ-85, which offers ambidextrous control levers and now both models are manufactured with firing pin safeties.

Another extremely well-made and well-designed fighting pistol in 9mm is the Heckler & Koch P7M8 or P7M13. Most often known by the term "Squeeze-cocker", the P7 has a large lever positioned on the front portion of the pistol grip. When this lever is squeezed, the pistol action is cocked, and when the grip is released the pistol action uncocks, thus

The Heckler & Koch P7M8 is a small 9mm Parabellum pistol designed for the self-defense market. It is an unusual design in that it utilizes a 'squeeze-cocker' action. PHOTO CREDIT: HK INC. USA

being rendered 'Safe'. After the grip is squeezed on the HK P7, the trigger pull is light and easy. This makes it an extremely accurate pistol, and the squeeze cocker system is fast. I mean really fast if you are heavily trained and have used it extensively. Unfortunately, it is so different from any other handgun operating system out there prudence demands that if this is your choice for a self-defense pistol, then let it be your only one. Otherwise you may forget to squeeze the grip in the proper manner during presentation, remaining inert when you need it to fire. The HK P7 is an extremely reliable pistol when fed good, jacketed ammo, but it will not function for long with lead bullet loads because it is a gas retarded action and lead shavings will eventually plug the gas port making the gun malfunction. The HK P7 is described by HK personnel as a "gunfighter's pistol". That is true, but beware; it takes dedication and heavy training to operate this design well. Few shooters are good enough to switch back and forth between the HK P7 and other designs.

The Heckler & Koch P7 squeeze-cocker is one of the faster pistols available to get into action from a complete state of rest. All one has to do to fire the pistol is squeeze the grip, aim at the target, and pull the trigger. PHOTO CREDIT: HK INC. USA

The HK P7M13 was a high-capacity version of the Heckler & Koch P7M8 and PSP pistol. The front portion of the grip must be squeezed before firing and for many operators this requires extensive training to maintain safe gun handling habits. PHOTO CREDIT: HK INC. USA

Even though the Heckler & Koch P7 design is an excellent piece of engineering, the firm also recognized after some years the market resistance to its innovative operation. The result was Heckler & Koch designed a whole series of new pistols that were more traditional in their operation and function. The Universal Service Pistol or USP was the result. The USP is a relatively large pistol that employs a polymer frame, and a Browning-style dropping barrel action. The USP is available in a number of different calibers. Various models have been produced for select military units, which featured threaded muzzles for the quick installation of sound suppressors. The USP can be found in different variants (10 for some models) based on the different trigger mechanism available for this pistol. The USP Compact is a compact version of the same basic pistol. It is the one I used for a number of years and it remains one of the most accurate pistols I've encountered in .40 S&W caliber. The USP Compact LEM was introduced in 2002 and features a unique DAO trigger mechanism with a decreased trigger pull of between 7.5 pounds to 8.5 pounds in pull weight. The HK2000 is yet another new pistol from HK that is meant for the law enforcement and concealed carry self-defense market. It has an interchangeable back strap option similar to the Walther P99 providing the consumer with the ability to match the gun's grip size to an individual's hand size. Yet, the HK2000 remains a DAO design offering the minimum in terms of manual safeties and other operational controls.

It was the concern over mechanical safeties that made the introduction of the Glock 17 and the various SIG 'Classic' pistols so revolutionary when they were introduced during the early 1980s. Neither the Glock design nor the SIG 'Classic' pistol have the traditional slide- or frame-mounted manual safety lever.

◀ **Smith & Wesson introduced the S&W Sigma in 1994. It featured a striker-fired mechanism and a polymer frame. Unlike the Glock, however, the magazine employed a metal tube instead of one made from polymer.**

The Heckler & Koch P2000 is their latest 9mm design that follows popular convention in that it features a double-action mechanism as well as interchangeable inserts to change the grip size to fit different size hands.

The Glock design features what Gaston Glock calls a "Safe Action." It has three mechanical safeties. The first is found on the face of the trigger. It's a little lever that protrudes from the middle of the trigger and it must be depressed before the trigger will fully operate. The two remaining safeties are the firing pin safety and the drop safety. The Glock design is striker-fired. That means it doesn't have a traditional hammer, but rather a striker assembly that is partially cocked when the slide is closed. However, it takes a pull of the trigger to complete the cocking of the striker assembly, as well as the release of the striker to fire the pistol. It's all done in one trigger pull and that's why the Bureau of Alcohol, Tobacco, Firearms and Explosives (BATFE) has classified the Glock design as a double-action-only (DAO) semi-auto pistol.

Most importantly, because the Glock design has no manual frame-mounted or slide-mounted safety, it is an extremely fast pistol to get into action and professionals the world over have recognized this, plus one other facet of the Glock. They are extremely reliable. In a short phrase, Glocks work! I don't care what the caliber or the specific model; seldom does a Glock pistol malfunction. If they do, my personal experience has shown it was probably due to either one of two outside factors; the first was poor or substandard ammunition, or the owner had installed after-market parts not made by Glock in order

▶ **The Glock semi-auto pistol has revolutionized the world of concealed carry handguns. It is available in variety of calibers and different frame sizes and many feel it is a pure fighting pistol. The mid-size Glock Model 19 shown here initially came with a 15+1 magazine capacity.**

The Glock 29 was a reduced size 10mm pistol with a 9+1 capacity and an overall size equal to an average mid-size 9mm compact pistol.

The Glock pistol is truly a simple design. Shown here are all the component parts that make up a Glock pistol, in this instance a Glock Model 19, but they are essentially all the same internally.

The Heckler & Koch P7M8 was an innovative pistol that did not sell well in the American market. It was expensive in comparison to other pistols in the same caliber range and unorthodox in its operation. Experts agree, however, it was a reliable, accurate and well made handgun.

to achieve some imagined advantage, which was not only unnecessary, but downright dumb. Both Smith &Wesson and Springfield Armory offer pistols that, like the Glock, have no frame- or slide-mounted safety levers yet remain safe to carry and easy to fire.

Prior to the implementation of the 1994 Crime Bill and its restrictions on 'ammunition feeding devices capable of holding more than 10 rounds of ammunition', the Glock design boasted some of the highest magazine capacities for any pistol of an equivalent size. As these words are being written this restriction is still in effect, but it appears it may very well expire within the next few months due to its embedded 'sunset' provisions. If it is allowed to do so, that bodes well for the concealed carry handgun consumer. It would allow the consumer to realize the full potential of these pistols.

The SIG pistols that are so popular in law enforcement and military applications are all hammer-fired designs. They don't feature a manual safety. Rather, they employ a hammer-decocking lever. The first shot can be fired via the double-action trigger pull quickly without manipulation of any lever or safety. It is fast. Of course, the pistol can be fired single-action on the first shot if the hammer is manually cocked. After the first shot, all subsequent rounds are fired single-action and the hammer remains cocked at the completion of firing. Before holstering the pistol the decocking lever must be engaged to lower the hammer back to a position of rest for safe handling and holstering of the pistol. The SIG system has been in use for more than two decades and SIG has taken to

SIG 'Classic' pistols have proven popular with many different law enforcement agencies across the United States and around the world. The SIG Model 228 (lower left) was once the issued pistol for the FBI. The SIG Model 229 (center) is a .40 caliber version of the SIG 228 featuring a made-in-America blackened stainless steel slide. The SIG Model 226 (upper right) was the close competitor to the Beretta Model 92F in the U.S. military service pistol trials of the 1980s. It lost only because of a slightly higher cost.

calling these pistols "SIG Classics". The SIG pistol is a good pistol and it has served as the duty pistol for a number of federal agencies, state and local departments throughout and across the United States, but a complaint about this system centers around the decocking lever. Officers and troopers sometimes forget to engage it after a firefight. I've seen this happen during a live fire training session where the officer was so focused on performing the exercise correctly, he forgot to decock his SIG duty pistol at completion. It makes everyone uneasy.

Smith & Wesson and Beretta are two major 9mm handgun manufacturers who first ignored the speed advantages offered by absent manual safeties or decocking devices. Smith & Wesson introduced their first 9mm semi-auto pistol in 1955. It was a double-action semi-auto with a slide-mounted safety, an alloy frame and it was known as the Model 39. The world didn't beat a path to their door in pursuit of the Model 39. In fact, in 1955 S&W assembled just 298 Model 39 pistols and the following year they produced only 797 examples. The Model 39 continued in production as it went through a continual series of upgrades to improve its reliability and accuracy. For a number of years the early examples were plagued with deficiencies, almost to the point it became a joke within the industry. During the Vietnam War (1968) the U.S. Navy requested a 14-shot version of the Model 39. A design that was developed earlier (1964) was dusted off and supplied to them for examination. The Navy soon decided they wanted stainless steel construction for corrosion resistance as well as a number of additional features. Pistols were manufactured for the Navy by an experimental department with S&W, but production of a high-capacity pistol didn't begin until 1971 and the resulting handgun was the S&W Model 59. The Model 59s were redesigned and upgraded to what many collectors refer to as the 'Second Generation' pistols around 1980. Among the changes made at this time was the addition of a firing pin safety and the introduction of a smaller, but high-capacity 9mm pistol, the Model 469.

During the late 1980s the interest in high-capacity 9mm pistols exploded due in large part to the publicity gained by the FBI-Miami Shoot Out as well as the advances made in handgun and ammunition technology. Smith & Wesson soon realized they were losing their dominant position in the law enforcement market, which they had enjoyed previously with their .357 Magnum revolvers. I was flown to Springfield, Massachusetts in August of 1988 for the introduction of their 'Third Generation' auto-pistols. The 9mm models consisted of a number of variations off the same basic pistol featuring a 15-round magazine. A smaller version of the same basic pistol was the Model 6904 and it featured a 12-round magazine. The Smith & Wesson "Third Gen" guns as they came to be called were eventually made available in 9mm Luger, .40 S&W, 10mm and .45 ACP and their model numbers became so confusing as to features; calibers, size and magazine capacity the company made a slick cardboard computer 'whiz wheel' to help the dealers and consumers keep them straight.

Over the years I have conducted two "melt-down" endurance tests of Third Generation Smith & Wesson auto-pistols. The first involved shooting 7,000 rounds of 9mm ammo through a Model 5906 in just over five hours. The second test fired 10,000 rounds of full-power 10mm ammo through a Model 1006 in less than eight hours. It was amazing what these guns would endure in terms of functional abuse and still keep running. Today, the Smith & Wesson 9mm auto-pistol product line is much different than that seen prior to the high-capacity magazine ban. Many of their current designs are more refined variations of the Third Gen auto-pistols, even if they only come with single-column magazines featuring the politically correct less than 10-round capacity.

Smith & Wesson recognized the success of the Glock pistol and in 1994 they introduced the Sigma, but it was seen almost immediately as an S&W clone of the Glock.

The author once endurance tested a Smith & Wesson Model 1006 through a melt-down test of 10,000 rounds. It took just under eight hours to shoot all that ammo and required the services of several shooters. All things considered the Smith & Wesson Model 1006 survived the experience in relatively good shape. It is shown here on top of 10,000 pieces of empty 10mm auto brass.

The Sigma featured a DAO trigger mechanism and a polymer frame with a comfortable grip profile. The Sigma, like the Third Gen DAO pistols, did not have repeat striking capability if the round didn't fire. This is also true of the Glock and the Springfield Armory XD series pistols. Without a restrike ability, the slide has to be retracted to re-cock the firing mechanism. The theory is if the pistol has chambered a bad round, the proper thing

The Glock Model 26 and 27 are the smallest Glocks yet to be introduced. Because they are Glocks, however, they are superb handguns. The Glock Model 27 (right) in .40 S&W caliber features a 9+1 ammunition capacity while the Glock Model 26 (left) in 9mm caliber offers one more round of capacity.

The big differences between the SW99 (left) and the Walther P99 (right) can be seen at the front of each polymer frame and at the very back. The Walther P99 features a prominent 'hook' to its frame that impacts the web of the hand in recoil with stout loads. The 'hook' is missing on the SW99 for exactly that reason.

to do is get rid of it, but to do so the shooter must train heavily on the immediate action drill to be instinctively responsive when this malfunction occurs. Sigma pistols were the first S&W auto-pistols in recent memory not to have a magazine safety. (A magazine safety renders the pistol inert and incapable of firing whenever the magazine is removed from the pistol.) The Sigma was made in both full size and compact models and the latest catalog from Smith & Wesson indicates they offer four different full-size models in both 9mm and .40 S&W calibers.

Just a couple of years ago Smith & Wesson formed a working alliance with Walther in Germany. Smith & Wesson became the import agent for Walther and a number of cooperative ventures came out of this business relationship. Not the least of these ventures was a new pistol patterned after the Walther P99, which was called the SW99. Smith & Wesson manufactures some of the components of the SW99 in Springfield, MA and imports the frame and other parts from Germany. The interesting thing is the SW99 is assembled on the Sigma production line at the factory. The SW99 is available in both full-size and Compact versions and is available in either 9mm or .40 S&W calibers.

Walther introduced the P99 in 1996 when the Alexandria, Virginia based Interarms Co. was still importing them. The Walther P99 is an excellent pistol and one I personally appreciate. Like the Glock, the Walther P99 lacks a traditional manual safety, and like the Glock it is a striker-fired design, but it operates and feels like a hammer-fired pistol in terms of its trigger control. It has a long double-action first shot and a very short, quick to reset, single action for all the following rounds. De-cocking the cocked striker on the P99 is accomplished by depressing a button located on top of the slide and near the back. The really great thing about the Walther P99 in my view is it comes with three different interchangeable back straps for the grip that allows the consumer to 'custom' fit the grip size to just about any hand size. This has always been possible with revolvers but prior

The Smith & Wesson SW99 is the result of cooperation between Smith & Wesson and Walther in Germany. Although the SW99 borrows heavily from the Walther P99, they are not exactly the same. The SW99 has different frame features, some of which prove important when shooting 'hot' .40 S&W caliber loads.

to the Walther P99 the general attitude on the part of most auto-pistol manufacturers was one size fits all. Well, it doesn't work in shoes or underwear and it has never been true with auto-pistols. For those who don't appreciate the long first shot double-action trigger pull Walther has another version of the P99 called the Quik-Action which features a consistent shot-to-shot double-action trigger pull. Walther has just recently come out with a Compact version of the Walther P99 and there are several things about it I like over the SW99 counterpart. The Walther P99 Compact has a different set of control levers as well

The Walther P99 features a polymer frame, a striker-fired mechanism that operates like a hammer-fired pistol, a high-capacity magazine for law enforcement, grip inserts to fit different hand sizes and it's chambered for the 9mm Parabellum round.

The author appreciates the design of the Walther P99 in 9mm caliber and is seen here during training at the Thunder Ranch facility. He is in the 'simulator' called THE TERMINATOR. The gun functioned perfectly even if he didn't.

as an abbreviated accessory rail on the dust cover of the frame in front of the triggerguard. It maintains the Walther P99 heritage by offering different size grip inserts to help the pistol fit the consumer's hand better. All in all, I am a big fan of the Walther P99.

Beretta built their first 9mm Parabellum pistol after World War II. It was called the Brigadier, or the Model 951. The design of this particular pistol was not all that spectacular. It was a single-action design utilizing the same barrel locking principle as the Walther P-38. Beretta learned from this pistol, and years later the offspring of the Model 951 would shake the small arms world when it replaced the 1911 pistol in U.S. military service. The Beretta Model 92 quickly evolved over a short period of time in order to win the military acceptance trials that every military small arms manufacturer treasured. Initially offered with a frame-mounted safety, the Beretta Model 92 became the Model 92S when a slide-mounted safety was substituted. It operated exactly like all other slide-mounted safeties, but this pistol eventually became the Model 92SB which was the pistol submitted to the U.S. Government trials. In terms of performance during the U.S. trials it was almost a dead heat between the Beretta Model 92 and the SIG Model 226. The final arbiter was the price and here Beretta had the advantage. The Beretta Model 92 SB turned into the Model 92F, which became known in the U.S. military as the M9, and then later as the M10.

SIG wasn't left out entirely though. A trial was held a few years later to find a compact, high-capacity 9mm pistol for military investigators and secret agents. SIG won with the Model 228 and it became known as the M11.

Controversy has surrounded the Beretta pistol for a number of reasons. First of all, it's natural to anticipate a considerable amount of antipathy from those within the military to any 9mm pistol. (And in the view of the author for good reason.) Secondly, some military Beretta pistols, under circumstances that are still vague and controversial, suffered the embarrassment of having their slides come apart and injure the shooters. Beretta immediately denied their pistol was at fault, but whatever the cause, the guns now feature a 'slide catch' which is a device to capture the back of the slide should it separate

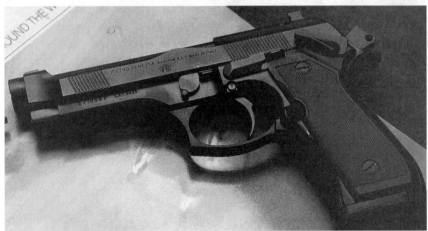

The Beretta 'Stock Gun' was an accurized Beretta service-style pistol featuring a frame-mounted manual safety, a heavier slide and an accurized barrel bushing. It was intended for shooting competitions, but then never imported to the American market.

The Beretta Vertec differs from the previous Model 92 in two important respects; the first is the different grip size and angle and the second is the forward frame rails for the easy installation of accessory devices like tactical lamps and lasers. The Vertec offers a slightly shorter trigger reach than that found with the standard Beretta Model 92.

Many police agencies following the 1985 adoption of the M9 service pistol purchased the same pistol for their law enforcement officers – Beretta Model 92.

The Colt All American 2000 was Colt's attempt to manufacture and market a polymer-frame 9mm pistol. It failed – miserably. Although the initial design was valid, Colt's interpretation suffered from a severe lack of quality control and a misdirected emphasis on a larger size for the entire envelope.

and move rapidly to the rear during firing. These pistols have earned a good reputation for accuracy and have been chosen by a wide number of state police agencies in the United States and around the world.

Beretta introduced the Model 8000 Cougar series of semi-autos in 1995. The big difference with the Cougar is in its method of operation. It features a short recoil system with a rotating barrel. It offers a trigger mechanism very similar in style and operation to that seen with the Beretta Model 92. The overall size of the pistol is much reduced. The Cougar employs a double-stack magazine in calibers like 9mm, .357 SIG, or .40 S&W and there is even an 8+1 version chambered in .45 ACP called the Model 8045. Beretta has expanded the Cougar line in recent years by adding 'mini' versions of the larger pistol. The big advantage to the Beretta Cougar is all of these models come in a smaller overall size than the Beretta Model 92 or its military equivalent the M9 service pistol.

Springfield Armory was one of the last of the handgun manufacturers in America to offer a polymer-framed 9mm pistol and the pistol they now import for sale is manufactured in Croatia. Springfield calls it the XD-9 when in 9mm caliber or XD-40 when chambered for the .40 S&W round. This pistol has excellent ergonomics and features a trigger safety like that found on the Glock and a grip safety like that seen on the 1911 pistol. This pistol was formerly imported by another firm and known as the HS2000. Whatever name it goes by the XD-9 is a striker-fired design which many assume is yet another pistol operated with a DAO trigger mechanism. It is NOT. It is a single-action design as the striker assembly can only be in one of two positions, fully cocked and ready to fire, or fully forward in an 'uncocked' condition. The trigger mechanism is completely incapable of fully cocking the striker assembly. The striker assembly is cocked by action of the slide being drawn to the rear. This is important for a number of reasons; safety being the first one.

The second reason is any shooter using this design in competition will have a competitive advantage over those using true DAO designs because the trigger pull on the XD-9 can be lightened to a significant degree with the minimum of effort. Thirdly, there are many police administrators who will openly ban 'single-action semi-autos', but fall in love with any DAO type pistol. Let's be clear about this, the Springfield XD-9 is NOT a DAO pistol. It's a single-action pistol that is different from the 1911A1 pistol only in the sense it is a striker-fired design and not a hammer-fired design. It is a good pistol and so far it appears to be an extremely reliable design. Just know it is a single-action semi-auto and requires all the care and attention that use of any single action semi-auto demands.

The high-capacity 9mm pistols, often called 'Wonder Nines', ruled the marketplace during the 1980s and early 1990s, but increasing legislative restrictions like the prohibition of magazines holding more than 10 rounds in the United States and the outright ban on all handguns in the United Kingdom changed the picture drastically. The emphasis following the 1994 federal law resulted in smaller pistols that were easier to conceal and better able to utilize the 10-round restrictions. Two brilliant examples of this result are the Glock Model 26 and the Kahr K9. The Glock is a radically reduced version of

The Springfield Armory XD-40 employs a polymer frame and is a single-action design with a striker-fired mechanism. It is often compared to a Glock, but offers some of the features found on the 1911 pistol like the grip safety and the fact it is a single-action semi-auto. The SIG P-226 shown above it illustrates the fact the Springfield Armory XD-40 is slightly smaller in overall size and both have established a good record for reliability with good ammunition.

The Kahr K9 is a semi-auto pistol chambered for the 9mm Parabellum cartridge. Its trigger mechanism is double-action-only, but extremely smooth and easy to operate. This particular example is made of all steel and therefore somewhat heavier than its contemporaries, but the Kahr design wins accolades for its reliability and ease of concealment.

the compact Glock Model 19 featuring all the same attributes of the larger pistols like a polymer frame, the Glock Safe Action and uncommon reliability in such a small pistol. Using Federal's 115-grain jacketed hollowpoint ammo, "9BP", my personal Glock Model 26 is also as accurate as many centerfire target pistols and for a pistol so reduced in size that is an unusual accomplishment. The Kahr K9 is an all-steel pistol, but albeit one with greatly reduced dimensions. Testing has indicated they are reliable pistols. They operate with DAO trigger mechanisms that set standards for smoothness and ease of operation. The most recent models from Kahr feature polymer frames that really reduce their weight from the same versions using steel frames. The Kahr pistols although from a relatively new manufacturer are good enough the New York City Police Department has approved many models for off-duty use by their officers.

The 9mm pistols will remain popular because they offer the defensive firearms consumer an easy entrance into the world of self-defense handguns. There is a wide selection of models from many manufacturers. A diligent consumer can find an affordable pistol that fits both his hand and lifestyle perfectly. This is likely the biggest advantage to the 9mm pistol.

CHAPTER SEVEN

The 1911 Pistol

More than a hundred years ago, the poor performance of the .38 caliber Colt double-action revolver used against the Moros in the Philippines spurred the search by the U.S. military for a better fighting pistol. The prior success of the Colt SAA in .45 Colt (often incorrectly referred to as the .45 *Long* Colt cartridge) prompted many to request a .45 caliber fighting pistol, but one in a self-loading format. John Browning, working in cooperation with Colt's Manufacturing Company, provided the answer and the world of gunfighting has relied on it ever since.

The pistol was and is the Model 1911 chambered in .45ACP (Automatic Colt Pistol). It was named after the year in which it was adopted by the United States military forces and served as the official sidearm of the U.S. Army, Navy and U.S. Marine Corps for more than 74 years. Many feel it was a dreadful mistake to abandon it. The Model 1911 was used in the trenches of World War I, and carried by hundreds of thousands of GI's in World War II. It has seen action in Korea, Vietnam, and almost all of the American military engagements since the close of World War I. The 1911 pistol has been a tool used by Texas Rangers, and early FBI Special Agents. While no longer authorized for the majority of FBI Special Agents, it is important to note the issued handgun to the FBI HRT (Hostage Rescue Team) and Regional FBI SWAT team members is once again a highly developed version of the 1911 pistol.

The Colt .45 Automatic was adopted by the U.S. military in 1911, giving it the name the "1911 pistol". John Browning designed it and it stands as one of history's all-time best fighting pistols. The Colt pistol shown here is a return to the guns produced during World War II by the millions.

Jeff Cooper is acknowledged as the father of the 'Modern Technique' for shooting a combat pistol. His writings and commentaries have influenced multiple generations of self-defense oriented firearms owners. He also created Gunsite, the firearms training center near Paulden, Arizona.

Les Baer was formerly a custom pistolsmith that decided to get into the manufacturing business. He is shown holding a Para-Ordnance 1911-style pistol that his firm modified and sold to the FBI for a short period.

The mere mention of the words "Forty-five" creates an image of no-nonsense power and purpose. The 1911 pistol has been called old slabsides, old ugly and the Government Model. It has saved many a man's life and for this faithful duty more than a few consider it the perfect fighting pistol.

Essentially, the 1911 pistol in most of its forms and variations is a semi-automatic, recoil-operated, with a detachable magazine pistol. It is recoil-operated because the barrel moves, and during the first part of the movement the barrel and slide are locked together for a short distance. After this short distance, however, the barrel drops down from the

The Springfield Armory "TRP" model 1911A1 pistol is very similar in terms of its extra features to the pistol produced by them for FBI SWAT teams and used nationwide. It is an excellent .45 caliber semi-auto pistol and clearly built for use as a fighting handgun, most often a concealed carry fighting handgun.

When it comes to handguns, there are few things more intimidating than the muzzle of a .45 caliber auto-pistol. The author is seen here with his Novak custom Colt Lightweight Commander.

slide through action of the 'link' positioned under the barrel. The link is the connection between the barrel and the frame at the rear. The front of the barrel is held in place by the muzzle bushing. On target-grade pistols the fit between the muzzle bushing and the barrel is often so tight a bushing wrench is required to complete the removal of the bushing from the slide and barrel.

The 1911 pistol is fired by means of a short, single-action trigger pull after the hammer has been cocked. The 1911 also features a frame-mounted manual safety, and a grip safety. The grip safety must be depressed before the pistol will fire. Most of the Colt-manufactured Government Models since the 1980s also have an internal, but passive

Smith & Wesson many years ago produced so many different semi-auto models in various calibers like .45 ACP, .40 S&W, 10mm auto and 9mm Parabellum they produced a 'whiz wheel' to help the consumer and their dealers keep their respective details straight according to the model number.

firing pin safety. (Those 1911 pistols manufactured previously or in the style of the 'Series 70' guns do not have the passive firing pin safety. The Series 80 passive firing pin safety has received a great deal of criticism from purists and experts because it complicates the trigger pull on any 1911 pistol.) Some authorities consider the half-cock notch on the hammer a safety feature. It is in the technical sense, but it's best if the shooter ignores this aspect of the mechanism and practices better and more sound safety habits than lowering the hammer to the half-cock notch over a loaded round. (The Series 80 Colt pistol does not have a half-cock feature as seen previously. On a Series 80 Colt if you put the hammer at the half-cock position and pull the trigger the hammer will fall, but the pistol should not fire.) The 1911 design also features a disconnector, which prevents the gun from firing out of battery or whenever the slide begins to open. Many authorities feel the disconnector is a safety device that should be included in any listing of 1911 safety features.

Normally, the single-column tube magazine holds seven rounds of .45 ACP ammunition. The growth of action-oriented shooting competitions over several decades fostered the development of a number of after-market magazines holding eight rounds of

.45 ACP ammo. Chip McCormick markets his magazines with the 'Shooting Star' follower, which was originally developed by the late Charles Kelsey, an innovative thinker who first figured how to stuff an extra round in the normal 1911 magazine. Kelsey created a cleverly designed follower that replaced the original factory follower and when used in combination with a magazine spring developed by Walter Wolf Sr. added one more round to the normal seven-round .45 ACP 1911 magazine.

On most 1911 pistols currently on the market all the controls are on the left side. This works well for right-handed shooters, but creates problems for the 10 percent of the population that is left-handed. A solution for the left-handed shooter is the installation of ambidextrous manual safety levers allowing the operation of the pistol in the same manner as a right-handed person. The remaining controls can be used in the normal manner by a 'lefty', but it requires a slightly different technique.

All 1911 pistols should lock open after the last round has been fired. The left-handed shooter after inserting a fresh magazine into the butt of the pistol has only to pull the slide slightly to the rear to release the slide and chamber a fresh round in the barrel. As for the magazine release most left-handed shooters should use the trigger finger of their left hand to depress the frame-mounted magazine release and drop the single-column magazine from the gun. The metal magazines used by all 1911 pistols, if not damaged or deformed in some way, should fall freely upon release from the pistol.

However, even the best parts in anything man-made will malfunction. The film *Way Of The Gun* starring Ryan Phillippe and Benicio Del Toro has a scene in it where actor Ryan Phillippe, who is armed with a Colt 1911A1 70 Series pistol, has a magazine that hangs up after the slide has locked open following the last round. Philippe's character has only one good arm due to an injury and he correctly uses his teeth to pull the empty magazine from the butt of the pistol. Hollywood often gets the manipulation and operation of a self-defense pistol wrong, but this film is one of the few that gets it right. Of course, both of the lead characters in this film are armed with Colt 1911A1 pistols and they carry and use them most of the time the way a real-world professional would. Del Toro even performs a 'tactical reload' correctly for the camera by catching the partially spent magazine between his fingers and then quickly reinserting a fully loaded magazine into the gun with the same

All .45 caliber 1911-style pistols are classified in IDPA competition as "Custom Defensive" class. The author is shown here shooting off the right side of a barricade with the Kimber Super Match 1911 pistol.

hand, all without dropping or misplacing the partially spent magazine.

The 1911 pistol will stand as a testament to the genius of John Browning. The 1911 pistol was the last of a series of .45 caliber pistols Browning designed around the turn of the 20th century. As for the cartridge, the earlier 1905 .45 caliber automatic pistol cartridge featured a full-metal-jacket bullet weighing 200 grains and the American military requested this be increased to 230 grains. These changes, plus evolutionary changes to strengthen the design resulted in Browning's 1911 pistol. Norway produced the 1911 pistol during World War I as the '11.25mm Aut. Pistol M/1914', but they were not a combatant in the war. The Nazi occupiers of Norway also produced their own .45 caliber 1911 pistols during World War II. Colt supplied different models to Argentina during the 1920s until Argentina eventually produced their own examples, first under license and then in Buenos Aires by a large manufacturing firm. These later pistols were of a slightly different design and many of the parts are not interchangeable with the Colt pistols.

The HK-produced SOCOM pistol is a high-capacity .45 auto pistol that is designed to work with higher-pressure ammunition. It features a frame-mounted safety and can be fitted with a sound suppressor for covert activities. PHOTO CREDIT: HK INC. USA

In 1926, a number of small changes at the behest of the American military were incorporated into the basic 1911 design to create the 1911A1 pistol. Among the changes made to the gun were the addition of an arched mainspring housing at the back of the grip, a shorter trigger, a slightly longer tang on the grip safety, and clearance cuts were made to the frame just aft of the trigger. There were also slight changes made to the rifling dimensions of the barrel, but it remained a .45 caliber pistol. During World War II more than 2.5 million 1911A1 pistols were manufactured by six different companies, including Remington-Rand Company, Union Switch and Signal Company, Remington Arms Company, The Ithaca Gun Company, The Singer Manufacturing Company, and Colt's Manufacturing Company. Those production numbers are amazing when you understand the 1911A1 pistol produced during World War II required 728 machining operations and 187 checks and inspections before final assembly. The guns made by the Singer sewing machine company are models highly sought after by collectors because only 500 or so were ever produced during the war.

For years after the war these 'war surplus' 1911A1 pistols were used by sport shooters just as they were built or as the basis for a custom project to tailor the pistol to the competitive shooter's needs. It should be noted the problem in 1985 that precipitated the need for a new military pistol was the fact all the 1911A1 pistols in military service had been built either during World War II or immediately prior to the war which ended more than 40 years previously. Those 1911A1 pistols the military wanted to retire so badly were all old and when you think about the abuse they had withstood as a group, it's hard to imagine another pistol design that would have served for so long and in such a durable fashion.

'CONDITIONS' OF THE 1911 PISTOL

The 1911 design can be carried in one of four operating conditions and they are given the designation of 'Condition One' through 'Condition Four'. The shooter investigating the 1911 design is advised to learn these four operating conditions thoroughly. They all relate to the status of the pistol in terms of whether or not it's loaded or unloaded and whether or not it is ready for immediate action.

Condition ONE means the magazine in the butt of the gun is fully loaded, there is a round in the chamber, the hammer is cocked and the frame-mounted manual safety is engaged. This is commonly referred to as "cocked and locked". This is also what makes the 1911 pistol the choice of professionals because it remains an easy pistol to deploy, aim and engage an armed aggressor. It is also fast as many IPSC and IDPA competitors can easily prove. As the operator grips the gun in the holster, usually carried on the strong side ('strong side' means whichever hand the shooter uses to shoot the pistol one handed), the pistol is gripped high with the trigger finger pointed forward and kept straight. Many trainers advise the beginning shooter to place the trigger finger along the slide.

This is an important part of the safety system because the shooter should never put his trigger finger on the trigger until the sights are on the target and he is preparing to fire.

Just through the act of gripping the gun firmly the grip safety on the 1911 pistol will be disengaged before the pistol is removed from the holster. The thumb on the firing hand goes 'high' to be placed atop the manual safety lever on the left side of the frame. As the shooter acquires the target then the decision to fire or not can be made. If the decision

is fire, the thumb pushes downward – taking the pistol OFF Safe and pressure is applied to the trigger face by the trigger finger, which has already moved smoothly to the trigger as the safety is disengaged. Believe me, it works far faster than it takes you to read this procedure and is the main reason the 1911 pistol remains at the head of the class.

Condition TWO describes a 1911 pistol that has the magazine loaded, the chamber loaded and the hammer is down with the manual safety in the OFF position or down location. Firing the pistol in this condition requires the hammer to be thumb-cocked in the same fashion as the old single action revolver. It was a practice that was favored prior to World War II by many shooters who were used to the old Colt 'cowboy' revolver, but the truth is it is a procedure that can lead to accidental discharges. It does nothing to insure a firm firing grip of the pistol because the firing hand really doesn't maintain a good purchase of the grip while the thumb is cocking the hammer. Those who practice the Condition Two draw often refer to the half-cock notch in the hammer as being a safety preventing an unintentional discharge. In my view, that theory simply does not hold water and anyone recommending carrying any 1911 pistol in Condition Two simply lacks the intelligence or experience to know better.

Condition THREE has the magazine fully loaded, the chamber empty, the hammer down and the manual safety OFF. To fire the pistol from this condition the slide must be retracted to chamber a round and cock the hammer. This is the condition the military demanded of all its personnel prior to the adoption of the M9 and M10 service pistols, which replaced the 1911A1 pistols, even if the practice continues with the newer double-action/single-action M9 and M10 pistols. Although it is a time-consuming process, those in charge of multiple young men armed with 1911 pistols, which were carried in full-flap military holsters, preferred this method to any other. Military troops who wanted to improve their reaction speed under these circumstances developed a draw stroke that lifted the holster flap in one motion with the strong hand while also acquiring a grip on the pistol. The pistol was drawn from the holster and as it was brought up to the line of sight the off-hand would move over the top of the gun, gripping the slide and pulling it to the rear in one smooth motion. Of course, this requires the shooter to point the gun one handed at the target. It is literally the best anyone can do when they are essentially equipped with an empty semi-automatic pistol. Another method perfected by experienced soldiers armed with the 1911 pistol involved their partially drawing the pistol from the military holster and turning the pistol 90 degrees sideways to trap the slide inside the holster. They then pushed the pistol down into the holster to retract the slide and chambered a round upon removal from the holster.

Condition FOUR has the magazine out of the gun, the chamber empty and it really doesn't matter whether the hammer is down or cocked and the safety is ON or OFF, but traditionally the hammer is down. The gun is empty – completely. It would be of little use if needed in a hurry unless, of course, you practiced the charging procedure for the Condition Three draw from a military flap holster after inserting a loaded magazine into the pistol.

◀ **The Gunsite Training Center was founded by Jeff Cooper. Cooper is no longer involved with the daily operation of the facility, but the Gunsite Gunsmithy produced an excellent example of a fighting pistol in .45 ACP.**

THE MOST SERIOUS CRITICISM OF THE 1911 PISTOL

The most serious criticism in my view of the 1911 pistol is the fact the pistol can NOT be loaded with the safety engaged. This is easily accomplished with any traditional double-action/single-action semi-auto pistol featuring a slide-mounted safety. The safety can be engaged and thus guarantee the chamber can be loaded without the possibility of an accidental discharge. For many this isn't a big deal because they understand you must always point the pistol in a SAFE direction as the slide is released over a loaded magazine and a live round is chambered in the barrel.

Problems develop when amateur or untrained gunsmiths perform 'trigger jobs' on 1911 pistols and the subsequent operator fails to point the pistol in a safe direction as the slide is released. Loud noises are often the result and depending upon where the pistol was pointed, holes have a tendency to materialize in objects that do better if left unpunctured. Some military units had a barrel of sand outside the squad room and the soldier was told to charge his 1911 while pointing the muzzle of the gun toward the barrel. That is, if the soldier had a commander who allowed them to carry the 1911 pistol in Condition One, but few did. The big thing to understand is the 1911 pistol is capable of firing while the chamber is being charged. Once you get passed this point of concern and operation, the 1911 pistol design isn't any more difficult to operate safely than any other semi-auto and remains one of the best fighting pistols, if not the best ever created.

WHAT TO LOOK FOR ON A DEFENSIVE 1911 PISTOL

For years following World War II most competitive shooters used military cast-off 1911 pistols as the base vehicle for building the pistol they needed. Most of these shooters weren't building defensive pistols, but rather they were 'accurizing' the pistol for use as a 'Bull's-eye' gun in NRA 2700 known-distance competition. Today the government, courtesy of people like past Attorney General Janet Reno and similar politicians, feel the

The Kimber Super Match is a top-of-the-line target pistol that offers great accuracy and total reliability. It also features just about every extra a customer could wish for and as a result it is a delight to shoot. It also functions well as a concealed carry self-defense pistol with its .45 ACP chambering.

government should not be in the business of selling guns to citizens. So all surplus military firearms, whether eligible for civilian possession or otherwise, are routinely destroyed with the exception of the guns sold through the Director of Civilian Marksmanship program. Years ago that wasn't the situation as a former high school classmate of mine who served in Germany purchased an old Union Switch & Signal 1911A1 pistol from the Rod & Gun club at his Army base. The pistol to this day rattles like a BB in a boxcar, but it was sold to him in Germany as surplus by the military branch in which he was serving. Many others who served our country during those days were allowed the same privilege. These pistols were often sold once the soldier returned home and needed cash to buy a car, get married or generally return to civilian life. (My friend still has his and he won't sell it because I've asked a couple of times.) Of course, Colt Firearms continued manufacturing the 1911A1 pistol after the war. For more than a couple of decades their commercial product differed little from the military example and they both were found wanting by many seeking a truly good self-defense 1911-style pistol.

I purchased my first 1911A1 pistol from Dave Cook Sporting Goods in Denver, Colorado in 1973. I was living and working in the city at the time and the gun was a brand new Colt Series 70 pistol. Right out of the box it demonstrated a 9-1/2-pound trigger pull. I couldn't hit the side of a barn from the inside with the doors closed with the goofy thing. Fortunately I had a close friend from work, Ted Harris, who was a retired U.S. Army Ordnance armorer. Ted loved the 1911 pistol because he had used one in a gunfight in Germany a short year after the war with a former Nazi SS trooper who was armed with an MP-40 submachine gun. Later Ted came to the conclusion the man was part of the 'Der Spider' organization that supported former leaders and war criminals in their efforts to escape justice for war crimes. I gave him my pistol and in the course of one evening it quickly gained a trigger pull of just over 4 pounds. It proved to be a delight and I still have it.

Although the situation has changed drastically in terms of what's available to the consumer today as opposed to only two decades ago, anyone investigating the 1911 design should pay attention to the trigger pull. The ideal trigger pull weight for a self-

The author is seen here putting the Kimber Super Match through its paces at a local IDPA club match. The Kimber Super Match has to be shot in competition to be truly appreciated. It is a superlative pistol in every respect.

defense or 'duty' 1911 style pistol is just over 4 pounds. Most competition shooters want their trigger pulls far lighter. Some of the 'Master' class shooters will use 1911-style pistols with trigger pulls that will often scale between a pound and a pound and a half, but it takes a 'Master' class shooter to be safe with a trigger pull that light and they are NOT as a matter of routine in the practice of holding people at gunpoint. I personally don't want the trigger pulls on even my competition pistols under 3-1/2 pounds simply because I anticipate something in this range as I apply pressure to the trigger face. I don't want the trigger to go off unexpectedly when I am bringing the gun on target.

A big no-no with lightened trigger actions is seen when the hammer 'follows' as the slide is closed over an empty chamber. Usually this indicates a number of possible deficiencies. The most likely culprit is a poor hammer and sear engagement, if not a bad sear or a bad hammer or a combination thereof. The problem with the hammer following the slide is the operator is only an instant away from an accidental discharge during charging of the chamber from a loaded magazine. As a matter of safety, I won't carry, work with or shoot a 1911 style pistol that exhibits this characteristic. There simply is no need for it because Brownells, the gunsmithing supply people, offer a wide combination of good quality 1911 parts that after proper installation will give the consumer a superior quality 1911 pistol no matter how bad it was before repair.

As for the actual length of the trigger, that is a matter of personal preference. The original 1911 pistol had a 'long' trigger so called because of its length inside the triggerguard. The subsequent 1911A1 pistol had a 'short' trigger. The relative narrowness of the 1911 frame and the comparatively small circumference of the grip means many shooters find they manage quite well with the long trigger design while those who with a shorter trigger reach find they require a short trigger. The benefit of the 1911 pistol design is its ability to accommodate different hand sizes with relative ease when compared to almost any other design on the market today.

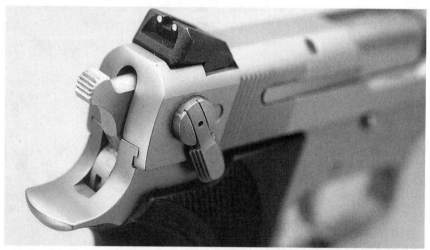

The Novak Lo-Mount rear sight is one of the more popular replacement sights used on 1911-style pistols. Its snag-free design enables users to perform malfunction clearing 'slide-swipe' drills without fear of cuts or abrasions. It presents a clear, clean sight picture to the shooter.

The original military-issue 1911A1 pistol came with what can only be described as 'minimal' iron sights. The front blade on the original 1911 was thin and small, and while the blade thickness was increased on the 1911A1 model it was still difficult to acquire for most eyes. The rear sight was even worse. It consisted of a blade that featured the smallest of notches and it offered nothing to those requiring the use of sights in low-light or bad lighting conditions.

The cottage industry developed over the last three decades that caters solely to the upgrade of all 1911 pistols has recognized this. There are an untold number of firms offering replacement or custom installation of after-market sights for any 1911 style pistol. The two I highly recommend are fierce competitors of each other, but they both are excellent. The first is from Wayne Novak and Novak's Lo-Mount sight is a really good design. The Novak Lo-Mount rear sight is also available with tritium inserts that can be used in combination with a custom dovetailed front sight blade featuring a single tritium front sight dot. The Novak Lo-Mount sighting system has no sharp edges and this is an important feature on any self-defense 1911 style pistol.

The second sight I recommend is the Heinie sight from Richard Heinie. Heinie Specialty Products offers both their traditional sight and the 'Slant-Pro' rear sight. I prefer his traditional sight simply because it hooks better on my belt when I'm doing one handed malfunction clearance drills with the 1911 pistol. The Slant-Pro is also available with tritium inserts for use with a tritium front sight blade. Heinie also makes a gold bead front sight Walt Rauch originally designed. I prefer gold bead front sights simply because gold has no 'half-life' like tritium does and gold reflects in bright daylight whereas tritium powered dots can only be seen in low-light or dark conditions. The Heinie gold bead front sight

The author prefers the traditional Heinie sight because it enables him to perform one-handed malfunction drills with any auto pistol equipped with this sight. He simply 'hooks' the front of the rear blade over the top of his belt and pushes downward to open the slide with one hand. Once the slide has been fully retracted he can use a thumb to lock it open and proceed to clear the malfunction with one hand.

features a hemisphere surface on its rear face and although some criticize this because the brighter reflection makes it hard to shoot really tight groups for bull's-eye shooting, I prefer it because the eye finds it much faster. Additionally, it works even on cloudy days or even in low-light conditions with artificial light like that provided by a streetlight.

Those who want a fully adjustable sight can have a Bomar rear sight installed on their 1911 pistol, but the rear of the slide has to be machined and then refinished. The most popular installation three decades ago was to have the fully adjustable rear sight from a Smith & Wesson revolver installed on the slide. I did and I encountered the same problems everyone else did, it kept flying off. The Smith & Wesson adjustable rear sight is held to their revolvers by a single screw securing the leaf spring to the frame. On a pistol with a reciprocating slide, the forces are sufficient to break that single screw and leave the shooter searching among the gravel or the weeds of the firing bay for the absent rear sight. Truly, rear sights for the 1911 pistol have improved in more ways than one.

In my opinion, one of the greatest improvements to the 1911 pistol came from IPSC competitors and that is the development of the 'beavertail' grip safety. Decades ago, it was the common practice to 'pin' the grip safety closed, or deactivate it. The goal was to eliminate the misspent draw when the 1911A1 grip safety wasn't properly engaged. When this happened the gun wouldn't fire because the grip safety must be completely depressed to allow the pistol to discharge. Pinning the grip safety to the firing position, however, was NOT the thing to do when you think about all the possible things that could and would often go wrong. Beavertail grip safeties are now made by a multitude of 1911 parts manufacturers and each has its own special features. The big thing is the increased size of the grip safety allows the shooter to grasp it quickly and disengage the safety in

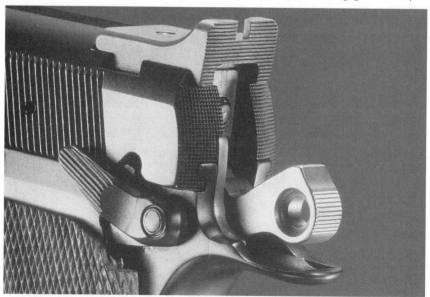

The beavertail is an extension welded to the frame of a Browning High Power as seen here on a .40 caliber Browning. On 1911 style pistols, the beavertail is an extension of the grip safety. A beavertail grip safety has many advantages and few disadvantages.

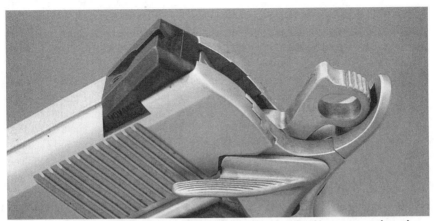

The installation of a beavertail grip safety on a 1911 pistol is a functional improvement the author endorses wholeheartedly. It is an improvement that was developed by IPSC competitors and gunsmiths.

one sure motion. Another great advantage is the center of the firing hand is positioned closer to the boreline of the pistol and that, pure and simple, increases control of the gun. Also, beavertail grip safeties do it without the accompanying 'hammer bite' where the rear of the pistol's hammer digs into the flesh of the hand pushed up tight against the grip safety. Of course the size of the beavertail grip safety can work against the concealed carry holder because it will 'print' against the covering garment the shooter is wearing. Therefore, it is wise to examine all the grip safeties available and choose a more subdued example for your concealed carry project.

In the minds of many, the perfect concealed carry pistol will have about as many sharp edges as a well-worn bar of soap. The reason is elementary. The pistol will be worn close to the body and next to the skin. If it has any sharp edges they won't take long to be noticed. Additionally, many shooters have discovered much to their regret that long hours on a live fire training range will reveal every deficiency the pistol is prone to and sharp edges, wherever they may be, will without fail slice and dice a number of fingers as you practice malfunction clearance drills.

The first place you are going to notice a sharp edge on any 1911 style pistol is the manual safety. The standard 1911A1 manual safety is simply too small to be used as efficiently as it needs to be. The exact size of what an extended thumb safety should be is, again, a personal decision. Some are intentionally made wide and long and are often referred to as 'gas pedal' safeties. The lever fitting this description is difficult to tolerate in concealed carry applications close to the body. The big thing is the complete absence of any sharp edge and the lever or levers (if ambidextrous) must not be overly large. I like the extended safety levers on my 1911 pistols to be approximately the same width as that found on the military 1911A1 pistol, but I want the lever longer and with smooth rounded edges featured on both on the top and the outside edges.

Many custom pistolsmiths install full-length guide-rods in the 1911 pistols they build and many factory-produced 1911 pistols from a variety of manufacturers feature them as well. I am a critic of the full-length guide-rod and I have come to this position after working for some time with a full-length guide-rod on my favorite 1911 .45 caliber pistol. Full-length guide-rod are supposed to help center the slide over the frame. Another alleged benefit is they help maintain a tight fit between the slide and the frame as well as better direct the energy of the recoil spring through the slide during the cycling process. I have seen no strong evidence for the validity of any of these arguments. Depending upon how the full length guide-rod is constructed, it will either (1) come apart unintentionally and unexpectedly, causing a major malfunction at the worst possible moment, or (2) they require the use of 'tools' to take the pistol apart for routine maintenance and cleaning. (The 'tool' required can be nothing more than a paper clip or something as involved as a hex head 'Allen' wrench, but without this 'tool' the gun can't be taken apart and cleaned as needed. The exception is the one-piece guide rod, which doesn't need a tool

Smith & Wesson recently unveiled its own version of the fabled 1911 pistol. It is shown here with an early production S&W Model 4506. The SW1911 has a stainless steel slide and frame and comes with a number of extras like a full-length guide-rod, beavertail grip safety and Novak Lo-Mount sights.

▶ The Para-Ordnance P-12 is a high-capacity .45 caliber auto-pistol in a small to medium size format. This custom P-12 from Richard Heinie sports fine-line checkering on the grip, a squared off triggerguard, Heinie's own rear sight and a number of other custom features to both improve its looks and performance.

for disassembly.) The presence of the full-length guide-rod also prevents one-handed retraction of the slide because you can't push the spring plug below the muzzle bushing against a door edge or hard corner to cycle the slide with one hand in the event of a dud round. John Browning designed the original 1911 pistol without a full-length guide-rod and I feel he knew more about the engineering of the gun than many who today tout the use of such devices.

Titanium firing pins and lightweight hammers are supposed to decrease lock-time and thereby help make the pistol more accurate. In a perfect world and if you are a Super-Master class shooter this would probably be true. For most of us these things are simply gadgets sold by people catering to the 1911 competition market to earn sales and increase profits. There are other areas of the 1911 pistol that need attention before one spends money on exotic metal firing pins.

Making sure the gun feeds hollowpoint ammunition reliably is a major concern and to their credit most of the 1911 pistols offered today by the American manufacturers satisfy this need quite well. However, polishing the feed ramp of a military 1911A1 barrel to feed modern hollowpoint ammunition is a job best left to the professional. It should not be attempted by the amateur because when performed improperly it creates a dangerous situation where the casehead of the cartridge is unsupported and prone to ruptures when fired. This can lead to catastrophic failures of the ammunition and the gun.

Checkering on the front strap of the grip is a popular custom touch and a point of pride by some owners as they exclaim it was 'hand' checkered. Whether the 30 line per inch checkering on the front of the grip was 'hand' checkered straight and true or it was achieved through use of a carefully programmed computer-driven machine is really beside the point to me. I appreciate fine checkering on this gripping surface. Others prefer courser checkering along the order of 20 lines per inch, but the main point is checkering increases the purchase of the gun if your hands become wet and slippery. Of course, most shooters don't experience wet hands until they step up to the shooting box for the first time and realize the eyes of all their friends and fellow competitors are focused on their performance. Then they develop a severe case of sweaty palms and this increases

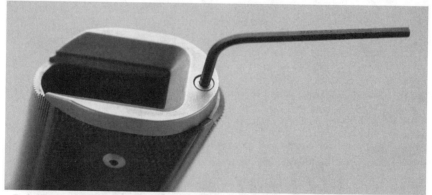

To facilitate a rapid reload with any 1911-style pistol, a magazine funnel is often installed. The example shown here is mounted on Kimber's Super Match competition and is secured to the mainspring housing through application of a hex-head screw.

the difficulty of maintaining control of the pistol when gripping smooth metal surfaces. If your hands sweat in competition, image what they will do in the face of a life-threatening encounter. An inexpensive alternative to checkering can be found by gluing a wide piece of coarse grain sandpaper or skateboard tape over the front of the grip frame.

The biggest advantage to the semi-auto pistol over the revolver is the easier manipulation of the former during the reloading process and to that end; it is also wise to 'funnel' the open end of the magazine well at the bottom of the grip. It used to be they all came with sharp edges at the magazine well and it was easy to snag the reload as the outside edge of the magazine tube collided with the sharp edge of the opening. Action competition shooters use wildly exaggerated magazine funnels on the bottom of the pistols to facilitate a rapid reload, but these devices prove counter-productive on a concealed carry pistol. Richard Heinie makes an excellent mag funnel for the 1911 pistol that works well on any 1911 pistol meant for concealed carry applications. Otherwise, these edges should be broken and feature an inward slope to help the insertion of a fresh, fully loaded magazine.

WHAT SIZE OF 1911 STYLE PISTOL?

For decades the 1911 pistol was available only in one size – the 5-inch-barreled Government Model, but then enterprising gunsmiths like Armand Swenson, Bob Chow, Jim Clark, Austin Behlert and others began (borrowing a phrase from the custom car trade) to 'chop and channel' the old Government Model down to a more manageable size during the late 1950s through the 1960s.

The first really successful and popular attempt to reduce the size of the Government Model came not from a custom pistolsmith, but Colt Firearms Company when they introduced the alloy-framed Commander in 1950. This new pistol really was the result of

The Colt Lightweight Commander is a reduced-size variation of the 1911 Government Model. It is lighter because of its alloy frame and the example seen here is a custom pistol made for the author by Wayne Novak. It features his sights with tritium inserts, a Bar-Sto barrel and thin custom Spegal grips.

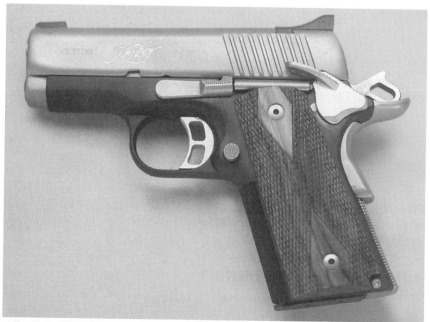

The Kimber Ultra II is an extremely small 1911-style self-defense semi-auto in .45 ACP. It featured an alloy frame and a 3-inch barrel with a dual recoil spring assembly. It is powerful and easy to conceal.

This Springfield Armory Compact .45 is from the shop of Heinie Specialty Products. As such it represents the ultimate in a concealed carry .45 auto pistol. It's reliable with a minimum of bulk and the maximum in caliber for its size and weight. PHOTO CREDIT: HEINIE SPECIALTY PRODUCTS

The Kimber 'Compact' is a 1911-style pistol in .45 ACP with a shortened grip frame and a 4-inch barrel. The shorter grip on the alloy frame reduces the magazine capacity by one round, but it also helps avoid the inadvertent 'printing' of this pistol when it is carried concealed.

For those wanting the smallest and lightest possible big-bore self-defense pistol there is the Colt Lightweight Officer's Model. This example has been customized by Wilson's Gun Shop and it is meant specifically for self-defense applications, not use as a competition pistol.

The HK USP pistol was a direct response by HK to the market demands in the American small arms market. The USP pistol features a frame-mounted safety lever that moves 'down'. The HK USP was one of the first pistols to come with an accessory rail for the mounting of a tactical lamp.

a search for a newer lightweight pistol by the American military immediately following World War II. The military eventually decided to stay with the guns they had and ceased further interest in any new lightweight pistols, but the law enforcement and sporting market quickly fell in love with the Colt Commander. The main difference in physical size between the new Commander and the previous Government Model was only three-quarters of an inch. The Commander featured a frame that was .75 of an inch shorter as was the slide and corresponding barrel. The alloy frame was lighter, with an empty weight of only 27 ounces for the entire pistol. The Colt Commander was the first significantly reduced size 1911 pistol to appear in commercial production.

In 1985 Colt introduced a much smaller version of the basic Government Model 1911 pistol and it was called the Officer's Model Series 80 pistol. It featured a 3-1/2-inch barrel length and corresponding short slide length and a reduced grip height. Here some would argue the point of diminishing returns was reached because slide velocities were significantly increased over that seen with the Old Government Model. The engineering on the 1911 style Officer's Model therefore required the use of a dual spring recoil spring system to help dampen the recoil forces unleashed when firing this pint-sized .45. (The dual spring recoil spring assembly had previously been patented by Leander Seecamp and he sued everyone who violated his patent, including Colt, and everyone paid him royalties until the patent expired.)

Remarkably, all of the manufacturers of 1911 pistols presently operating in the domestic American market have followed Colt's lead on this and produced their own versions in each of these three frame sizes with possible minor differences. Kimber Manufacturing, Inc. produces an entire line of different size 1911 style pistols and their Pro-Carry model is a close relative of the original Commander in terms of size and weight. The only difference between the two is the Kimber Pro-Carry features a 4-inch barrel length versus the Commander's 4-1/4-inch length. There are other differences as well, because the Kimber employs a firing pin safety that operates off the grip safety and therefore doesn't affect the trigger pull weight of the gun at all.

Although many manufacturers make their own 1911-style pistols in a size and format comparable to the original Colt Officer's Model, I am not completely comfortable with the size-challenged variations of the original Government Model. I base my reasoning on the following concerns. The first is the shorter barrel lengths often reduce muzzle velocity to a point below what I feel is absolutely mandatory to the round's effectiveness in terms of stopping criminal behavior. It is the second concern however that raises the biggest alarm in my view. The dual-spring recoil system and the high slide velocities of this class of self-defense pistol all raise concerns over reliability. I know some manufacturers specifically warn against the use of "+P+" ammo because it generates enough force to literally 'kill' the recoil springs in their pistols. In testing a number of these pistols from different manufacturers (no names will be given) I also have noticed that each pistol will develop a preference for a certain load and lot number of ammunition. The gun will work perfectly with a specific load and lot number, but substitute another and it won't work quite as reliably. The operation of these short pistols is also more sensitive to the strength of the magazine spring, because a weak magazine spring can induce malfunctions. In other words, these abbreviated 1911 style pistols require research to discover what each example likes and doesn't like. That's one reason why I still prefer the old full-size Government Model. Most of the models offered from a variety of manufacturers today work very well with a far wider selection of affordable self-defense ammunition.

The author's son, Michael, was fortunate enough to receive pistol shooting instruction from 10-time IPSC National Champion, Rob Leatham. The weapon chosen by the boy was a Springfield Armory 1911A1 Trophy Match pistol in .40 S&W caliber.

The Colt Delta Elite is no longer offered by Colt's Manufacturing Company, but this 10mm auto Colt built by custom pistolsmith Richard Heinie has been used by the author for more than a decade. It has seen extensive use in a variety of applications and performs beautifully. PHOTO CREDIT: HEINIE SPECIALTY PRODUCTS

CALIBERS OF THE 1911 PISTOL

The 1911 is primarily thought of as a .45 caliber pistol, but it has been chambered for a wide range of calibers, many of them applicable to the self-defense market. The .38 Super cartridge was the first alternative to the .45 ACP round when it was introduced in 1928. It was specifically developed from the old .38 Auto round to offer law enforcement more penetration against vehicle-mounted bank robbers during the 1930s. In 1931, a .22 Long Rifle version of the Government Model was introduced with the Commercial Ace and then four years later, the Service Ace. Over the course of its history Colt has manufactured various 1911A1 pistols in 9x19mm caliber and even the obscure 9x21mm caliber, but never on a continuous basis. In 1987, the Colt Delta Elite was introduced and this was a 1911A1 pistol chambered for the 10mm cartridge, but it was discontinued in the mid-1990s. For a short period of time Colt Firearms offered the 1911A1 pistol in 9x23mm caliber, but the numbers produced were small. Other firms producing 1911 style pistols made guns chambered for the .40 S&W cartridge, but most of these were meant for application in the action competition market as my son has one and its reliability with

Those interested in shooting a 1911-style pistol for purposes other than self-defense often select calibers other than .45 ACP. This Springfield Armory Trophy Match 1911A1 pistol belongs to the author's son and is chambered for the .40 S&W cartridge.

factory ammunition is not the best. However, if the ammunition is handloaded to the overall length of 10mm ammo, the gun runs flawlessly. It's a competition-oriented pistol and not one meant for more serious applications.

I will cover how to carry the 1911 in the chapter on holsters. One of its most endearing traits to my mind, besides it reliability and power, is the relative ease with which the 1911 pistol can be easily carried concealed.

IN SUMMARY

In the War on Terror currently being campaigned in Iraq and Afghanistan, it is easy to notice from the news video shown each evening that a number of our service personnel have procured 1911A1 pistols. It's hard to beat success and for effective handgun defense, one way to spell success is the "1911A1 pistol in .45 ACP".

CHAPTER EIGHT

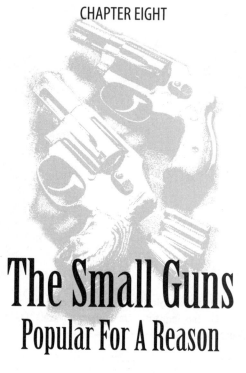

The Small Guns
Popular For A Reason

T he problem in selecting an effective handgun for concealed carry purposes is not a new one. It has been the same since Sam Colt first invented the fighting handgun. Comfort and ease of concealment are often at odds with power and terminal effectiveness. What follows in this chapter is not an all-encompassing treatise on small self-defense handguns, but rather a brief examination on some of the better examples available today. The criteria used in this admittedly subjective evaluation are the same as previously established. That is reliability, accuracy and terminal performance of the chambered caliber.

The history of the smaller guns requires some background explanation. Prior to the introduction of smokeless powder, the overall size of the handgun was a good indicator of the power of the cartridge for which it was chambered. The more powerful black powder cartridges all required large frames and large cylinders. The smallest revolvers could only be chambered for rounds like the .22 rimfire, the .32 rimfire cartridges or rounds of a similar low power. The introduction of smokeless powder in the mid-1880s spurred the interest in self-loading firearm designs. Naturally, the initial interest in this new technology was geared toward military applications and resulted in the development of higher-velocity, but smaller caliber military rifles and machine guns. These were used to a devastating effect during World War I.

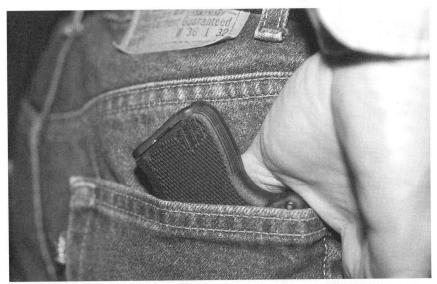

The Kel-Tec P-32 has a width of only .748 of an inch. This slim width means it rides easily and covertly in the back pocket of a regular pair of blue jeans.

More than a few small arms designers, however, realized this new propellant technology could be used to build ever-smaller handguns. These handguns possessed power and penetration greater than anything seen previously in a small black powder handgun. They came to be known as "pocket pistols".

The .25 ACP cartridge was used by John Browning to create the first semi-auto .25 caliber pistol in 1905. The pistol was built in Liege, Belgium by Fabrique Nationale des Armes de Guerre (FN) and patented in Belgium the same year. Three years later, Colt started production on this pistol using a license from Browning who received a U.S. patent for it on Jan. 25, 1910. Called the Colt Pocket Auto, this pistol was manufactured by Colt from 1908 until 1941 and it was the first of a class of small automatics to be called "Vest Pocket" pistols. With a loaded weight of only 13 ounces and an overall length of 4-1/2 inches, the Colt Pocket Auto would easily fit inside the front pocket of a vest worn by gentlemen of all ages.

John Browning, soon after developing the Colt Pocket Auto, created an even smaller version that was marketed under the name "Baby Browning". The two pistols are quite similar, but the Baby Browning is half an inch shorter in barrel length and overall length. It has a loaded weight of only 10 ounces and an overall length of 4 inches. Both models used a single-column magazine holding only six rounds of ammunition.

These pistols proved highly popular because they were so easy and light to carry and conceal. They were not complicated mechanisms. Because of the low power of the cartridge, each utilized an unlocked blowback action. Manufacturers across Europe were soon producing their own imitations of these guns and everything would have been sweetness and light in the world of fightin' handguns, but for one small detail – the .25 ACP, also known as the 6.35mm Browning, was a terribly poor fight stopper.

John Browning actually created the entire class of pocket pistols when he introduced the 'Baby Browning'. With a loaded weight of only 10 ounces and an overall length of 4 inches the 'Baby Browning' soon proved to be an extremely popular 'self-defense' pistol even if it was chambered for the feeble .25 ACP cartridge. PHOTO CREDIT: WALT RAUCH

The Colt 1903 Model 'M' is shown above the Kel Tec P-32. The Colt 1903 in .32 ACP caliber was a popular self-defense pistol prior to World War II. Many were purchased by the military for issue to General Officers and by the OSS for use by wartime secret agents. Of the two pistols seen here the author states the Colt is the more accurate of the pair.

The next step up in the automatic pistol continuum is the .32 ACP, otherwise known as the 7.65mm Browning round. It was developed for the Browning Model 1900 which proved to be one of the first truly successful semi-automatic pistols in the world of small arms. This cartridge was used to power an infinite number of 'pocket pistol' designs and was often discredited by many for the same reasons related to power and penetration as the disdained .25 ACP. Yet, it remained a popular chambering prior to World War II with the most successful version being the Colt Model 'M' 1903 Pocket Auto pistol.

The Colt Model 1903 Pocket pistol was designed by John Browning. It is a blowback, single-action, semi-auto pistol that was manufactured between 1903 and 1946. It was manufactured in four distinct model variations during those years. The last variant was purchased in significant numbers by the United States Government for use by the OSS and high-ranking military officers during World War II. The Colt 1903 Pocket pistol is an accurate gun even with a cartridge that was never known for great target performance. It is an extremely well-made and well-designed pistol. It is also one of the few factory pistols that have about as many sharp edges as the hypothetical well-worn bar of soap. Because the Colt 1903 is relatively thin, it is an easy gun to carry in a coat pocket. (Hey, if Humphrey Bogart continued to use it in so many movies, the gun had to have some class.) Even with its all carbon steel construction, the Colt Model 'M' only weighs 24 ounces. The magazine is held in place on the Model 'M' by a heel clip and holds eight rounds of ammunition.

I own a Type III Colt 1903 Pocket pistol and I like it. My gun is equipped with the optional 'German Silver' front sight, which consists of a low, thin, silver-colored blade, featuring a reverse ramp with rounded edges. The rear sight is a thick blade with a very narrow, but well-rounded, extremely small u-notch at its center. Evaluating the sights by modern standards, the rear notch and the front blade are miniscule, but the surprising fact is how well they work for shooting tight groups if the light is sufficient. It's doubtful the Colt Model 'M' 1903 Pocket pistol could be marketed today with the legal atmosphere we presently experience in America. The Model 'M' has a rather small manual safety and it is equipped with a grip safety. I do have to say, however, that my experience with the grip safety on my personal Model 'M' is an encouraging one. It works perfectly as designed by John Browning. Even if the manual safety is left in the 'OFF' position, the gun will not fire under any conditions until the grip safety is fully depressed. About the only sources for a good 1903 Colt Model 'M' pistol today are gun shows, the "previously owned" section at large firearms retailers and the websites that cater to the used gun market.

The biggest drawback to the Colt 1903 Pocket model, besides the lack of appropriate leather and its non-production status, is the limited availability of good quality spare magazines. Some after-market firms offer magazines for the Colt 1903, but my experience has been none of them work well with modern hollowpoint ammunition. Only the original Colt magazine for my pistol will feed the Federal Hydra-Shok, the Speer Gold-Dot and the Winchester Silvertip hollowpoint ammunition reliably in my pistol.

It was the introduction of the Winchester Silvertip hollowpoint round together with the development of the Seecamp LWS 32 in 1985 that brought new life to the .32 ACP cartridge as a self-defense pistol. Disparaged by many as ineffective, the extremely small size of the LWS 32 from Seecamp gave the cartridge a rebirth of sorts.

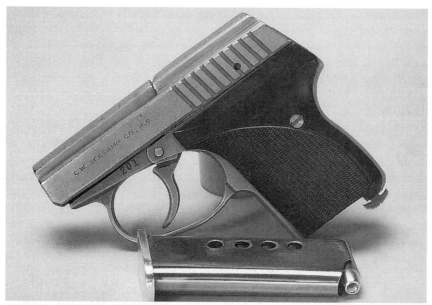

The pistol that started all the interest in extremely small self-defense pistols, the Seecamp LWS 32, is designed to work with only one type of ammunition – Winchester Silvertip. The Seecamp LWS 32 is virtually handmade and there is a waiting list of some duration for those who want to own this exclusive little pistol. **PHOTO CREDIT: WALT RAUCH**

With a 6+1 capacity and at a distance of 7 yards the North American Guardian in .32 ACP is able to keep all rounds within 3 inches. While not big bore target accuracy or performance it is still more than adequate for close range self-defense.

The Seecamp LWS is a double-action-only design made from stainless steel, but it is a very small pistol. It weighs only 11.5 ounces and has a 2-inch barrel. It has a six-round magazine capacity. It is strongly recommended by the manufacturer that only Winchester Silvertip ammunition be used in this pistol. The Seecamp pistol was designed specifically for the Winchester Silvertip round and it will work with no other round. It has no sights. (The idea being, it would be deployed at such short distances, sights will not be needed.) The main difficulty is the Seecamp LWS 32 is virtually a handmade handgun. The production rate for these exclusive and well-made, tiny handguns is low.

Over the years since the introduction of the Seecamp LWS 32, other firms like Kel-Tec and North American Arms have produced pistols nearly equal to the heralded Seecamp in both size and reliability and at more affordable prices. The Seecamp enjoys a perpetual back-order situation from the manufacturer.

The North American Arms Guardian in .32 ACP caliber is a double-action-only design and is manufactured from stainless steel. It has a six-shot magazine and weighs 13.5 ounces. The barrel length on the Guardian in .32 ACP is 2.185 inches, but it is available with sights. Unlike the Seecamp, the Guardian works with all types of .32 ACP ammunition. The example I carry in extremely warm weather has a set of XS sights on it with a big tritium dot in the front blade. Normally, most experienced shooters want the magazine release to be a push button located on the left side of the semi-auto pistol at the junction where the triggerguard meets the frame. This is exactly what is found on the N.A.A. Guardian in .32 ACP. For a gun this small, there have been instances where this release was inadvertently activated by something else in my pocket, like a small flashlight or a pocket knife and the magazine was partially released even when carried in a protective 'pocket' holster. This results in a one-shot pistol. The European-style heel clip magazine catch is a better idea for pistols this small. Few shooters are going to be performing a speed reload with a gun this tiny in any firefight.

The North American Guardian in .32 ACP joins the Seecamp LWS32 and the Kel Tec P-32 in being a deep cover, easy-to-conceal pocket pistol. Many police officers purchase pistols like these as back-up pistols.

The Kel Tec P-32 is a .32 ACP semi-auto pistol that utilizes a locked breech. Unusual for a small pistol, the locked breech is necessary because the slide is light and the whole gun weighs only 6.6 ounces!

Both the North American Guardian (left) and the Kel Tec P-32 (right) are .32 ACP pocket pistols. The Guardian because it is smaller has one round less magazine capacity than the Kel Tec product.

When it comes to lightweight self-defense pistols, it's hard to beat the Kel-Tec P-32, even if it is a .32 ACP. The Kel-Tec P-32 weighs only 6.6 ounces! It is light enough that even the most experienced, concealed carry holder will forget he has it in his pocket or on his person. It has happened to me more than once. Being slightly larger than the NAA Guardian or the Seecamp LWS 32, the P-32 has a magazine that holds seven rounds of ammunition. The Kel-Tec P-32 also works with all types of .32 ACP ammo and it is not brand specific. The P-32 is also unusual in that it employs a locked breech operating mechanism, which is virtually unknown in small caliber, pocket pistol design history. Locking the breech has nothing to do with increased power or pressure, but rather it is an easy way to keep the breech closed on the lightweight slide. I have heard of some handloaders who felt because it was a locked breech design, they could handload 'hotter' .32 ACP loads for this pistol. This didn't work, as their loads proved excessive and broke the barrel. I do not fault the Kel-Tec P-32 for this, but rather question the judgment and intelligence of an individual who would do such a thing. The Kel-Tec P-32 is a little longer and taller than either the Seecamp LWS 32 or the N.A.A. Guardian, but it is by far the thinnest pistol of this class. The P-32 measures only .748" at its widest point. This, coupled with its light weight from its polymer frame and small slide, makes it an extremely easy pistol to carry with you under conditions that demand the most minimal of clothing.

The P-32 is a double-action-only design, but it lacks re-strike capability. That means if you pull the trigger and the pistol fails to fire, the slide must be cycled before the trigger will again work. The NAA Guardian has continuous re-strike capability and does not need to have its slide cycled to function on a subsequent trigger pull.

Some authorities feel it is better to immediately expel a dud-round and replace it with a fresh round. Others feel it is faster to simply pull the trigger a second time in hopes of getting the dud round to fire on the second strike. Human nature being what it is, I can say most operators will attempt the second trigger pull before cycling the slide unless they are extremely well trained in malfunction clearance procedures.

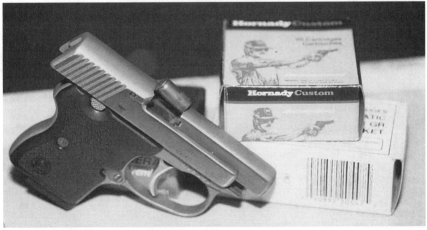

These small pocket pistols are more sensitive in terms of reliability than larger pistols. This small pistol trapped the ejected spent case in the breech opening when the shooter 'limp wristed' the pistol by not holding it firmly.

Before moving to the Pocket Pistols chambered for the .380 ACP cartridge, the Walther PPK needs examination. The Walther PP was the first successful double-action, semi-auto pistol in the history of small arms when it was introduced in 1929. It proved so successful, a smaller version was developed two years later for use by police and law enforcement. This smaller Walther was called the PPK and as every movie fan can testify it was also the chosen weapon of the Man With A License To Kill – James Bond.

The Walther PPK is too big to be considered a 'vest' pocket pistol, but still small enough for inclusion in the pocket category. Walther PPK pistols have been chambered in .32 ACP and .380 ACP, as well as .22 Long Rifle and a very few in .25 ACP. For a number of years the Walther PPK (actually the PPK/S because of American import laws) was considered the smallest and most practical self-defense pistol due to its availability in .380 ACP. Smith & Wesson is currently manufacturing the Walther PPK/S under license at their plant in Maine because all German production was halted in 1999. The Walther PPK and PPK/S are blowback operated with the traditional double-action/single-action trigger pull. This pistol has influenced the design of a number of similar pistols, the most notable being the Russian Makarov.

The Walther PPK is a historic pistol, but the truth is, in my opinion, it is often over-rated. When chambered in .380 ACP, the Walther is a hard-recoiling pistol with too many sharp corners on the frame near the grip. Additionally, on all but the latest models the reciprocating slide will cut 'tracks' across the web of the firing hand as the outside edges of the slide dig into the flesh bunched up by a firm grip. True, the Walther PPK is a relatively thin pistol for one chambered in .380 ACP. It was the first successful double-action semi-auto, but Bond, James Bond, would have been equally served with a number of other designs.

The Walther PPK is the gun used by the spy with a license to kill, Bond – James Bond. The PPK was the first successful double-action semi-auto pistol design, but the author feels it is somewhat over-rated considering what's available. PHOTO CREDIT: WALT RAUCH

The Colt Model 1908 is another product from the imagination of John Browning. It is chambered for the .380 ACP round and it is, like its little brother the 1903 Model 'M', a single-action semi-auto design. Production of this wonderful gun stopped in 1940 so don't look to find one in the 'new' gun section of your local gunshop. **PHOTO CREDIT: WALT RAUCH**

The Kahr Micro 9 is an extremely small semi-auto that easily joins the ranks of pocket pistols, but in a more serious self-defense caliber like 9x19mm. The Surefire 6P flashlight is shown for size comparison purposes.

The author considers the Kahr MK40 to be the smallest pocket pistol available in .40 S&W caliber. Surprisingly, it is also extremely accurate for so powerful a cartridge in so small an envelope.

Lacking the mystique of the Walther PPK, or its modern operation, the Colt Model 1908 is another product from the imagination of John Browning. It is among the larger examples of the pocket pistol class of defensive handguns. The Colt Model 1908 is very similar in design and operation to the Model 'M' 1903 Colt Pocket pistol in .32 ACP. The big difference between the two is the Model 1908 is chambered for the .380 ACP cartridge. It features a 3.75-inch barrel I and was produced in three different variations between 1908 to 1940. Like its smaller caliber predecessor, the Colt Model 1908 is notable for its lack of sharp edges.

The modern alternative to a .380 ACP pocket pistol is provided by Seecamp, North American Arms and Kel-Tec as each has a .380 ACP equivalent to their previously mentioned .32 ACP pistols. Naturally, each larger caliber model from the respective manufacturers is slightly larger than the smaller caliber predecessor. Yet, they remain small enough to be easily classified as 'pocket' pistols.

There is a new manufacturer that started operation in 1993 whose products should be included in the small pistol/pocket pistol category. Kahr Arms produces what can only be described as an innovative double-action-only, locked breech, semi-auto pistol that is available in either 9x19mm or .40 S&W caliber. Even though the majority of Kahr models are small pistols in size, the guns that I would include in the true 'pocket' category are the "Micro" Kahrs. I have had a MK40, the micro compact version of the Kahr is an amazingly well-made, reliable, self-defense handgun. The double-action trigger is unusual in that it is smooth and glitch free. The MK40 is a stainless steel gun that weighs 22 ounces empty. The pistol comes with two magazines; the flush-fitting model holds five rounds of .40 S&W ammo, while the extended magazine holds six rounds. The factory sights are excellent. The MK40 is an accurate pistol and an extremely reliable one. I carried mine in the left front pocket of some cut-off pants, during a long beach vacation, and felt very secure with its power, accuracy and reliability. The main shortfall of the MK40 was its weight. That has now been rectified with the introduction of the PM40, a polymer-framed version of the same pistol. The PM40 weighs only 17.1 ounces and it is a true pocket pistol, but one offering a significant increase in power over that seen with its historical predecessors.

Although the Glock Model 26 is too large to be considered a true pocket pistol, it is still a small pistol. It is also accurate as this target shot by the author at a distance of 50 feet demonstrates.

THE SNUB-NOSE REVOLVER

Colt introduced the modern snub-nose revolver in 1928. There had been many small double-action, swing-out cylinder revolvers built prior to this, but none were chambered for the .38 Special cartridge. All the previous chamberings were of a far inferior nature in terms of power, bullet diameter and muzzle velocity. Simply shortening the barrel on the already popular Colt Police Positive double-action revolver to 2 inches created this new revolver. Colt called the new revolver the "Detective Special". It weighed 21 ounces and featured a six-shot cylinder.

Colt previously introduced a line of small, double-action revolvers called 'Pocket' revolvers in 1895. In 1905 the name was changed to Pocket Positive to reflect the upgrade in the internal safety system. This prevented the hammer from being cocked whenever the cylinder was not completely closed and locked into the frame. The Colt Pocket Positive revolver was chambered for a number of .32 caliber cartridges including the .32 Short Colt, the .32 Long Colt, the .32 S&W and the .32 New Police. None of these .32 caliber cartridges earned accolades for stopping power. Colt ceased manufacture of the Pocket Positive revolvers during World War II and never resumed their production following the war.

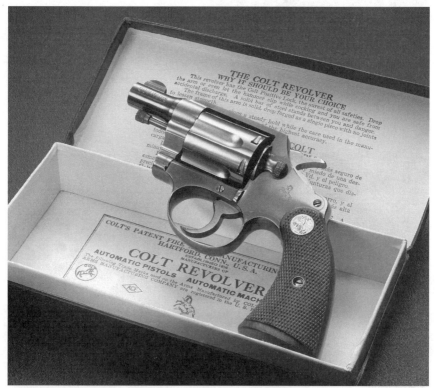

The Colt Detective Special created the concept of the snubnose revolver. Introduced in 1928, the Detective Special soon became known as the "Dick Special" and its possession was synonymous with plain clothes police work.

There seems to be a bit of confusion as to what actually came first. There are authorities who feel the first snubnose revolver was the Colt Banker's Special. It was chambered for the weaker .38 S&W cartridge. It used a shorter frame than that found on the version chambered for .38 Special. Some say the Banker's Special was introduced in 1928 while other sources cite the year as 1926. In any event, by the close of 1928, Colt Firearms Co. was the only source of small-frame revolvers sporting 2-inch or shorter barrels in .38 Special caliber. There are also references that state the Banker's Special was built at the request of the U.S. Postal authorities for use as a pocket gun for railway postal clerks.

The Colt Detective Special has endured a history of change. The Detective Special has always been a six-shot small-frame revolver, most often chambered in .38 Special caliber, but the first examples had an exposed ejector rod and skinny wood grips. In 1972, a shroud was added to the design to protect the ejector rod. In 1986, Colt discontinued the Detective Special only to bring it back in the 1990s and then discontinue it again in 1998.

The Detective Special earned the nickname 'Dick Special' and was extremely popular with plain clothes police officers back when they routinely carried revolvers. This example has been equipped with after-market grips as a means of increasing its control during routine police qualification courses.

This new class of self-defense revolver immediately received its share of criticisms. The combination of the short sight radius (the distance between the front sight and the rear sight), the relatively small size and the comparatively powerful caliber made the Colt Detective Special a difficult revolver to shoot well. It was, however, a trendsetter as it established the viability of the classic snub-nose revolver.

Smith & Wesson was the big competitor to Colt prior to World War II. It is well to remember during the period before World War II, Colt was absolutely dominate in terms of popularity among law enforcement and military personnel, as well as the general perception of overall quality. Following World War II that perception changed. It began slowly, but Smith & Wesson began to introduce a number of new and exciting designs in self-defense revolvers.

The first was the introduction of the Chief's Special, the first revolver to be manufactured on Smith & Wesson's new J frame. The year was 1950, but it would be two more years before the Chief's Special reached regular production status. The Chief's Special was a double-action, swing-out cylinder revolver. It had a fluted five-shot cylinder and weighed approximately 19 ounces. It had a 2-inch barrel and was received by law

The changes Colt made to the Detective Special were a response to reduced market share. The large rubber grips increased control but reduced concealability. The shrouded ejector rod achieved little more than an attempt to duplicate the look of their competition.

The Taurus Model 85 is a five-shot snubnose revolver in .38 Special. It is a good choice for those not wanting to pay premium prices for more expensive products offering more or less equivalent performance.

enforcement officers with great enthusiasm. The Smith & Wesson Chief's Special was at its introduction the best combination of light weight, small, easy-to-conceal size and power ever created in a defensive handgun. Needless to say, it was a success and over the subsequent years Smith & Wesson followed the introduction of the Chief's Special with a number of additional defensive revolvers based on the J frame.

The *Airweight* version of the Chief's Special was the next model to be unveiled by the handgun manufacturer in Springfield, Massachusetts. The Airweight Chief's Special had a frame and originally a cylinder made from an aluminum alloy and it weighed only 10.75 ounces empty. Unfortunately, the aluminum cylinder demonstrated excessive wear and by 1954 a steel cylinder was substituted on the Airweight Chief's Special. The gun now weighed 12.5 ounces and remained one of the lighter defensive handguns available for a number of decades.

Smith & Wesson in the 1880s pioneered the safety hammerless design of revolvers. These guns were top-break revolvers, featuring a concealed hammer and a grip safety at the back of the grip frame. They were true double-action-only revolvers, referred to as 'lemon-squeezers' because they required the same gripping action as one would exercise when squeezing the fruit. The idea behind these revolvers was to create a gun that would not snag on the lining of a pocket as it was being drawn. They were successful designs but by 1940, they were also antiquated and out of date in a number of ways.

Smith & Wesson re-introduced the concept with the Centennial Models in 1952. The Centennial Models, later were known as the Model 40 and Model 42 revolvers, were built on the J frame. They used the same swing-out cylinder operation as all the other double-action revolvers and five-shot fluted cylinders and double-action-only trigger mechanisms. The big difference was the hammer was concealed within the frame of the revolver. The Airweight Centennial weighed 13 ounces when it was fitted with a steel cylinder. The first models were fitted with an aluminum cylinder and weighed 11.25 ounces. However, the aluminum cylinders were discontinued due to excessive wear concerns at the same time as the Chief's Special.

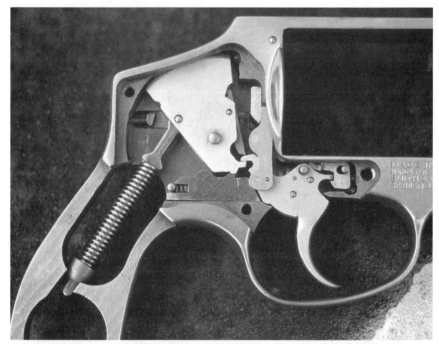

The Centennial revolver design from Smith & Wesson is not a hammer-less design. It has a hammer. It is just that is contained completely within the frame. This allows the operator to fire the revolver from within a pocket without fear of a malfunction or the hammer snagging on the lining of the pocket containing the handgun.

Because the hammer was contained within the frame the design proved especially popular because it allowed the gun to be fired from within a coat pocket without fear of fouling the action. I have interviewed more than one law enforcement officer or private sector armed professional, who acknowledged using a Centennial in a coat pocket to covertly cover a known dangerous suspect without their knowledge. The Centennial and the Centennial Airweight revolvers also featured a grip safety like their Safety Hammerless predecessors.

The Bodyguard Airweight and the Bodyguard revolvers were the next models to be introduced by Smith & Wesson. The difference found with them was a shrouded hammer design. The shroud was built as part of the revolver's frame and it protected the hammer from snagging on the lining of a coat pocket. The advantage over the Centennial design was the Bodyguard was capable of both double-action and single-action firing. The hammer spur could be manually cocked. It was exposed at the top and back of the protective shield allowing access to the thumb. The success of the Bodyguard models overshadowed the Centennial models for a while and in 1974 Smith & Wesson discontinued all the Centennial revolvers.

In 1991 the Centennial revolvers were reintroduced, but the new guns were slightly different than the old. First of all, many were made with stainless steel. Smith & Wesson had pioneered the concept of using stainless steel for personal defense handguns with the Model 60. The Model 60 was a stainless steel version of the Chief's Special and it was introduced in 1965.

Another big difference with the re-introduced Centennial revolvers was the missing grip safety feature seen on the earlier models. Smith & Wesson over the ensuing years produced a whole series of Centennial models in a variety of calibers and barrel lengths. Some of these revolvers included models chambered for the 9x19mm cartridge (the Model 940) and the .32 H&R Magnum round. Eventually, the field was narrowed to those models chambered for .38 Special. In 1999, they introduced a series of revolvers built with Scandium frames and titanium cylinders that were stressed for "+P" pressures in the .38 Special chambering. Many of these revolvers weighed between 10.8 ounces and 12 ounces.

The Smith & Wesson Model 640 (top) and the Model 638 (bottom) are both made from stainless steel. Smith & Wesson pioneered the use of stainless steel in handgun construction with the Model 60, another member of the J-frame family. Stainless steel eliminates many of the worries and complaints associated with maintenance on a handgun that is carried close to the body in humid or wet weather conditions.

The Smith & Wesson Centennial was first introduced in 1952 as the Model 40 (top left). It featured a grip safety which can be seen sticking out the back of the grip. The Model 42 (top right) was the same revolver, but one featuring an alloy frame and corresponding lighter weight. The revolver seen on the lower right is a custom made Model 640 from the Smith & Wesson Performance Center while the Model 642 at the lower left is an alloy frame revolver with a stainless steel barrel and cylinder.

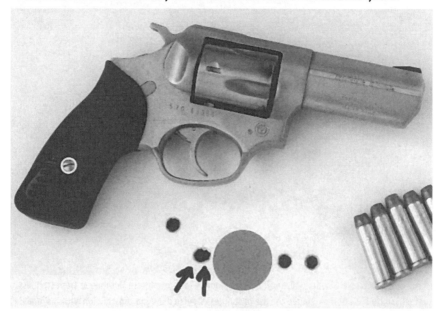

The Ruger SP-101 was the first small-frame snubnose class of defensive revolver to be chambered for the .357 Magnum cartridge. The early production example seen here has a 3-inch barrel and a santoprene grip that helps cushion the felt recoil in this 25-ounce gun.

Smith & Wesson next took the scandium frame one step further by chambering the same small, light revolvers in .357 Magnum. S&W was not the first to build a small-frame snub-nose .357 Magnum revolver; Sturm, Ruger & Co. earned that honor with the SP-101. The SP-101, however, was an all stainless steel revolver that weighed 25 ounces and even then it was handful when firing full-power .357 Magnum loads. Many did not find the experience pleasant. With that being the case you can just imagine what the reaction was when everyone learned the Smith & Wesson Model 360 weighed just 12 ounces, or less than half what the Ruger SP-101 weighed in the same chambering.

Sturm, Ruger and Co. was the first revolver manufacturer to offer a five-shot small-frame .357 Magnum revolver with the introduction of the SP-101. Ruger however warned against using any bullet heavier than 125 grains with an engraved warning on the side of the barrel. PHOTO CREDIT: STRUM, RUGER & CO.

The introduction of scandium-framed revolvers featuring titanium cylinders by Smith & Wesson has enabled them to create extremely lightweight self-defense revolver in serious calibers. Many of these revolvers weigh less than 12 ounces.

The Glock Model 26 is too large to ride in the author's pockets so he carries in a DeSantis Apache ankle holster, but the Smith & Wesson Model 442 rides regularly in an offside pocket of his trousers. Both are among the better examples of good quality self-defense handguns.

The truth is, shooting any of the 12-ounce .357 Magnum scandium/titanium/stainless steel revolvers manufactured by Smith & Wesson with *any* .357 Magnum load is just flat **painful.** It is not fun. Having said that, it is obvious Smith & Wesson has demonstrated a superior engineering feat by building a gun that will outlast all, but the strongest of shooters.

I will be criticized by some when I say this, but I feel the Smith & Wesson Model 442, now discontinued, but the stainless steel alternative, the Model 642 which is still available, represent the most practical (almost perfect) combination of easily concealable size versus power presently available. Even when loaded with 158-grain lead hollowpoint ammunition, these 15-ounce revolvers are not difficult for all, but the beginning revolver shooter to manage over a long course of fire for training purposes. Additionally, the huge popularity of these revolvers is mute testimony to the practicality of them for concealed carry permit holders.

Even though the Model 340PD represents the same package at 3 ounces less weight and in a more powerful chambering, I have to admit the recoil is sufficient to prevent me from practicing with the latter gun and ammo combination to any level of proficiency.

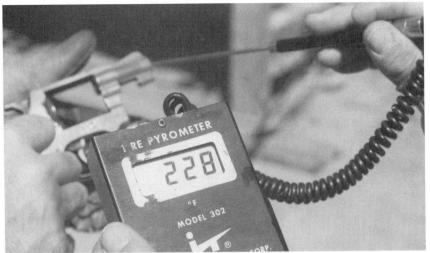

How durable are small revolvers? The author discovered they are pretty tough when he and a group of shooters ran 5,000 rounds through a Smith & Wesson Model 60 in just over four hours. This pyrometer states the highest reading he was able to register throughout the test – 228 degrees F.

POINT OF DIMINISHING RETURN?

The critical assessment and one every concealed carry permit holder must face is, will my selected gun and ammunition combination allow me to maintain or improve my proficiency? I feel the manufacturers, while demonstrating superior engineering in these products, have reached the point of diminishing returns in concealed carry handguns. Simply put, these guns are too light for so powerful a cartridge, making reasonable practice and training sessions for the majority of folks all but impossible. It would be appropriate at this point to return to the original vest pocket pistol John Browning designed in .25 ACP. It weighed 13 ounces loaded, which is a full ounce heavier than the Model 360 that Smith & Wesson currently produces in .357 Magnum weighs when empty. Those who use these lightweight 'magnum' revolvers on a regular basis remain a realm populated by a dedicated and select few. I am not one of those few. The 15-ounce revolvers and a "+P" loading of a .38 Special cartridge, in my view, remain within the parameters of reasonable recoil if not the upper limits that can be used for training, practice and duty use.

CHAPTER NINE

Carry And Concealment
A brief look at Fashion and Holsters

A s a practical matter for those new to the idea of carrying a concealed handgun daily, this chapter should be the first one studied. It is located in the back of this work for a reason. All of the subjects examined previously are necessary for a thorough understanding of the dynamics of effective handgun defense, especially one carried close and concealed throughout the workday.

The clothes, the lifestyle, the climate, the work atmosphere, the amount and degree of contact with the outside world and even the gender of the concealed carry permit holder will have a most critical influence on how a person will carry a defensive handgun comfortably and securely for long hours. What is the daily dress? Is it business attire or is it more casual and informal? What is the average temperature and humidity where they reside? How often does the permit holder have contact with the general public and to what degree? Does the general public in the subject area routinely wear an outer (covering) garment or do they exhibit a more casual style of dress indicative of a sun-drenched vacation resort community? How strenuous in terms of physical activity is the permit holder's employment? How clean is the work atmosphere in terms of dust, soot or other factors that can disable a firearm if it isn't routinely examined and cleaned? Does the employment require extensive travel and if so, is it by automobile or commercial airlines? What are the employer's rules pertaining to personally owned or employer-owned

When it comes to choices the beginning concealed carry permit holder will soon learn he can quickly be overwhelmed by the number of different holsters and styles available for the armed self-defense market. All of these holsters are built to fit just one gun, the Colt Magnum Carry shown here in a Galco horizontal shoulder holster and ammo carrier system.

defensive firearms in the workplace? Does the work require frequent visits to courthouses or other facilities with mandated security screening processes before entry?

All of these questions must be addressed before one contemplates how to carry and conceal the defensive handgun. The optimum mode of carry will often determine the exact type and style of defensive pistol.

YOUR PERSONAL THREAT ASSESSEMENT

While the first rule of a gunfight is 'Have A Gun', there are times when you will have to disarm as a result of circumstances beyond your control. Examples include entering the secured area of an airport, or a federal courthouse. The truth is you are at greater personal risk in these 'high security' areas because anyone targeting you or someone near you knows this is a target-rich environment with designated and predictable response personnel. The armed personnel within these areas are almost always in a uniform of some description and easily seen. In the minds of some, their presence is a 'deterrent' when in fact it makes the reaction plan more easily understood. Defending yourself within these restricted areas requires skill, cunning and more than a little training, but unarmed combat against a determined foe in a restricted area is outside the purpose of this text.

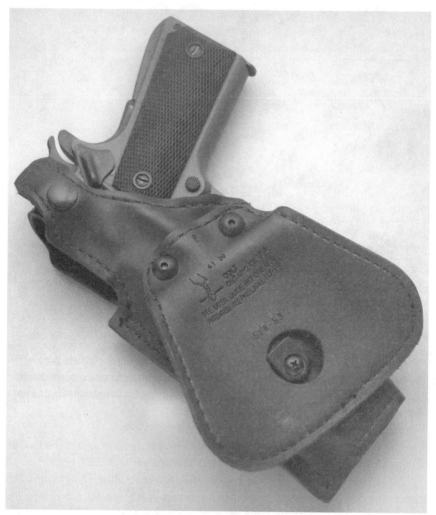

Many concealed carry permit holders who work or travel at times with no outer covering garment may be forced to select some form of a paddle holster as shown here with this Safariland holster. Paddle holsters as a general rule are easy to remove, but sometimes difficult to put on quickly.

Studies have shown that individuals or groups targeted for assault by criminals or political terrorists are in the gravest risk when either entering or leaving their homes or places of business and employment. The reasons are many and they involve the targeted individual being distracted while the attackers are able to wait in anticipation of the attack. For most, this scenario involves a vehicle of some description and depending upon the laws and regulations covering the concealed carry permit the vehicle-mounted firearm remains a viable option. One should consider what legal liability will result, should the vehicle be burglarized and the firearm stolen.

The best option is to always carry the personal defensive handgun on the person.

For women, this can prove exceedingly difficult and I won't for one minute pretend to be an expert on how a woman should carry a concealed firearm, but I will recommend one. Gila May-Hayes is an accomplished firearms trainer, writer and shooter based in the Seattle, Washington area and she has written a good book for both genders, but especially so for women, entitled "EFFECTIVE DEFENSE, THE WOMAN, THE PLAN, THE GUN." Kathy Rauch is another writer who is knowledgeable about the problems women face in carrying a concealed handgun and she has contributed many articles to *Combat Handguns* and other magazines.

BELT GUNS

Those familiar with "Class Three" firearms often use this term to refer to medium and heavy belt-fed machine guns, but here it is being used to refer to all holsters mounted on the trouser belt. Another term often used to describe this type of carry refers to the holster positioning; i.e. hip-holster. The belt gun will most likely be mounted on the 'strong' side. Unless you are a Hollywood film director or screenwriter, this is the most commonly encountered method of carrying and concealing a handgun. (Shoulder holsters or underarm holsters are often used in films because they are more 'visual'.)

Belt guns can be carried either outside the waistband, inside the waistband, or in the cross-draw position. If the operator is even faintly interested in a handgun 'action' oriented form of competition it is recommended they research and purchase some form of strong-side belt holster or hip-holster. Due to concerns over safety just about every firearms sanctioning organization in existence endorses the use of only strong-side holsters. Cross-draw holsters and shoulder holsters are universally prohibited as they allow the competitor to carry and draw a loaded firearm that is, at different stages of the draw, pointed up range or outward toward indicated safety areas for range officers and spectators.

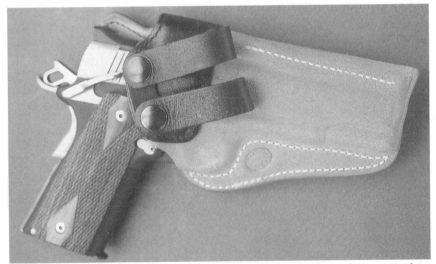

The Summer Special 2 from Milt Sparks as used by the author has two belt loops. They are secured at the top of each loop with a thumb snap. The snaps allows the user to quickly remove the holster should the need arise, but the dual loops guarantee the holster doesn't change position during a long day.

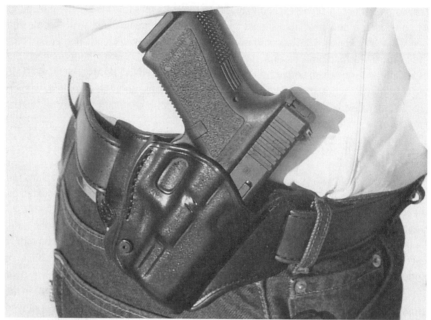

The Model CC-AT from Milt Sparks is a good hip holster for pistols like the Glock Model 19 (seen here). It offers good gun retention and positions the gun tight against the body to avoid unnecessary 'printing' of the gun and holster under a covering garment.

The first item one should investigate for a good belt holster is not the holster, nor the gun, but the belt. Without exception, the belt should come from a reputable holster maker. The reason is simple. Dress belts sold by fashion stores are not strong enough to support the weight of the gun and holster. They sag, fold and wear to a point of non-performance rather rapidly, even under the slightest use. Even when lightest self-defense pistol is placed in a good holster on a fashion house belt, the result can only be increased fatigue for the user because of the constant need for re-adjustment, and in the worst cases, loss of the firearm or its inadvertent exposure.

Hip-holsters and strong-side holsters for belt guns can be classified according to the material used in construction, their slant and whether or not they offer security retention against 'gun-grab'. Law enforcement officers as a general rule need a holster with some form of retention or security device, even if it is nothing more than a cross-over thumb snap strap. Civilians don't need to be as concerned about a gun-grab because if the gun is truly concealed, no one should be aware of its presence. However, there are those who recommend some form of retention device or design on the strong-side holster even for civilians. The concern is obviously someone noticing the gun, then grabbing the gun from behind the permit holder. The situation can degrade in various degrees from that point on with the worst case being the permit holder getting shot and killed with his or her own self-defense firearm.

The big problem with any kind of retention device is it will slow the draw, or at best complicate the draw stroke. It is a personal decision and one every permit holder

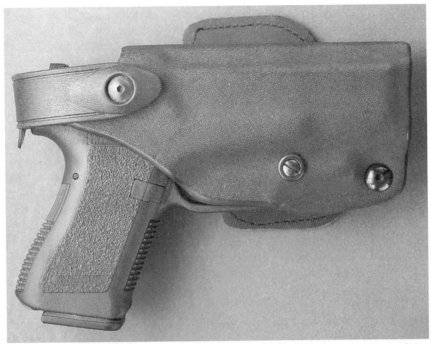

This Safariland holster is meant for use by those who want a higher level of gun retention on their concealed carry pistol. This cross-over strap operates via thumbpiece located on the body side portion of the strap. It must be pushed down and rotated forward for the gun to clear the holster. It works better in practice than the explanation sounds.

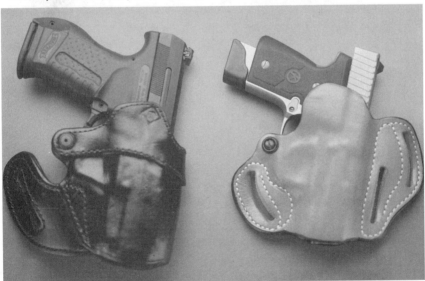

Most everyone who makes a hip holster angles the butt of the pistol forward as seen here on the Aker product for the Walther P99 (left) and the DeSantis holster for the Kahr MK9 (right).

must face when choosing the proper holster. For years, I used nothing but some form of retention/security holster for concealed carry. However, in recent years I've become less concerned about the security aspects of a holster's design and more concerned about its ability to carry a handgun comfortably and, more importantly, discretely.

A good concealment holster should not allow 'printing'. Printing occurs whenever some aspect of the handgun's general outline is revealed through the covering garment. An observer doesn't have to see the actual gun or the overall outline of the gun, but some part of it to know a person is carrying. Printing primarily occurs with the gun butt, but some designs reveal the barrel profile through the trousers if it's an inside the waistband design. Printing of the concealed carry defensive pistol must be avoided at all costs. The problem is no concealment holster for a handgun will work for everybody. There are some that work better than most for a greater percentage of concealed carry holders and some that work exceedingly well with a certain type of handgun, but not so good with others.

For concealment purposes all strong-side holsters should tuck the butt of the gun in to the body, approximately in the area of the kidney. This is a somewhat relative requirement because if they tuck the gun butt in too tightly then it is possible the muzzle and bottom portion of the holster will stick out or print badly against the covering garment.

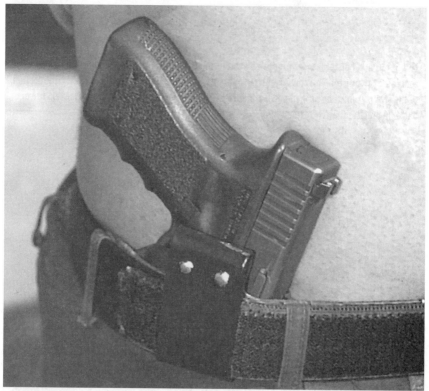

Many manufacturers of Kydex holsters also offer an IWB version of the same basic holster. The advantage is the same holster a weekend competitor will use for competition will serve them well throughout the week as the means of concealing the concealed carry self-defense handgun.

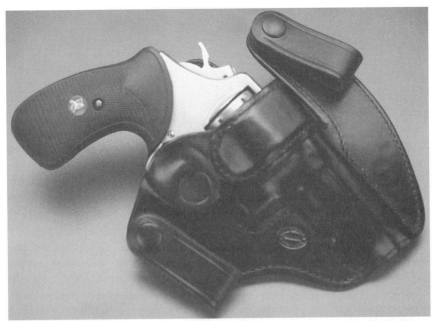

Milt Sparks offers this inside-the-pants holster for revolver shooters and recommends it over the revolver version of the Summer Special. The NP-2 features dual retention snap loops that allow the gun and holster to be removed without removal of the pants belt. The gun shown holstered in this photo is a Smith & Wesson Model 65 with a 3-inch barrel and after-market Pachmayr grips.

Milt Sparks made this hip holster and single magazine pouch for the author many years ago and it has served him well. The main design advantage is the metal reinforced mouth of the holster which guarantees it won't collapse when the pistol is removed. This allows for easier re-holstering.

Additionally, a big concern with the belt holster despite its style and manufacturer is the need for a covering garment with sufficient length for the hem of the garment to extend well below the bottom of the holster.

With all this in mind it is easy to recommend some holsters and manufacturers from personal experience. One of the oldest firms in the business of building custom concealment holsters is Milt Sparks Holsters, Inc. It is now owned and run by Tony Kanaley, who started with the firm in 1983. I have used both their Model CC-AT for a Glock Model 19 and the Model NP-2 for a Smith & Wesson Model 65 revolver with a 3-inch barrel. The quality of both holsters is top notch and they worked well at keeping the profile subdued under a covering sport coat. Additionally, the people at Milt Sparks have a long history with combat handgun competition so they understand the need for a practical, easy-to-use holster for your favorite blaster while at the same time providing a design that enables an efficient draw stroke. Milt Sparks also pioneered the Summer Special, but more on that design in a moment.

Lou Alessi operates Alessi Holster Incorporated in Amherst, New York and I've used his holsters for a number of semi-auto handguns. If you examine my Alessi holsters you will notice they are scuffed and have less than a perfect appearance. There is a reason for that. I've used them extensively for a long time because they are well-designed, well-

The D.O.J. holster is manufactured for Heinie Specialty Products by Alessi. It is a design that offers no cant forward or rearward, but sits the holster straight up. It keeps the gun close to the body and works exceedingly well at presenting the gun butt to the firing hand.

▶ Lou Alessi makes a number of very fine holsters. Even though the one seen here holstering a Smith & Wesson Model 4506 appears scuffed and beat up there is a reason. The author used it for many years because it was an excellent holster.

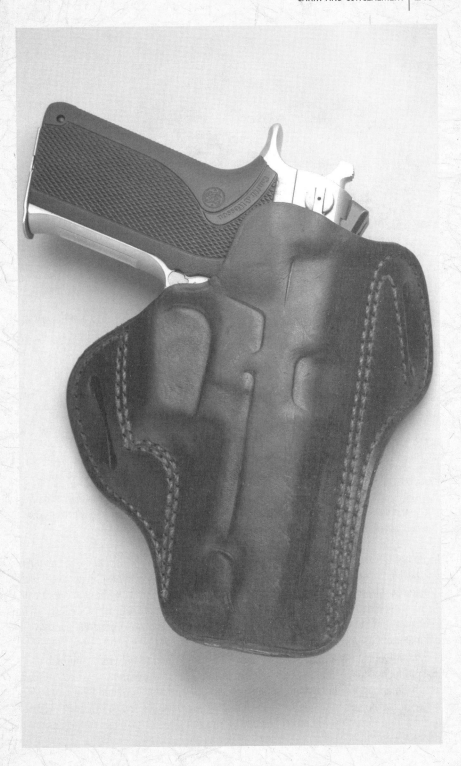

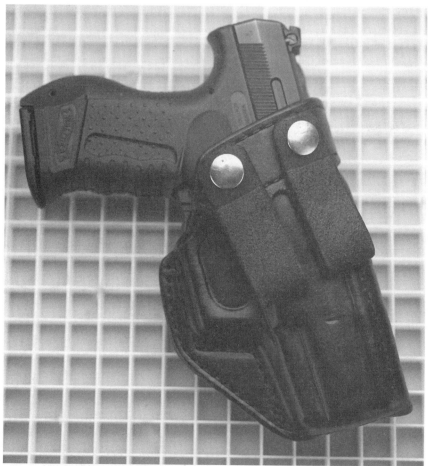

Matt Del Fatti, a retired Wisconsin Sheriff's Deputy, made this IWB design for the author's Walther P99. It is well-made and rides comfortably on the ball of the hip. Del Fatti is quickly establishing himself as one of the 'young lions' in the concealment holster trade.

made holsters that tuck the gun into your side yet still provide for a good purchase of the grip during the draw stroke. Heinie Specialty Products also offers the D.O.J. holster, which is made by Alessi for Heinie. The Heinie D.O.J. is available with or without a thumbreak. There is even a version made for the ladies. The D.O.J. is made primarily for 1911 style handguns and the Glock series of pistols, but it is one I have used with good success for a number of years.

Matt Del Fatti is a retired deputy sheriff in Wisconsin and he runs a one-man shop that produces some of the best concealment leather available anywhere. His holsters have as a hallmark an extremely tight fit between the gun and leather. I found the fit so good between the holster he made for my Smith & Wesson Model 657 with a 3-inch barrel that it adds another level of protection against the gun grab. It's that tight. Yet, it remains a discreet holster that easily presents the gun during the draw stroke.

INSIDE THE WAISTBAND

Milt Sparks pretty much established the Inside the Waistband holster as a viable concept when he started manufacturing the Bruce Nelson-designed Summer Special. The Summer Special positions the bulk of the handgun inside the pants. Because of this only the butt of the handgun needs to be covered and concealed by the covering garment. The result is the common blue denim jacket will conceal a large pistol like the 1911 Government Model and do so in an extremely comfortable fashion. If the weather is too warm for a short-hemmed jacket, then the whole affair can be concealed under nothing more than an untucked shirt. There had been inside-the-pants holsters prior to this design, but the late Bruce Nelson, who was an undercover drug agent with the California Department of Justice for many years, added a steel reinforced mouth to the top of the holster. This enabled the concealed carry holder to draw and reholster with one hand without having to unbutton, unzip and adjust his jeans in public during the attempt to replace the handgun in the holster. It was a revelation when it was first introduced and proved so popular that just about everyone who makes concealment leather offers one or a dozen different models.

One thing should be mentioned at this point. The 1911 Government Model and the Browning High Power pistols, because of their flat, smooth sides and relatively narrow slides are extremely comfortable handguns to carry in a good IWB holster. The original Nelson design has the rough side of the leather on the outside of the holster because of the better adherence to the surrounding garment, but the truth is having an IWB holster with the smooth side out is a more comfortable holster over the long haul. As for the positioning and movement issue, that can be controlled through the location and number of belt loops that secure the holster to the pants belt.

The Browning High Power seen here is holstered in a Summer Special holster from Milt Sparks. Orginally designed by the late Bruce Nelson, who was an undercover agent with the California Department of Justice for many years, the Summer Special works well with single-action semi-autos like the Browning or the 1911 Government Model.

The original Summer Special made no provision for the protection from the manual safety on the 1911 pistol or the Browning High Power and if the gun was equipped with an extended manual safety it would soon make its presence known to the carrier by digging into the person's side. Milt Sparks Holsters recognized this shortcoming with the introduction of the Summer Special 2. The Summer Special 2 provides an extension of leather that covers the manual safety and is positioned between the gun and the body of

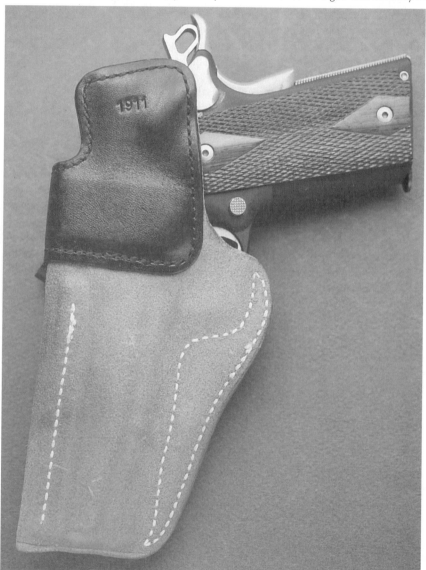

The Summer Special 2 from Milt Sparks Holsters is one IWB holster the author has used for many years. Shown here is the inside of the holster and the upper portion of the holster protects the body from contact with the manual safety of the 1911 pistol.

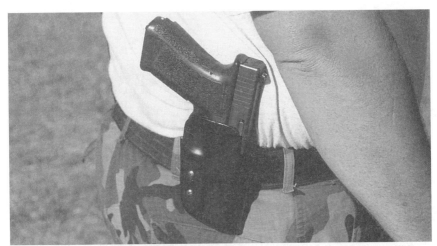

The IDPA organization stipulates that only holsters from an approved list can be used in competition. Fortunately, many different kinds of Kydex holsters are on that list and they are proving popular as this competitor has selected one for use with his Glock pistol.

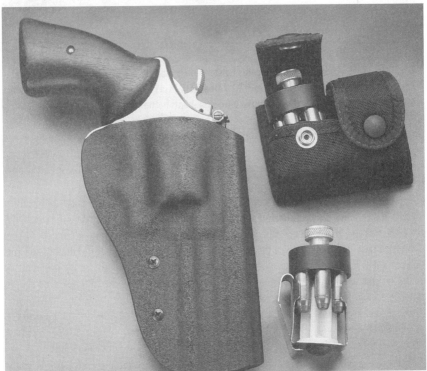

This Kydex holster from Blade-Tech works well for IDPA competition. The advantage to IDPA competiton is it doesn't require a big investment for the concealed carry self-defense advocate. All that is needed besides the usual eye and hearing protection is a gun, a holster, a couple of speedloaders (if a revolver) and some sort of pouch for carrying the speedloaders.

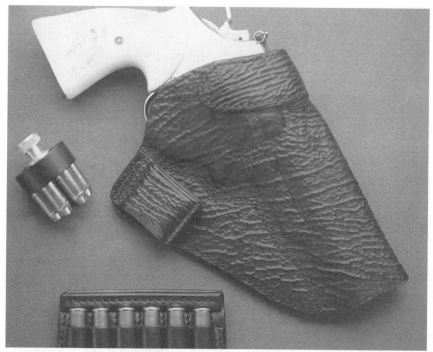

The Mitch Rosen ARG is an inside-the-pants holster mainly built for use with semi-auto pistols, but Rosen made this ARG holster for his 5-inch S&W Model 657 in .41 Magnum. The main design feature of the ARG is the belt loop at the rear of the inside-the-pants holster.

the wearer. Additionally, it is available with two loops for more secure positioning of the holster and I have used one for more than a decade with many of my 1911 pistols. If you use a 1911 style pistol, this is an easy holster to recommend, even for those with more robust body styles.

Another good IWB design is the Mitch Rosen ARG design. ARG used to stand for 'Ayoob Rear Guard' as it was designed at the request of noted gunwriter Massad Ayoob, but since the tragedy of September 11th, it has been changed to 'American Rear Guard.' The big difference here is the location of the belt loop, which is positioned behind the holster. This positioning of the belt loop makes it easy for a draw stroke, but difficult for the gun grabber as the holster will 'rock' to the rear and prevent or at least slow the attempt. This should provide enough time for the wearer to execute the proper defense to the gun-grab. Mitch Rosen also makes an ARG holster with a second belt loop on the outside of the holster to position it more securely, but it is favored more for competition shooters in IDPA. One thing about Mitch Rosen products, they are not inexpensive, but the quality is first-rate.

There is a whole range of synthetic holsters, both hip-holster and IWB designs, made from Kydex that are proving extremely popular in IDPA competition. (IDPA competition rules mandate the competitor's holsters come from an approved listing.) The big thing with the Kydex holsters, available from a number of manufacturers like Michaels of Oregon Co., Blade-Tech Industries, Fobus USA, and others is their speed in terms of the draw stroke.

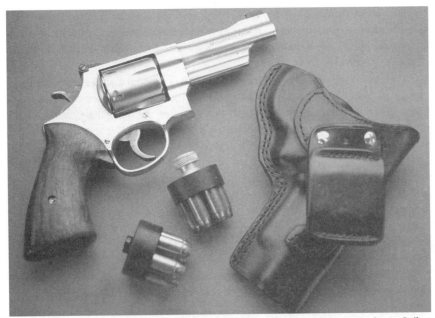

The Kramer Thomas Perfectionist is an extremely good holster for large-frame revolvers. Built specifically for the Smith & Wesson Model 657 Mountain Gun shown here, the Thomas Perfectionist is an inside-the-pants design that works unusually well.

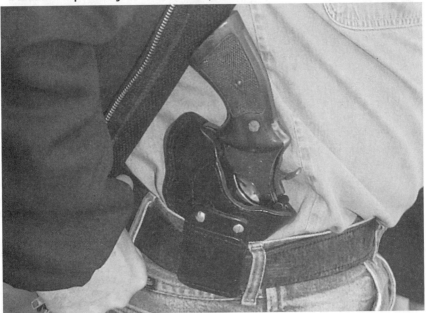

The Kramer Thomas Perfectionist shown here with a pre-Model 29 Smith & Wesson .44 Magnum positions the cylinder of the revolver above the belt and cants the gun butt forward in a very aggressive fashion.

Yes, they make a noise when you holster and draw the gun, but in IDPA competition Kydex holsters are proving more popular than any conventional leather holster. Some of these Kydex holsters are so inexpensive and affordable that even the most budget-minded shooter will appreciate them.

Carrying a medium to large revolver in an IWB holster has always been a challenge that few enjoyed. The big problem was the width of the cylinder, particularly on the large-frame revolvers. There are three products I've used over the years that achieve a level of success others have found somewhat elusive. The first would have to be the revolver version of the ARG from Mitch Rosen. He made one for my 5-inch Model 657 years ago and it has worked well, but it only works well with those trousers where the waistline is larger than need be because it takes up additional space.

Another really good design for an IWB holster for use with a large-frame revolver is available from Kramer Handgun Leather and it is the Kramer Thomas Perfectionist. Doug Kramer and gunwriter Dwayne Thomas designed this inside-the-waistband holster jointly. It is a high-riding design that positions much of the cylinder above the belt and angles the butt well forward in a radical cant, but quite close to the body. The result is both comfortable and easy to conceal under most any covering garment. I've found it works especially well with any 4-inch Smith & Wesson N-frame revolver in my inventory.

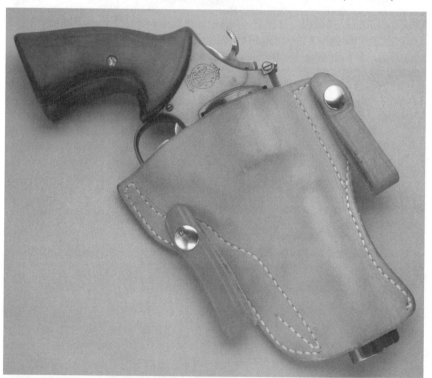

'CABO' stands for "Carry A Big One." The CABO holster is an extremely well thought out, yet simple IWB holster for carrying large revolvers. It positions the cylinder of the revolver above the belt and uses two snap belt loops to securely position the holster inside-the-pants.

The last holster I am recommending to those wanting to conceal a large-frame double-action revolver is available from CABO Holsters, LLC. CABO stands for 'Carry A Big One', so that should give you a clue what this company is all about. The CABO is a simple design and again it positions the cylinder above the belt. It features two snap loops and a forward cant. I've found the one I've been working with for several months works better with a 5-inch N-frame than shorter barrel lengths. It balances a heavy revolver quite well and keeps the gun close to the body. It is a high-riding design. About the only criticism I have of the CABO deals with the screws used to secure the snaps to the leather. They keep coming loose and the cure I discovered was to use a liquid metal fastener to keep the internal screws from backing out.

THE TUCKABLES

There is another category of strong-side concealment holsters that is fast gaining popularity with concealed carry permit holders and this is the 'tuckable' holster. The idea with a tuckable is the holster is secured to the pant's belt via a snap loop or a sewn loop, but there is a gap between the leg the loop is attached to and the holster itself. The idea

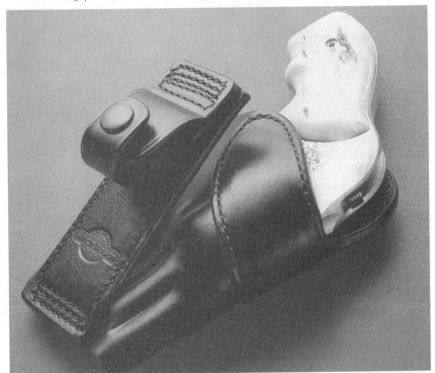

The Mitch Rosen Workman holster is a "tuckable" design that carries the gun under the covering of the shirt in warmer climates. The snap belt loop fastens to the pants belt with the holster being positioned inside the pants. The shirt is then 'tucked' between the holster and the pants. The model shown here holds a shrouded-hammer Airweight Smith & Wesson revolver with stag Eagle Secret Service grips.

being once the gun and holster have been mounted and secured to the belt, the shirt is tucked between the snap and inside the pants, but over the holster, providing complete concealment of the pistol. The snap loop on the belt can provide additional camouflage through use as a retainer for a set of keys. Mitch Rosen Leather has a model called the 'Workman' and I have used two examples of this holster from Mitch Rosen; one for a Glock Model 26 and a second for a J-frame Smith & Wesson revolver with a 2-inch barrel. Of the two, I prefer the one made for the small Smith & Wesson, but in truth I feel the whole range of tuckable holsters is an acquired taste. They simply don't work well with my slightly abundant waistline. Things are tight enough to make it hard not to experience printing under a cotton shirt. That's not to say they won't work for you.

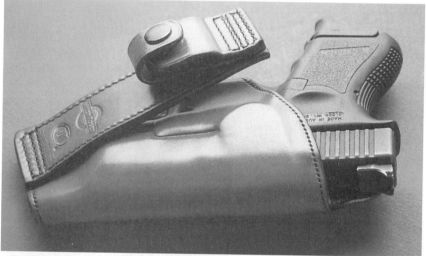

The idea behind any "tuckable" holster like the Mitch Rosen Workman is the ability to carry a more potent self-defense pistol with the minimum of a covering garment. The model shown here was built for the Glock Model 26.

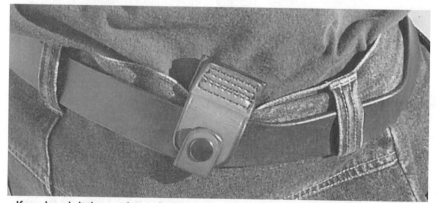

If user has a belt that matches perfectly the color of the snap loop on the tuckable it camouflages itself to a point where few would notice it. Adding a set of car keys or work keys explains the presence of the snap loop without raising the suspicion it is used to secure and locate a holster.

SHOULDER HOLSTERS

When it comes to the subject of shoulder holsters most experienced concealed carry veterans either hate them or love them. Seldom do you find someone who is ambivalent on the subject of shoulder holsters. I have used them in various styles for many years and overall I am a strong advocate of a shoulder holster system. There are deficiencies with

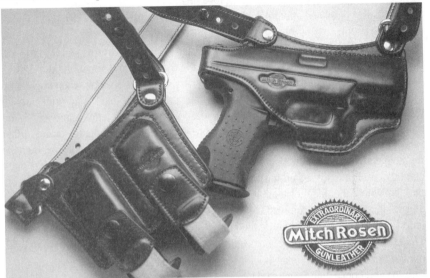

If quality is more important than cost, it's hard to beat the products from Mitch Rosen. This shoulder holster for the author's Walther P99 is finished in cordovan color and is an extremely high quality product.

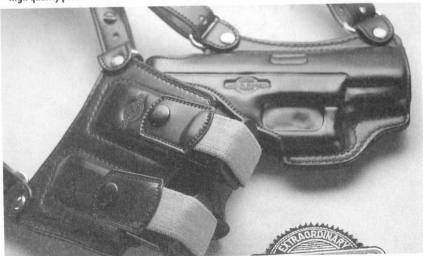

Like all horizontal shoulder holster systems the Mitch Rosen system employs a dual spare magazine carrier on the off-side. Unlike others, however, Rosen uses a tailored elastic material to guarantee the spare magazines remain in their carriers until the reload.

any shoulder holster, the biggest one being you can't use them in competition because of the concerns over safety during the draw stroke. Secondly, those with a large middle section often have a hard time acquiring a good grip on the gun simply because the gun is hard to reach. And, thirdly, even for those with a slim body profile, the draw stroke from any vertical-mounted shoulder is pretty much a two stage affair. The first stage allows sufficient purchase of the grip to withdraw the gun from the vertical holster and the second stage, usually completed after total withdrawal from the holster, involves getting a higher grip on the pistol.

Another big difficulty with a shoulder holster is securing or not securing it to the pants belt. If the shoulder holster is secured to the pants belt and you work at a desk or are driving for a long period of time, the whole affair changes position when you get up from the seat. The support and positioning straps crossing the back may print through the fabric of a tailored coat at this point. The best of them have a tendency to 'climb' up the shoulders, thereby positioning the gun more toward the rear of the torso and further away from the strong hand. If the shoulder holster is not secured to the pants belt then the problem with the holster changing position remains, but to a far lesser degree. It is more comfortable if you are seated for long periods either at a desk or while driving. The big problem with a shoulder holster that isn't secured to the pants belt is if you have to run for any distance. When you run with it – it flops – badly. This makes it easier to lose the gun unless it is securely fastened inside the holster.

With all these difficulties you would think I would be a great critic of the design, but the truth is I generally like shoulder holsters because they provide a good means of carrying and concealing large handguns.

Shoulder holsters come in two basic styles; the vertical scabbard and the horizontal carry. The vertical scabbard was the first shoulder holster developed and El Paso Saddlery

The retention straps on all horizontal shoulder systems cross between the shoulder blades of the user and to keep the two sides equal a retainer must be employed at the crossing point. Mitch Rosen uses this brass retainer which carries the Rosen company logo.

Co. makes faithful reproductions of two of the more successful designs from Western history. If the shoulder straps and the vertical scabbard holster are made carefully it's easy to conceal a large-frame Smith & Wesson revolver with a 5-inch or 6-inch barrel under nothing more than a zipper-front sweat shirt. I know because I've been doing it for more than 30 years.

Unfortunately, I could never find the exact shoulder holster I wanted so I made my own decades ago and in truth it is a very simple idea. It is nothing more than a pouch holster, similar in many ways to the El Paso Saddlery 1879 Texas shoulder rig, but with some subtle differences. It is an unsecured shoulder holster in that it does not attach to the trousers belt. It also differs from the original Texas-style pouch design in that the holster

The Bianchi X-15 is a vertical shoulder holster and it is a secured design in that it must be fastened to the pants belt. It works well for a number of different handguns due to its front metal reinforced opening. The author has carried both semi-autos and revolvers in this holster, but the new versions come with a retention strap the older models like this one lacked. He feels it is needed.

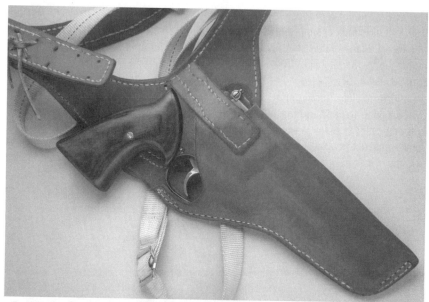

Frustrated that he couldn't find the shoulder holster to meet his needs, the author made this one by hand almost 30 years ago. It is a pouch design which has the gun butt canted forward approximately 5 degrees. The Model 57 with the 5-inch barrel holstered in this rig is retained by a single cross-over strap with a thumbsnap.

itself is angled butt forward at approximately a 5-degree cant. This provides an improved access to the butt of the gun during the draw and for security purposes; the revolver is kept in the holster with a cross-over strap equipped with a thumb-snap. This rig works well with loose-fitting outer garments, zippered-front sweat shirts or any form of outdoor work clothing. It was not meant for use with a tailored sport coat.

Probably the most popular vertical scabbard shoulder holster has to be the Bianchi X-15. It is a spring-clip design that will accept a number of different pistol styles. This is possible because the spring clip at the front opening of the holster body is what keeps the gun in position. The Bianchi X-15 is a secured design in that it must be fastened to the pants belt and it is basically available in three different sizes; small, medium and large. I found the medium size works equally well for both medium size auto-pistols and revolvers. For several years now there has been a retaining strap added to secure the handgun inside the holster because on the older models (like mine) it was possible for the pistol to fall from the holster because of the momentum built up when one jumps down from a reasonable height. When your feet hit the ground, you stop but the gun doesn't. That's why the retaining strap is needed.

Jackass Leather Company pioneered the horizontal shoulder holster concept and the concept has been carried even further with additional refinements by Galco International, Ltd. It is a design that has proven popular with many besides the Hollywood film set for a number of reasons. First of all to balance the weight of the pistol on one side of the body, there are pouches for spare magazines or extra ammo on the opposite side. This makes for a complete system and allows the concealed carry operator to grab the gun, holster and spare ammo in one motion before slipping the rig on. Designed for both revolvers and auto-pistols, this style of shoulder rig is best remembered from the television show "MIAMI VICE" as it adorned the shoulders of Don Johnson.

Aker International, Inc. makes a good horizontal shoulder holster rig for revolvers in the Aker Comfort-flex. It is an unsecured design that balances the revolver with two speedloader pouches on the opposite side. I've used an Aker Comfort-flex with a Smith & Wesson Model 27 with a 3-1/2-inch barrel for some time and found it a quick and easy way to carry a revolver and spare ammo. If I have a complaint about the Comfort-flex it would concern the tight fit between the HKS speedloaders I use and the pouches as the lack of extra space makes it difficult to withdraw them quickly for a timely reload. Additionally, the holster employs a cross-over thumb snap, but there is only sufficient length for a narrow hammer on the model I've been using. If your gun is equipped with a wide target hammer, I would recommend special ordering a longer cross-over strap.

Probably the most innovative and simple shoulder holster systems are those offered by Ken Null. Made from synthetics, the Model SMZ is ideal for small revolvers and double-action semi-autos. Its design will work for a number of different pistols without modification. The holster on the Model SMZ employs a breakaway snap that fastens through the front of the triggerguard on the pistol. The pistol is designed to hang butt-down/muzzle-up and the gun is drawn by grasping the butt and then twisting it sideways

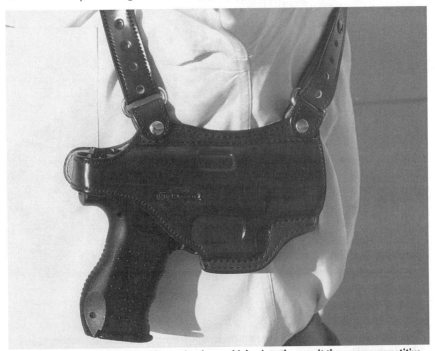

The Mitch Rosen horizontal shoulder carries the gun higher into the armpit than many competitive designs. Depending upon the build of the permit holder this could be an advantage or a disadvantage. The author felt this positioning aided greatly in increased concealment of the handgun.

to break the retaining snap. The straps used to position the holster are narrow and go around the back of the neck under the collar of the covering garment. The suspension strap can be secured to the pants belt on the off side by means of a loop or through use of the provided alligator snap that can be fastened to the waistband or even an undergarment. Built for lightweight handguns, this system is slick and works exceedingly well. If it has a weak point it is the tendency by the user to holster too heavy a gun in it and thereby create discomfort problems with the narrow suspension straps across the shoulders. It is impervious to moisture because of the heavy use of synthetics and it is an ideal deep-cover shoulder rig for both professionals and civilians.

ANKLE RIGS

The 1971 film "THE FRENCH CONNECTION" was a revelation in one respect. It was the first time the general public witnessed an ankle holster in regular use by a celluloid police officer. Gene Hackman portrayed Popeye Doyle who was a character based on Eddie Egan. Egan was a real New York plainclothes police officer who did use an ankle

The ankle holster is a specialized holster and carries with it many deficiencies. The inability to draw the pistol quickly is the main deficiency. Yet, the DeSantis Apache ankle holster is a good ankle holster for use with a Glock Model 26. The model shown here is the author's second Apache, as he wore the first one to threads from heavy use.

holster as a means of covert carry. Ankle holsters work well at concealing a handgun with certain stipulations. The first is don't wear 'high-water' pants. That may seem to be an obvious statement, but wait till the permit holder with an ankle rig sits down in the waiting room of a doctor's office. If his pants legs aren't long enough, everyone will notice the gun metal just above his shoe.

Secondly, unless the permit holder is flat on his back, there is no easy way to draw the pistol from an ankle holster. However, having said that, most who have been through a physical altercation of some sort know it is really easy to wind up horizontally in the mud. From this position the ankle holster makes sense. It also makes sense for someone who drives a lot because usually it is easier to draw the pistol while positioned behind the steering wheel. Unlike the hip holster, seat-belt engagement should not impede the draw stroke from an ankle holster. You simply raise the leg bringing the holster and gun to the strong hand.

Ankle holsters are most often positioned on the inside of the off-side leg and to aid in the concealment of the holster it is recommended the user use two socks on the foot carrying the holster. The first sock is for normal use and the second sock should be the matching sock to the one on the opposite side. It is used to cover the gun and holster and it goes on after the holster has been positioned around the ankle.

One of the best ankle rigs currently available is the Apache from DeSantis Holster & Leather Goods. I've used one with my Glock Model 26 for so long I wore the first out and I'm now on my second holster for the same gun. Although I have no personal experience with it, I've been informed by various users that Renegade Holster & Leather Co. makes an extremely good ankle holster for small J-frame Smith & Wesson revolvers. Ankle holsters are a universal design now and most of the manufacturers listed in the Appendix offer one version or another. Obviously, ankle rigs don't work well with boots, tall cowboy boots in particular. The big thing to remember with an ankle rig is it is a specialized holster and one that for most people does not offer the opportunity for a timely acquisition of the defensive handgun in a threat situation.

POCKET HOLSTERS

For the small defensive handguns, there is an excellent alternative to the ankle rig for deep concealment and it is nothing more than the front trousers pocket on a pair of men's pants. It should be stipulated, however, that because most blue denim jeans are cut too tightly, pocket carry doesn't work well with them. The sole exception would be the baggy denim pants worn by some gang members in various inner-city locations.

The main idea for the permit holder is while choosing their wardrobe they select casual and dress trousers that offer large roomy front pockets. This is one reason why the Royal Robbins 511 pants are proving so popular with many firearms instructors and those who routinely work with defensive handguns. Besides the stylish appearance and great fit, these pants offer the concealed carry user an off-side pocket that easily conceals a small 2-inch snubnose revolver.

A holster is recommended for pocket carry for a couple of reasons. It helps break up the outline of the gun in the pocket. A holster also keeps the intrusion of pocket lint and dirt into the firearm to a bare minimum. The standard practice for many, me included, is to

The author's favorite method for carrying this North American Guardian is a pocket holster made from exotic leather. It is small enough it works well even with tailored clothing and never 'prints'.

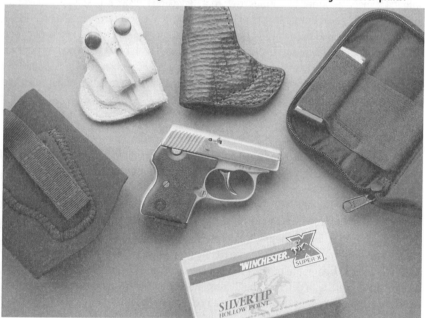

Small pistols need holsters. This North American Guardian can be carried in an ankle holster (far left), an inside-the-pants holster (upper left), a pocket holster (upper right) or an office-like 'organizer' (far right).

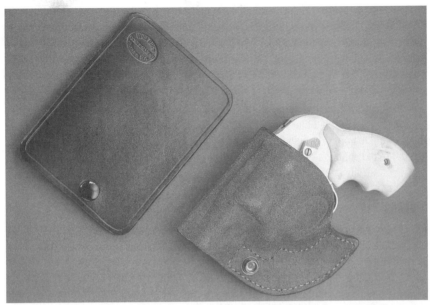

Wild Bill's Concealment offers this unique rough-out leather pocket holster. It comes with a snap-on flap to help break the contour and outline of the gun and holster once it is carried in a front pants pocket. The five-shot revolver is an Airweight Smith & Wesson with custom stag grips and a shrouded hammer design.

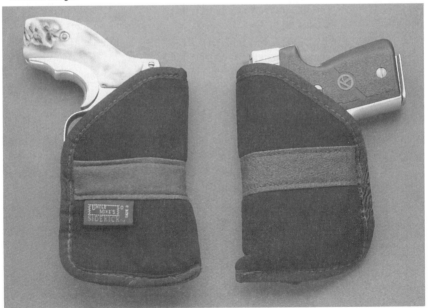

For those on a limited budget Uncle Mike's offers an extremely affordable pocket holster for just about any size pocket pistol. The holster on the left holds a Smith & Wesson Model 442 with stag grips and a Tyler T-grip adaptor, while the pocket holster on the right holds a Kahr MK40.

carry the gun in the off-side pocket and carry nothing else in the front pocket. That means if you're right handed you will be carrying this small handgun in your left front pocket. Naturally, a reload is recommended and if you use a revolver with speedloaders be sure to keep the speedloaders in a pocket by themselves. Don't put the speedloader in the same pocket as your small change because invariably a small coin will get stuck between the cartridges in the speedloader and thereby malfunction the reload.

While on the subject of pocket holsters and pocket pistols, it is recommended the gun be equipped with a hard, smooth set of grips to avoid adherence between the grip of the gun and the pocket lining. I've found stag works exceedingly well, but since stag grips are in limited supply a number of other grip materials can be substituted for the factory rubber or heavily checkered wood grips.

SUMMARY

Focus on choosing a holster and handgun combination that fits well with your fashion and lifestyle. For instance, ankle holsters won't work if you like to wear cowboy boots. The same is true for a pocket holster if you prefer Western-style jeans and obviously if you live on a beach, a hip holster and gun combination that requires a goose-down vest to conceal isn't going to work all that great either. I didn't touch on the subject of fanny packs quite simply because the general population is educated sufficiently to suspect a gun is hidden inside if you look at all out of place for the surroundings. Yeah, fanny packs work well if you're hiking on a nature trail, but a grown man wearing one in a shopping mall raises eyebrows on even the most naive of observers.

If you work in an office environment with those who object to the presence of a defensive firearm, you may very well be forced to a compromise in the sense you will have to select a holster that is easily removable like a paddle design. Paddle holsters are offered by a multitude of manufacturers and they represent the best compromise for someone who must remove his outer or covering garment during office visits. Just put the gun in a briefcase and lock the briefcase while visiting the restroom upon arrival and remove it in the same manner upon departure from the worksite.

The big thing is to remember to reholster the handgun upon departure. Otherwise, you end up violating the first rule of effective handgun defense.

CHAPTER TEN

Attitude Is Everything

L ike most shooters age 50 and older, I grew up on the writings of Elmer Keith, Skeeter Skelton and Bill Jordan. Keith was never officially a lawman, although he did carry a badge in his wallet when I visited him in his home in August of 1975. Keith was an outdoorsman. He made his living outdoors through ranching, guiding big game hunters or working various state projects like building fish ladders in the streams of Idaho.

Skelton was kind of a combination of an outdoorsman and lawman as he worked for numerous law enforcement agencies in the southwest and at one time operated his own cattle business. If you read much of his writing it is plainly obvious he didn't spend a lot of his time pushing paper around the top of a desk. He, too, was an outdoorsman.

Bill Jordan was a U.S. Border Patrolman and a fine gentleman. I state the last in every sense of the definition. He was also an outstanding handgun shooter. After his retirement from the Border Patrol, he spent a good part of his time putting on shooting exhibitions for the National Rifle Association. I never witnessed one of his demos first hand, but I have seen films of them and the feats he performed were inspiring. Even though he spent his entire professional life in law enforcement, he was also an outdoorsman. He was a man, like the two others, who in earning his living spent the major portion of his life outdoors.

Being a farmer, I believe those who earn their living outdoors are a breed apart from those who work indoors, because climate and its hazards can make life difficult, if not miserable, in the blink of an eye. Sometimes it takes a tough mindset just to survive what

The author believes that of all the old gunwriters Elmer Keith was the best at conveying the influence weather had on small decisions with regard to working outdoors. Mindset is a critical element in survival whether it involves a gunfight or a snowstorm. The author is seen here with Elmer Keith in the living room of the Keith home almost three decades ago.

the weather can deliver. I believe Keith was the best of these three writers in conveying the influence weather had on even small decisions and their results. What has this got to do with a book on effective handgun defense? It is about mindset, and mindset has everything to do with self-defense.

I was fortunate enough to grow up around men who worked outdoors; a few in law enforcement, but most were farmers and cattlemen. The three writers mentioned above and many of the men I knew as a child were from the generation raised before World War II. Some will point out they experienced the Great Depression and this contributed to a hard-headed view of things, but it is my belief their tough attitudes were the result of working on a daily basis with large livestock. Society prior to World War II was far more agrarian than people realize or remember. Few people are built big enough to 'man-handle' a large four-legged mammal. People have to dominate large working animals through shear force of will. My grandfather, Rufus James, was, at 5 feet tall, an extremely small man and he never weighed more than 130 pounds, but he was the fiercest human being I have ever encountered in my entire life. He had to be. He farmed with horses well into the early 1950s and they were not the gentle, kiddy-park, old-age riding horses many think of today. Those working horses were tough, often wild, with a tendency to be unruly and while they were not treated with cruelty, they learned as colts who was the boss. He ruled these animals with an iron will. He did this not through violence, or yelling or screaming but with a low, guttural tone of voice that made them shiver in fear when he reprimanded them. He made sure they were fed and watered and had their harness sores and other ailments treated every evening before anyone even thought of supper. Sunday was always a day of rest for all the draft animals.

Throughout his life, he was unwavering. He was a hard man.

As long as the guns used in 'practical' competition remain the same as those used for concealed carry self-defense, these competitions hold the promise to advance the state of marksmanship But when the interest shifted to turning this discipline into a 'sport' many of the reality-oriented shooters were left behind. Walt Rauch is seen here finishing his reload at an USPSA Nationals of long-forgotten vintage.

I believe that each of the three gunwriters mentioned at the beginning of this chapter were in their own way, hard men. Their written work certainly conveys an element of a hard edge. For those of us living in the 21st Century, with every creature comfort one can imagine, it makes for extremely interesting and entertaining enjoyment. What they wrote weren't just stories, it was life as they lived it and few today can duplicate their experiences because the physical circumstances are so different in terms of daily technology, transportation, medical care, laws and legal regulations of a far more developed civilization.

This doesn't mean, however, the hard-headed attitude of these men toward life and those who disobeyed the rules are out-of-date or even out-of-fashion. Far from it, a strong mental attitude is needed as much now as it was years ago. It's just that now it is harder to define and explain to the general populace as opposed to six decades ago when it was easy to explain someone who had 'jumped the fence' and gone astray, sometimes violently. Our current society has lost the link and experience of working with big, hard-to-handle livestock. It tends to see these creatures with 'Disney' colored glasses as friendly, docile, harmless beasts, often with the human-like abilities to reason and debate issues. The result is our common language emphasizes phrases like "warm and fuzzy" and "politically correct" as opposed to the language of my grandfather who spoke of neighbors who were as "tough as whang leather" and refused to be "buffaloed" by animal or man. The adjectives and phrases of yesterday referred to a mental attitude necessary for success, if not simple survival. It's still true today.

WHAT LIES AHEAD

Human beings have a history of conflict that goes back beyond Cain and Able in the Bible. Wars are fought on a daily basis somewhere in the world. Acts of violence are reported constantly on front pages and from the talking heads repeating the evening news on television. Politicians are continually pledging to do something to make our streets safer, and to the surprise of many some politicians in state legislatures have actually done something that lowers the crime rate.

They have written and passed laws allowing the carrying of concealed firearms by law-abiding citizens. According to different sources the count stands somewhere between 31 and 33 states that allow this practice. (The difference depends upon the definition used for a 'Shall Issue' concealed carry permit in the different states.) This means that well over 60 percent of the states in the Union have established a legitimate process whereby honest citizens can go about their daily business while legally and quietly armed.

When this trend started in America, anti-gun alarmist shouted from editorial pages and through wide access to the generally anti-gun, anti-responsibility television media that blood would run in the streets. America would be returning to the days of Dodge City because violence and lawlessness would run rampant.

The opposite has happened.

IDPA competition places a greater emphasis on the use of cover as well as a covering garment for the concealed carry self-defense handgun. It is not a perfect form of competition but it has renewed interest in pistols that are more oriented toward real self-defense applications.

Prof. John Lott, Jr., Ph.D. of the University Of Chicago School Of Law conducted a two-year study covering the years from 1977 to 1992 clearly demonstrating when honest civilians carry concealed weapons violent crime decreases.

To many involved with firearms training and law enforcement the reasons are self-evident. Criminals prey upon the weak. Like all predators, criminals avoid the strong. Predators realize any animal that fights back can do them harm and they wish to avoid such harm. Criminals are the human predators of modern society. Not everyone is born to weigh 240 pounds or stand 6 feet, 8 inches tall for defense against those who would take physical advantage of them in a brutal, violent assault.

A woman who weighs no more than 110 pounds dripping wet and stands no taller than 5 feet 2 inches doesn't have much of a chance against a male deviant who is 100 pounds heavier. Give that woman training in armed self-defense and a .38 Special revolver and the situation changes drastically.

The cliché is "You Can't Rape A .38!"

Well, it's true.

Dr. Lott found in those areas where laws were enacted allowing civilians the right to carry concealed firearms homicides went down 8.5 percent, incidents of rape declined 5 percent, and aggravated assault dropped by 7 percent.

He also concluded that had the entire United States enacted concealed carry laws for average honest law-abiding citizens in 1992, at least 1,570 murders and more than 4,177 rapes would have been avoided by the time his report was released in 1996.

PARABELLUM PEOPLE

In my view, there are three kinds of people in the world today; the prey, the predators, and those who take responsibility for their own actions and their own safety.

You could call this last group the *Parabellum People*, "If You Want Peace, Prepare For War."

Can you shoot on the move? Any armed self-defense training should involve some degree of shooting on the move. Learning to move in the face of a threat is a sure survival skill because a stationary target is easier to hit than a moving one.

Some will find this message too harsh for their sensitivities. Yet, the Supreme Court of the United States has already ruled the police in the United States are under NO legal obligation or responsibility to protect any citizen. Many of these people believe they can reason with a violent criminal when violent confrontation threatens.

Sorry, but violent criminal attacks don't work that way. Most of the time, it is a quick and dirty deed. It hurts for a long time afterwards – if you live.

Law enforcement has always given attention to proper firearms training and teaching tactics, but for years now some observers have noticed those who survived really violent confrontations had something extra in their make-up beyond good shooting techniques and great marksmanship. What made some men and women survive repeated violent armed encounters, while others perished? Was it their tactics, their marksmanship, or their mental attitude?

The answer is they needed all three essential skills, but it was their mental attitude that most often made the difference between living and dying. These people, both male and female, had a love for life and in almost every case demonstrated a hard-headed refusal to give up, either mentally or physically.

That many of them were in good physical condition helped as well, but their physical conditioning could be used as a yardstick of their mental outlook. They had the discipline to stay in shape, to run 4 miles every morning, or to get up an hour early for the work-out in the gym while others enjoyed only slumber. These survivors as a group were not couch-potatoes.

Something inside every gunfight survivor made them want to survive by defeating the deadly threat facing them. They cared enough about the people and the world around them to give it their all in eliminating this threat. Traditional firearms training and competitions have a hard time teaching this or even recognizing it, but in the past years dedicated individuals like Walt Rauch and others have researched training and competition venues that begin to scratch the surface.

The first attempt was the National Tactical Invitational (NTI), which was an annual "shooting contest" conducted under strict supervision to prevent 'gaming' the event. The NTI mandated concealed carry firearms and holsters with only uniformed officers

The National Tactical Invitational was an attempt to return handgun competition to more reality oriented scenarios and courses of fire. Some of the early NTI competitions put the contestant in an automobile and ambush situations. How they reacted was the essence of the problem.

permitted to wear exposed holsters and guns in regulation duty rigs. The NTI was a surprise course of fire, that is, there was no walk-through or stage briefing prior to competition as seen in USPSA, IPSC, or IDPA competitions. It also mandated street guns, not the enhanced competition-venue pistols that turn IPSC champions into supermen. The NTI was an attempt to replicate the real world.

The 1993 NTI has a stage that simulated a robbery in a strange restaurant. The competitor, in this shot Ken Hackathorn, was unarmed so he had to seek cover and then find a weapon.

The use of black-out goggles by the NTI organizers simulated night time experiences. In this scenario, the competitor is in a strange motel room when he hears someone enter. What is his response, if no one answers his calls for assistance or help?

It was a step in the right direction, but mistakes were made and the next step in the evolution of the process was the Advanced Tactical Group (ATG). The ATG placed an emphasis on good shooting, good gun handling, and good tactics in serious interpersonal confrontations, but here technology helped to a great extent with the introduction of Simunitions.

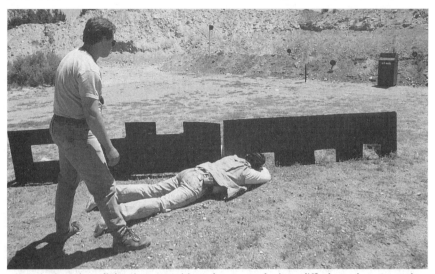

Many 'action-oriented' shooting competitions place an emphasis on difficult or what seem to be improbable shooting situations, but the truth is survival will demand a variety of shooting skills if shooting is warranted and no one knows what skills will be needed to survive, so develop all the skills at shooting you can.

Simunitions has brought a greater degree of realism to self-defense firearms training because it enables the trainee to work against targets that SHOOT BACK. This Glock 17 has been modified to shoot only Simunitions marking pellet ammunition. It is still dangerous and requires all due care before use, but through the use of Simunitions a trainee can safely experience a real gunfight without severe injury.

The NTI allowed only fully-sworn police officers to wear an exposed holster and then it had to be part of a duty belt. This police officer competing in the 1994 NTI held at Gunsite Academy is using a Glock Model 21 that was hidden in the sand before he started the course of fire.

Simunitions is a Canadian firm that converts real guns to fire a soap-based dye-marking pellet from what appears to be a modified cartridge case. The pistols used are real guns modified to shoot this nominally 'non-lethal' ammunition. I say nominally because it is always possible an accident could occur if the supervision was in any way the slightest bit lax.

Scenarios are created that replicate real world events in the life of almost every police officer, but the big difference with the ATG and some other Simunitions-based training events is the targets SHOOT BACK! Tactical errors yield real world pain, not life-threatening pain, but it is real nonetheless.

When the NTI started doing this, one of the shortcomings was the supervisors allowed the contestants or trainees (whichever the case was in each instance) to 'armor up' too much. The result resembled a children's snowball fight and good tactics quickly went out the window. Some armor is necessary to keep injuries to a minimum; especially serious ones to the head and chest area, but pain is essential to teaching good tactics with the Fightin' Handgun. Poor tactics must be punished and pain, regardless of the intelligence level of the student, is a great inducement for improving the student's personal performance.

The first ATG match was held in June of 1996 during the now-discontinued annual Secret Service Pistol Match at the United States Secret Service Training facility near Beltsville, Maryland. The lessons learned from the event paralleled the lessons drawn from real life events. The people who won were most often those who were the most 'tuned in' or totally focused on the task at hand. They were highly trained and their training clearly showed. Some even ignored the pain from incoming hits and continued forward

The Advanced Tactical Group had two different stages of Simunitions-based scenarios at the 1996 Secret Service Pistol Match. The team event shown here involves a car-jacking scenario.

An interesting test performed by the ATG role players involved a re-enactment of the El Presidente Drill, the difference here was the targets shot back. It proved impossible to survive. Of the various skilled test shooters who shot two rounds to each target, none of them made it to the third live target before they themselves were ruled neutralized by opposing the gunfire.

to destroy the threat, while some fell away completely disoriented once they were struck with painful pellet strikes.

The contestants and role players wore helmets and full-face protection, but once into the problem they often suffered the same problems people do in real gunfights. Things like auditory exclusion and tunnel vision were frequently mentioned in the debriefing after each stage. Participants forgot to focus on their front sights, and they failed to scan their peripheral vision for threats from their flanks while facing the one in front.

There have been many lessons to be learned from these events, but one of the more lasting impressions I gained personally is just how quick and how short in duration a gunfight really is. It's not like in the Hollywood movies where everything goes into slow

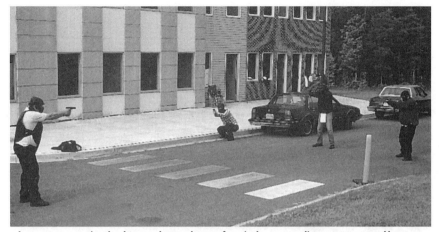

In an attempt to give the shooter a better chance of survival, a greater distance was created between the targets and the shooter. It was all to no avail, the third live target in the line had the advantage even if the shooter fired only one round at each of the two previous live targets. The best result ended in a draw and in a gunfight that still means death.

motion. It does in your memory as you replay the sequence of the event afterwards, but during the action you find you can't move fast enough.

More importantly, you can't even *think* fast enough and you realize it while it's happening. It's frustrating. Yet, those who were well-trained were able to react in many instances faster than the offender. (Yes, the reaction did beat the initiating action, but it didn't happen often.) The lesson was driven home if you want to survive, you have to train, and the harder you train, the better your chances are of surviving unscathed.

I found my reactions were based entirely upon reflex or training. The truth is I'm still not sure which was which, but the point is even the most trained participant related about how unprepared mentally he was and they were anticipating trouble. After all, the organizers wouldn't have put the body armor and protective helmet on them for nothing. Even the most feeble-minded among the contestants should have recognized this fact as a clue to coming events.

The problem with violent attacks is shock. It creates its own numbness or an inability to move. This shock-induced numbness can get you seriously injured or dead. Training reduces your reluctance to respond and overcomes shock when violence strikes. Once, you get started with your response, however, many things fall into place. The Big Rule for anyone facing violence is "DO SOMETHING. ANYTHING." It will work in your favor.

For all the positive trends in terms of armed self-defense and accepting responsibility for your self-protection, there are many countries in the world, like Great Britain, Australia and other places, that have disarmed their populace and left them powerless to the whims and wishes of the criminal elements in their societies. Of course, in many of these countries their citizens, or rather their subjects, had no right to start with to armed self-defense when threatened with violent aggression. I was once was told by a European the only way he could justify shooting someone in self-defense was if the criminal killed him first.

The Single Stack Classic is a once-a-year shooting competition devoted to the 1911 pistol and only 1911 pistols with single-column magazines may be used in it. It is a match that appeals to many who use a 1911 pistol as their concealed carry self-defense handgun.

It is my firm belief when free men are disarmed they are no longer free. They become dependent upon the state for their own safekeeping, and the state is usually governed by a privileged few who make their own rules. Whether these disarmed men want to admit it or not, they are no longer Parabellum People, but have become instead, simply, Prey.

It was my great privilege in life to be raised by a family, both parents and grandparents, who believed it was a lot better to have a gun and not need it, than to need a gun and not have it. They were exclusively people of the soil and to them a firearm was nothing more than a tool. It was neither good, nor evil. It was a gun, a tool, an object to be employed as necessary. As farmers, they routinely owned and employed many tools for a wide variety of purposes. The tools were used as needed. If a tool was misused by someone in the family, it was the family member who was punished, not the tool. Punishing the tool or restricting its use did little good to the welfare of the farm, repair of the tool, or to the future instruction of the family member.

I view *Effective Handgun Defense* in the same manner. It is a tool. It can be used by good people, or it can be used by bad people, but my hope is if bad people are misusing a firearm a good person who is well-trained and well-armed will be present and pro-active.

This, I believe, will solve the problem for society in a positive way as well as put forth the message that behavior of this type won't be tolerated.

It has been said that an armed society is a polite society and this too is true. After all, Parabellum People have accepted responsibility for their own actions and their own welfare.

I leave you with this question, what are you; Prey, Predator or a Parabellum Person?

BIBLIOGRAPHY

BOOKS

Bianchi, John, Blue Steel & Gunleather. North Hollywood, CA, Beinfield
Publishing, Inc., 1978.
Bloodworth, Trey and Raley, Mike, Hidden In Plain Sight.
Boulder, Colorado, Paladin Press, 1998.
Boothroyd, Geoffrey, The Handgun. New York, Crown Publishers, Inc., 1970.
Brandt, Jakob H. and Erlmeier, Hans A., Manual of Pistol and Revolver
Cartridges, Vol. 1. West Germany, Journal-Verlag Schwend GmbH, 1980.
Manual of Pistol and Revolver
Cartridges, Vol. 2. West Germany, Journal-Verlag Schwend
GmbH, 1980.
Cooper, Jeff, Cooper On Handguns. Los Angeles, CA, Petersen
Publishing Company, 1974.
Ezell, Edward C., Handguns Of The World, Harrisburg, PA,
Stackpole Books, 1981.
Fjestad, S.P., Blue Book of Gun Values, Fifteenth Edition. Minneapolis,
Minnesota, Blue Book Publications, Inc., 1994.
Hogg, Ian and Weeks, John, Pistols Of The World, Third Edition.
Northbrook, IL, DBI Books, 1992.
Hornady Handbook Of Cartridge Reloading, edited by
Todd Georgi, Grand Island, Nebraska, Hornady Manufacturing Co., 1991.
James, Frank W., S.W.A.T. Magazine Presents: SUB-GUNS & FULL-
AUTO GAMES. Cottonwood, AZ, Turbo Publishing, Inc., 1987.
Jordan, Bill, No Second Place Winner. Shreveport, Louisiana,
by W. H. Jordan, 1965.
Josserand, Michel H. and Stevenson, Jan. Pistols, Revolvers and
Ammunition. New York, Crown Publishers, Inc., 1972.
Keith, Elmer, SIXGUNS. Harrisburg, PA, The Stackpole Company, 1955.
La Garde, Col. Louis A., Gunshot Injuries. Mt. Ida, Arkansas, Lancer
Militaria, 1991.
Morris, W.R., The Legacy of Buford Pusser. Paducah, Kentucky, Turner
Publishing Co., 1994.
Mullin, Timothy J., The 100 Greatest Combat Pistols.
Boulder, Colorado, Paladin Press, 1994.
Neal, Robert J. and Jinks, Roy G., Smith & Wesson 1857-1945, A
Handbook for Collectors. South Brunswick, New Jersey, A.S. Barnes and Co., 1966.
Newark, Peter, Firefight!. Devon, England, David & Charles Publishers plc, 1989.
Pirates, edited by David Cordingly. Atlanta, Georgia, Turner Publishing, Inc., 1996.

Rauch, R. Walter, Real World Survival: What Has Worked For Me.
Lafayette Hill, Pennsylvania, Rauch & Co., 1998.
Practically Speaking: An Illustrated Guide To IDPA
and Defensive Handgun Shooting, Lafayette Hill,
Pennsylvania, Rauch & Co., 2002.
Rosa, Joseph G., Wild Bill Hickok; the man and the myth. Lawrence,
Kansas, University Press of Kansas, 1996.
Ross, James R., I, Jesse James. Dragon Publishing Corp., 1989.
Ruger, edited by Joseph B. Roberts, Jr., Washington D.C., a
publication of the National Rifle Association of America, 1990.
Sommer, Robin Langley, The History Of The U.S. Marshalls.
Philadelphia, Courage Books, 1993.
Stebbins, Henry M., Shay, Albert J.E. and Hammond, Oscar R., Pistols: a
modern encyclopedia. Harrisburg, Pennsylvania, The Stackpole Company, 1961.
Stiles, T.J., Jesse James; last rebel of the civil war. New York,
Vintage Books, 2003.
Supica, Jim and Nahas, Richard, Standard Catalog of Smith &
Wesson, 2nd Edition. Iola, Wisconsin, Krause Publishing, 2001.
Taylerson, A.W.F., Revolving Arms. New York, Bonanza Books, 1967.
Thompson, Leroy and Smeets, Rene, Great Combat Handguns.
London, Blandford Press, 1987.
Walter, John D., Secret Firearms, an illustrated history of
miniature and concealed handguns. London, Arms and Armour Press, 1997.
Waters, Robert A., The Best Defense, True stories of intended
victims who defended themselves with a firearm. Nashville, Tennessee, Cumberland
House, 1998.
Webb, Walter Prescott, The Texas Rangers, a century of frontier defense.
University of Texas Press, 1974.
Wilson, R.I., Colt: An American Legend. New York, Abbeville
Publishing Group, 1985.

OTHER

Ayoob, Massad. "The Ayoob Files, Four-Minute Massacre: The FBI
Miami Shootout." American Handgunner, vol. 13, no. 73 (January/February 1989) : p.38
and p. 71-80.
"The Ayoob Files, FBI Miami Shootout: An Update."
American Handgunner, vol. 16, no. 93 (May/June 1992) : p. 68 and p.84-88.

APPENDIX

CUSTOM PISTOLSMITHS

Hamilton Bowen
Bowen Classic Arms Corp.
P.O. Box 67
Louisville, TN 37777
Tel: 865-984-3583
Email: bcacorp@nxs.net
Web: www.bowenclassicarms.com

Cylinder & Slide, Inc.
William Laughridge, President
P.O. Box 937
Fremont, NE 68026-0937
Tel: 402-721-4277
Fax: 402-721-0263
Email: bill@cylinder-slide.com
Web: www.cylinder-slide.com

Richard Heinie
Heinie Specialty Products
301 Oak St.
Quincy, IL 62301
Tel: 217-228-9500
Fax: 217-228-9502
Web: www.heinie.com

Wayne F. Novak
Novak's .45 Shop
P.O. Box 4045
1206-1/2 30th St.
Parkersburg, WV 26101
Tel: 304-485-9295
Email: wayne@novaksights.com
Web: www.novaksights.com

Tibbets Classic Customs
Victor Tibbets, Master Pistolsmith
933 CR 439
Berryville, AR 72616
Tel: 870-423-4645
Fax: 870-423-4610
Email: victortibbets@alltel.net

TK CUSTOM
Tom Kilhoffer, Pistolsmith
303 Indian Hills Drive
Rantoul, IL 61866-1456
Tel: 217-893-1035
Fax: 217-893-3838
Email: tkcustom@prairienet.org

Jack Weigand
Weigand Combat Handguns, Inc.
1057 South Main Road
Mountaintop, PA 18707
Tel: 570-868-8358
Fax: 570-868-5218
Email: sales@jackweigand.com
Web: www.jackweigand.com

SCHOOLS AND TRAINING ACADEMIES

Blackwater Training Center
850 Puddin Ridge Rd.
Moyock, NC 27958
Tel: 252-435-2488
Fax 252-435-6388
Email: training@blackwaterusa.com
Web: www.blackwaterusa.com

Defense Training International, Inc.
John S. Farnam, President
P.O. Box 917
Laporte, CO 80535
Tel: 970-482-2520
Fax: 970-482-0548
Email: JSFarnam@aol.com
Web: www.defense-training.com

Gunsite
Bob Young, Vice President of Operations
2900 W. Gunsite Road
Paulden, AZ 86334-4301
Tel: 928-636-4565
Fax: 928-636-1236
Email: bob@gunsite.com
Web: www.gunsite.com

Lethal Force Institute
Massad Ayoob, Director
P.O. Box 122
Concord, NH 03302-0122
Toll Free: 1-800-624-9049
Tel: 603-224-6814
Fax: 603-226-3554
Email: ayoob@attglobal.net
Web: www.ayoob.com

SIG Arms Academy
233 Exeter Road
P.O. Box 903
Epping, NH 03042
Tel: 603-679-2003
Fax: 603-679-1639
Email: sigarmsacademy@sigarms.com
Web: www.sigarmsacademy.com

Thunder Ranch
96747 Hwy 140 East
Lakeview, OR 97630
Tel: 541-947-4104
Fax: 541-947-4105
Web: www.thunderranchinc.com

Yavapai Firearms Academy Ltd.
Louis Awerbuck
P.O. Box 27290
Prescott Valley, AZ 86312
Tel: 928-772-8262
Email: info@yfainc.com
Web: www.yfainc.com

HOLSTER MANUFACTURERS

Aker International, Inc.
2248 Main St., Suite 6
Chula Vista, CA 91911
Toll Free: 1-800-645-AKER
Tel: 619-423-5182
Fax: 619-423-1363
Web: www.akerleather.com

Alessi Holsters, Inc.
2465 Niagara Falls Blvd.
Amherst, NY 14228
Tel: 716-691-5615

Bianchi International
100 Calle Cortez
Temecula, CA 92590
Toll Free: 1-800-477-8545
Tel: 909-676-5621
Fax: 909-676-6777
Web: www.bianch-intl.com

Blade-Tech Industries
2506 104th Street Court South
Suite A
Lakewood, WA 98499
Tel: 253-581-4347
Fax: 253-589-0282
Web: www.blade-tech.com

CABO Holsters
P.O. Box 5118
Chino Valley, AZ 86323
Contact: Lane Raab
Tel: 928-710-0318
Email: cabo@cableone.net
Web: www.CABOHOLSTERS.com

Del Fatti Leather
907 S. Main St.
Greenwood, WI 54437
Tel: 715-267-6420
Web: www.delfatti.com

DeSantis Holster & Leather Goods
149 Denton Ave.
New Hyde Park, NY11040
Tel: 516-354-8000
Fax: 516-354-7501
Web: www.desantisholster.com

Dillon Precision Products, Inc.
8009 E. Dillons Way
Scottsdale, AZ 85260
Toll Free: 1-800-223-4570
Tel: 602-948-8009
Fax: 602-998-2786
Web: www.dillonprecision.com

Eagle Industries Unlimited
400 Biltmore Drive
Suite 530
Fenton, MO 63026
Toll Free: 1-888-343-7547
Tel: 636-343-7547
Fax: 636-349-0321
Web: www.eagleindustries.com

El Paso Saddlery Co.
2025 E. Yandell
El Paso, TX 79903
Tel: 915-544-2233
Fax: 915-544-2535
Email: info@epsaddlery.com

FIST, Inc.
35 York St.
Brooklyn, NY 11201
Toll Free: 1-800-443-3478
Email: FIST98@AOL.com
Web: www.fist-inc.com

Fobus USA
1300 Industrial Highway
Suite B-3
Southampton, PA 18966-4029
Tel: 215-355-2621
Fax: 215-322-9223
Web: www.fobusholster.com

Galco International, Ltd.
2019 W. Quail Avenue
Phoenix, AZ 85027
Toll Free: 1-800-874-2526
Tel: 623-434-7070
Fax: 623-582-6854
Web: www.usgalco.com

Gould&Goodrich
709 E. McNeil St.
P.O. Box 1479
Lillington, NC 27546
Toll Free: 1-800-277-0732
Tel: 910-893-2071
Fax: 910-893-4742
Web: www.gouldusa.com

Heinie Specialty Products, Inc.
301 Oak Street
Quincy, IL 62301
Tel: 217-228-9500
Fax: 217-228-9502
Web: www.heinie.com

Kramer Handgun Leather
P.O. Box 112154
Tacoma, WA 98411
Toll Free: 1-800-510-2666
Toll Free: 1-888-KRAMER-1
Fax: 253-564-1214
Web: www.kramerleather.com

The Leather Arsenal
27549 Middleton Road
Middleton, ID 83644

Midway USA
5875 West Van Horn Tavern Road
Columbia, MO 65203
Toll Free: 1-800-243-3220
Tel: 573-445-6363
Toll Free Fax: 800-992-8312
Web: www.midwayusa.com

Mitch Rosen
Extraordinary Gunleather, LLC
300 Bedford Street
Manchester, NH 03101-1102
Tel: 603-647-2971
Fax: 603-647-2973
Email: holster@mitchrosen.com

K.L. Null Holsters, Ltd.
161 School Street N.W.
Resaca, GA 30735
Tel: 706-625-5643
Fax: 706-625-9392
Web: www.klnullholsters.com

Renegade Holster & Leather Co.
P.O. Box 31546
Phoenix, AZ 85046
Tel: 602-482-6777

Safariland
Armor Holdings Products Div.
3120 East Mission Blvd.
Ontario, CA 91761
Tel: 909-923-7300
Fax: 909-923-7400
Web: www.safariland.com

Second Chance Body Armor, Inc.
P.O. Box 578
Central Lake, MI 49622
Toll Free: 1-800-253-7090
Tel: 231-544-5721
Fax: 231-544-9824
Web: www.secondchance.com

Milt Sparks Holsters, Inc.
605 East 44th, #2
Boise, ID 83714
Tel: 208-377-5577
Web: www.miltsparks.com

Michaels of Oregon Co.
(Uncle Mike's)
P.O. Box 1690
Oregon City, OR 97045
Tel: 503-655-7964
Fax: 503-655-7546
Web: www.michaels-oregon.com

Wild Bill's Concealment Holsters
P.O. Box 1941
Garner, NC 27259
Tel: 919-779-9582
Fax: 919-773-9456
Email: WBConceal@aol.com
Web: www.wildbillsconcealment.com